THE BIG BOOK OF
HACKS

POPULAR
SCIENCE

THE BIG BOOK OF
HACKS

weldon**owen**

contents

HOW TO USE THIS BOOK

MAKER BASICS

GEEK TOYS

HOME IMPROVEMENTS

GADGET UPGRADES

TRANSPORTATION & FITNESS

How to Use This Book

So you want to hack stuff—to tear it apart, put it back together with other components, and make it new. We at *Popular Science* salute you, and we've put together these projects to get you started. Many of them come from our popular How 2.0 and Manual sections, and many come from amazingly inventive individuals out there making cool stuff. (Check out the "Thanks to Our Makers" section for more info.)

Before starting a project, you can look to the following symbols to decode what you're facing.

COST

$ = UNDER US$50

$$ = US$50–US$300

$$$ = US$300–US$1,000

$$$$ = US$1,000 AND UP

TIME

⊘ UNDER 1 HOUR

⊘⊘ 2–5 HOURS

⊘⊘⊘ 5–10 HOURS

⊘⊘⊘⊘ 10 HOURS AND UP

DIFFICULTY

● ○ ○ ○ ○ One step up from 5 Minute Projects, these tutorials require basic builder smarts, but no electronics or coding wizardry.

● ● ○ ○ ○ Slightly advanced building skills are a must for these projects. Turn on your common sense, and troubleshoot as you go—it's part of the fun.

● ● ● ○ ○ If you see three dots, it means an activity demands low-level electronics and coding skills, or it's pretty rigorous, construction-wise.

● ● ● ● ○ You likely need serious circuitry know-how and code comprehension to do these projects. That, or be prepared to sweat with heavy-duty assembly.

● ● ● ● ● Hey, if you're reading this book, we figure you like challenges. And projects marked with five dots are sure to deliver just that.

If you're just breaking in your screwdriver and have never even heard the word *microcontroller*, try out these projects first. Designed to be doable within five minutes—give or take a few seconds, depending on your dexterity—and to make use of basic household items, these tech crafts are the perfect starting ground for the newbie tinkerer.

These are the big ones—the ambitious projects that you'll want to sink some real time and cash into, and that will challenge your skills as a builder. How much time and cash, you ask? And just how challenging? The helpful rubric above will give you an idea.

Popular Science has been doing DIY for a very long time—almost as long as the 140+ years the magazine has been in print. Occasionally this book shares a DIY project from our archives so you can try your hand at the hilarious retro projects your grandfather and grandmother built back before, say, television or smartphones.

Everyone loves a good success story—tales of everyday individuals who created something so wild that it makes you say . . . well, "You built WHAT?!" You'll find several of these stories throughout the book, and it is our hope that they will inspire you to take your projects to the next level.

WARNING

If you see this symbol, we mean business. Several of the projects in this book involve dangerous tools, electrical current, flammables, potentially harmful chemicals, and recreational devices that could cause injury if misused. So remember: With great DIY comes great responsibility. Use your head, know your tools (and your limitations), always wear safety gear, and never employ your hacking prowess to hurt others. (See our Disclaimer for more information about how *Popular Science* and the publisher are not liable for any mishaps.)

MAKER BASICS

001 Get to Know Basic Woodworking Tools

Set up a proper shop with some essential carpentry gear.

You can do most woodworking projects without elaborate table saws and expensive machinery (though they're handy if you have them). But you'll probably want to have these essentials on hand.

MEASURING TOOLS Accurately measuring lengths and angles is essential. A simple tape measure and a combination square (which allows you to measure and check angles) help you mark your cuts accurately.

HAND SAW This is the most basic, inexpensive saw that most of us have stashed somewhere in our garages. You should have one on hand and sharpened for making cuts that don't need to be incredibly precise.

TABLE SAW Now you're cutting with power. This electric saw features a circular saw blade set into a surface, and to make a nice, straight cut in an item, you push it across the blade as it spins. If it sounds dangerous, that's because it is. Be very careful when operating one of these saws.

JIGSAW Use this power tool when you need to make a curved cut in wood or metal. The jigsaw can be difficult to control, and as a result is dangerous—use it only when you require irregular contours or artistic touches.

ROTARY TOOL This simple yet versatile device allows you to cut, drill, sand, and carve into all sorts of materials. It comes with a variety of bits.

BLOCK PLANE This hand tool is useful when you want to soften edges and plane flat surfaces.

DRILL This device is your old faithful—your basic tool for making holes in wood. The size of the hole depends on the bit that you choose.

ROUTER A more advanced cutting alternative, a router is a power tool that accepts a variety of bits and creates hollows in surfaces. It's useful for making different wood moldings and joints.

SANDING BLOCK To smooth wood by hand, outfit a sanding block with sandpaper.

RANDOM-ORBIT SANDER This power sander is useful for faster sanding and large projects.

CLAMPS You'll want to have a variety of clamps on hand to hold your project steady as you glue it together.

WORKBENCH You need a solid surface to work on as you assemble your project.

VISE Some workbenches have a built-in vise, and those designed for woodworking won't damage the wood.

SAFETY GEAR Especially when using power tools, goggles are essential to protect your eyes from flying wood chips, and earplugs or noise-blocking headphones protect your hearing by muffling the noise. A face mask will also keep fine sawdust out of your lungs.

002 Make a Straight Cut in Wood

Because sawing straight lines can be trickier than you might think.

STEP 1 Use a ruler and/or combination square to measure your cut. Don't forget to account for the width, or "kerf," of your saw blade.

STEP 2 Mark the cut with a pencil on all visible sides of the wood, using an arrow to indicate on which side to begin and in which direction you'll cut.

STEP 3 Place the blade of the saw on one of the marked wooden edges, drawing it backward to slowly create a notch.

STEP 4 Repeat step 3 a few times to deepen the notch, then slowly guide the blade of the saw to the top surface of the wood.

STEP 5 Repeat steps 3 and 4 on the opposite side of the wood.

STEP 6 On the initial top surface of the wood, finish sawing through the cut you began in step 4. Make sure to support the wood and tilt the saw back toward yourself to avoid splintering.

003 Assemble a Mortise and Tenon Joint

Strong and simple—that's why this joint is more than 7,000 years old.

STEP 1 To create this type of joint, you'll need to cut one piece of wood so that a section protrudes (the tenon) and another piece so that it has a hole (the mortise). First, measure and mark the tenon, making it wide and long enough to create a strong joint.

STEP 2 Use a saw to cut out the tenon. You'll need to cut away a rectangular chunk of wood on each side of a central piece of wood that will form the tenon.

STEP 3 Use the tenon to measure out the mortise on the other piece of wood. Mark a space for the mortise on both sides of the wood.

STEP 4 Choose a drill bit that just fits inside the marks, and drill a hole halfway through the wood. Flip it over, then drill the rest of the way through the wood, using the marks you made in the third step as a guide.

STEP 5 Use a hammer and chisel or a jigsaw to cut the mortise square.

STEP 6 Fit the tenon into the mortise. Depending on your project, you can use a dowel, glue, or a wedge to keep the joint locked together.

004 Master the Butt Joint

If "butt joint" sounds like a joke to you, grow up and learn this woodworking staple.

STEP 1 To join two pieces of wood at a 90-degree angle, you'll first need to mark each piece of wood with a line at a 45-degree angle, drawn from front to back at the corner of each piece. Mark this 45-degree angle on opposite sides of each piece, and join the bottom corners of those lines together with a straight line on the third side. This will mark out the triangular wedge of wood you'll be removing from each piece.

STEP 2 Start your cut at one of the 45-degree lines, cutting a shallow groove. Finish your cut carefully, checking that it lines up with both the end corner of the wood and the straight line that you drew. Repeat on the second piece of wood.

STEP 3 Once you've cut each end into a 45-degree angle, line the pieces up with the newly cut surfaces touching. Check to make sure this forms a 90-degree angle, then glue the ends together with wood glue to form a mitered butt joint. Clamp the joint while it dries.

005 Drill a Hole

Think this is easy? It usually is—especially if you use the right tools and techniques.

STEP 1 Choose a drill bit that's the right size and length for the hole you need to drill.

STEP 2 Mark the spot where you want your hole, then use a center punch to create a dent at the mark. This will help keep the drill bit in place as you work.

STEP 3 Clamp the material you'll be drilling in place.

STEP 4 When you turn on your drill, check to make sure that the drill bit is spinning clockwise.

STEP 5 Drill into the material. As you go, the drill should feel like it's moving smoothly without requiring too much pressure. If that's not happening, stop and check for materials that could be clogging the bit.

STEP 6 When you're drilling, put the drill in reverse (spinning counterclockwise) to back out of each hole you make. If the back of a hole isn't smooth, use a deburring tool or sandpaper to remove burrs and splinters.

006 Suit Up with Metalworking Tools

Ready for some metal? You will be— once you have these basics together.

A handful of this book's projects require you to do some metalworking—either shaping it, or fusing one metal piece with another. Now, we wouldn't want you to do that without the right gear, would we?

HOT-CUTTING TOOLS Hot metal is easier to cut than cold, which is why torches and hot-cutting chisels come in handy.

COLD-CUTTING TOOLS Cold chisels are often used to create grooves in metal, and hacksaws are useful for getting through thick, cold metal.

PLIERS These tools help you handle metal that's hot or coated in toxic materials.

VISES AND CLAMPS These secure the metal you're working on, and can also be used to hold multiple pieces of metal together.

FILE A file grates away excess metal, allowing you to reshape a project as needed.

SANDPAPER This is the go-to tool you'll need for smoothing rough patches.

SAFETY GLASSES When you're working with metal, wear welding goggles or a welding hood at all times.

EAR PROTECTION When using tools that make lots of noise, cover your ears to avoid damaging your hearing.

WORK BOOTS Steel-toed or other thick, hard-soled shoes are essential protective gear when you're working with sharp or hot metal.

HEAVY GLOVES Last, but not least, take this important safety precaution: Protect your hands with thick, insulated gloves. Some metal pros wear leather ones, as leather isn't especially flammable—and it looks cool, too.

007 Cut Metal Pipes and Sheets

If you're working on plumbing or with metal sheet, you'll probably need to make a cut or two. Here's how.

TO CUT A METAL PIPE

STEP 1 Wearing the appropriate eye protection, clamp the pipe in place on your work table, and mark a line on the pipe where you want to cut.

STEP 2 Place a hacksaw on the marked line, checking to make sure that the blade is perfectly aligned with the mark. Begin cutting, using your nondominant hand to put gentle pressure on the top of the saw as you move it back and forth across the pipe. Check the alignment periodically as you work to ensure a clean cut.

STEP 3 Carefully remove the cut pipe from the clamp or vise, and smooth the cut edge with a file as needed to avoid sharp edges.

TO CUT SHEET METAL

STEP 1 Place the sheet on your work table, with the section you want to cut protruding over the edge. Hold it in place with clamps, and mark the line where you'll cut.

STEP 2 Use a jigsaw or other cutting tool to cut along the line you marked (the appropriate tool will vary depending on the type and thickness of the metal you're cutting). Hold the sheet with one hand while gently pushing the cutting tool along the line. Slow down if the sheet starts to vibrate excessively.

STEP 3 When you're finished cutting, use a file to smooth the cut edge of the metal sheet, and then unclamp the sheet from your work table.

008 Learn to Weld

It goes without saying that welding is cool. It's also really useful.

Welding allows you to join metals by heating them, then melting or compressing them together. There are several types—such as arc, gas, and resistance. Here's some basic information on arc welding, the most common method.

STEP 1 Safety first. Welding fumes can be really unhealthy, so set up in a well-ventilated area. Arc welding generates UV rays that can easily burn your skin, and molten metal can fly up and hit you, so cover exposed skin and keep a welding hood on the entire time you're working. Wear insulated welding gloves to avoid burns and electric shock, and always use work boots with insulated soles. Finally, use a work table made of nonflammable material.

STEP 2 Before you begin welding, prepare the pieces of metal you want to join. It's a good idea to use an angle grinder to bevel the edges you'll be joining—it'll allow the weld arc to penetrate and create a strong bond. Clean the metal surfaces of all paint, rust, and other contaminants that could interfere with the current created by the welding machine. Once the pieces are prepped, secure them together with clamps.

STEP 3 Attach a ground clamp to the larger piece of metal you'll be welding. The clamp will complete the circuit and allow electricity to pass through the metal once you begin welding.

STEP 4 Choose the right electrode and amperage settings for your welding machine—this will vary depending on your project. Attach the electrode to its holder, called a *stinger*.

STEP 5 Turn on the welder, and hold the stinger by its insulated handle using your dominant hand. You should be wearing all your protective gear at this point.

STEP 6 To begin welding, you need to strike an arc. Choose where you'd like to begin the weld, and tap that point with the end of your electrode. Immediately pull the electrode back slightly: This should create an electric arc between the metal and your electrode. The amount of space you'll need between the metal and the electrode varies depending on your project, and it may take practice to hold a continuous arc.

STEP 7 Move the arc along the path of your weld. This will create a weld bead, formed by the metal from the melting electrode and the base metal. The weld bead forms the bond that will hold your pieces of metal together. Move the electrode in a zig-zag motion to shape the weld bead to the desired width.

STEP 8 Once your weld is done, chip off any excess slag and use a wire brush to clean up the bond. To avoid rust, paint the metal.

009 Put Together a Soldering Kit

Soldering is playing with fire, or at least with hot metal. So you need the right tools.

If you're working on electronics projects, chances are you'll want to connect lightweight metal objects like wires, and soldering is the way to get that done. You heat pieces of metal with a soldering iron, then join them together using a molten filler, or solder. Once it cools and hardens, you're left with a strong, electronically conductive bond.

SOLDER This is the good stuff—the material you'll melt to connect metals. Traditionally, solder was a mix of tin and lead, but these days look for lead-free types to avoid nasty health risks. Choose thinner solder for delicate projects, like attaching wires to a circuit board, and thicker solder for projects involving heftier wires or bulkier pieces of metal.

SOLDERING IRON This tool has a metal tip and an insulated handle. When it's powered on, the tip heats up so it can melt solder. There are low- and high-wattage versions: Low wattage is useful for fragile projects, while high wattage is better for projects involving bigger pieces. There are also different types of tips available for the soldering iron.

SOLDERING IRON STAND Buy a stand that fits your iron so you'll have a place to put it down safely when it's hot. (Leaving this thing lying around when it's turned on is a good way to burn down the toolshed before you've even made anything cool with it!)

WIRE-MODIFYING TOOLS You'll likely be soldering a lot of wire, so it's useful to have wire cutters, wire strippers, and needle-nose pliers on hand so you can manipulate the wire. Before connecting wires, you must peel back their insulation to expose the wires, so wire strippers are definitely a must.

CLIPS AND CLAMPS Soldering requires both hands, so you'll need something to hold the materials you're soldering in place. Clips, clamps, and even electrical tape can do the job.

LIQUID FLUX Soldering works best when the items being soldered are squeaky clean, so have liquid flux on hand—it chases away oxides and other goop that can make soldering difficult.

HEAT-SHRINK TUBING You can use plastic heat-shrink tubing to insulate wires before you apply heat and solder them. It's available in several diameters for projects with various wire sizes.

TIP CLEANER Your soldering iron's tip will get a bit nasty as you work, so keep a wet sponge on hand to periodically wipe down the tip.

EXHAUST FAN The fumes from soldering are not healthy to breathe, so you need good ventilation from a fan or an open window to help clear the air.

SAFETY GOGGLES Bits of hot solder can go flying as you work, so don't do it without wearing safety goggles.

010 Learn to Solder Wires

Now that you have your soldering gear together, here's how to solder.

At its most basic, soldering is simply attaching wires to wires. The process is a bit different when you're soldering directly onto a circuit board, but don't worry: We've got you covered with info for each.

STEP 1 In a well-ventilated space, with your safety goggles on, plug in your soldering iron to heat it up. Be careful not to touch the tip, which will heat up fast.

STEP 2 Prepare the materials you want to join with solder. If you're connecting two wires, peel back any insulation about ½ inch (1.25 cm), and twist the wires together. Place your materials on a surface you don't mind burning a bit, like scrap wood.

STEP 3 Cut a length from the spool of solder and coil it up at one end, leaving a short lead. You can hold on to the coiled end as you apply the solder.

STEP 4 Touch the iron to the point where the wires are twisted together. Leave it there until the wires are hot enough to melt the solder (about 10 seconds), then touch the solder to the wire joint every few seconds until it begins to melt. Allow enough solder to melt onto the wires to cover them, then pull the solder and soldering iron away. Don't touch the solder directly to the soldering iron during this process—that will melt the solder onto the wires, but won't form a firm joint.

STEP 5 When you need to fix a mistake, you can reheat your joint, melt the solder, and reposition the components. If you want to break the connection you made for any reason, you can desolder a joint. For connections like joined wires, you can often simply heat up the joint and pull the wires apart, or cut each wire below the joint and resolder as desired.

011 Solder to a Circuit Board

Once you've masted soldering wires to wires, level up and solder to PCB.

STEP 1 Place the component that you wish to solder in the correct spot on the circuit board and clamp it down, then push the leads for each component through the holes on the board.

STEP 2 Solder the leads to the bottom of the board. (This is easier to do with a fine-tipped, low-wattage soldering iron.) Press the soldering iron to the lead and the metal contact on the board at the point where you want them to connect. Once they heat up enough to melt the solder—just a few seconds—melt a small amount of solder at the connection point (too much can cause a short, too little won't make a strong connection).

STEP 3 Pull the solder away, then remove the soldering iron a second or two later. Once you've soldered all the leads onto the circuit board, trim off excess wire with a wire cutter.

012 Study Circuit Components

To build a circuit, first you've got to understand its building blocks.

Maps of how current flows through a circuit are called *schematics*. Each component is represented by a labeled symbol, which is connected to other components by lines to represent the current's path.

In this book, we use several circuitry diagrams to show how to attach projects' components, so here we'll introduce you to some of the main circuit components that show up on these diagrams.

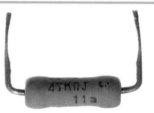

RESISTORS A circuit needs resistance to function. Without it, you'll end up with a short circuit, in which the current flows directly from power to ground without being used, causing your circuit to overheat and otherwise misbehave. To prevent that from happening, resistors reduce the flow of electrical current. The level of resistance is measured in ohms, so check those numbers to make sure a component's resistance matches the level indicated in the circuitry diagram.

TRANSISTORS A transistor amplifies energy flowing to its base pin, allowing a larger electrical current to flow between its collector and emitter pins. The two basic types of transistors, NPN and PNP, have opposite polarities: Current flows from collector to emitter in NPN transistors, and flows from emitter to collector in PNP transistors.

CAPACITORS These store electricity, then release it back into the circuit when there's a drop in power. Capacitor values are measured in farads: picofarads (pF), nanofarads (nF), and microfarads (μF) are the most common units of measure. Ceramic capacitors aren't polarized, so they can be inserted into a circuit in any direction, but electrolytic capacitors are polarized and need to be inserted in a specific orientation.

POTENTIOMETERS When you need to vary resistance within a circuit, use a potentiometer instead of a standard resistor. These have a controller that allows you to change the level of resistance: "B" potentiometers have a linear response curve, while "A" potentiometers have a logarithmic response curve.

SWITCHES Switches open or close a circuit. Some are normally open as a default; others are normally closed.

BATTERIES These store power for a circuit, and you can use more than one to increase voltage or current.

WIRE These single strands of metal are often used to connect the components in a circuit. Wire comes in various sizes (or gauges), and it's usually insulated.

DIODES These components are polarized to allow current to flow through them in only one direction— very useful if you need to stop the current in your circuit from flowing the wrong way. The side of a diode that connects to ground is called the *cathode*, and the side that connects to power is called the *anode*. Light-emitting diodes, or LEDs, light up when current flows through them.

INTEGRATED CIRCUITS These are tiny circuits (usually including transistors, diodes, and resistors) prepacked into a chip. Each leg of the chip will connect to a point in your larger circuit. These vary widely in their composition, and will come with a handy data sheet explaining their functions.

TRANSFORMERS These devices range from thumbnail-size to house-size, and consist of coils of wire wound around a core, often a magnet. Made to transfer alternating current from one circuit to another, they can step the power of the current up or down depending on the ratio of wire windings between one coil and another.

013 Build a Circuit

Now that you know what goes into a circuit, you can make one.

STEP 1 Assemble all the components that appear on your schematic, along with any tools you'll need to make connections, clamp parts, or trim wires.

STEP 2 To test your circuit before you solder it together, set it up on a breadboard first. Breadboards are boards covered in small holes that allow you to lay out and connect components without soldering them in place.

STEP 3 Once you're ready to construct the circuit, it's best to start by installing the shortest components first. This helps you avoid having to move taller components out of the way, and allows you to flip the board over to hold the component you're working on in place. As you install components, orient their labels in the same direction so they're all legible at once.

STEP 4 Many components have lead wires that you can insert into a circuit board. Bend these leads before you insert the component so that you don't stress the part or the board.

STEP 5 You'll need to hold your parts in place while you solder the circuit together. You can do this by clinching lead wires (bending them slightly on the other side of the board to hold them in place), using tape, or bracing the parts against your work surface.

STEP 6 As you solder, check that each component is aligned correctly after you solder the first pin or lead—it's easier to make adjustments at this point, before you've finished soldering the part in place.

STEP 7 When everything's soldered in place, trim all your circuit's lead wires and test it out.

Learn Programming Basics

Take a superquick programming primer to move onto computer-enabled projects.

To program one so it does what you want, start with a task, then break it into smaller steps until you end up with actions simple enough for a computer to do. Then you explain those actions in a way that a computer can understand. That means speaking a computer's language. There are dozens of popular computer languages out there, but they all share concepts.

SPECIAL PUNCTUATION Minding your dashes carries more weight in programming than in English class. Using a comma instead of a period can stop a program dead. Here are some common examples of special punctuation:

- **COMMENTS** These are used as a chance to inject plain English into your code and are ignored by the computer. They often start with # or // and end at the end of the line, or begin with a /* and end with */.

- **CODE BLOCKS** These are handy for grouping a bunch of code together as a single unit. This is usually done with curly brackets, but some languages group code by how far the line is indented.

- **END OF LINE** This is commonly indicated by a semicolon, while some languages are smart enough that you can just hit return.

VARIABLES The labeled boxes of coding are variables. You can put a single thing in the box—for example, a number or word. Then you can do things with the boxes, like compare or add their contents without knowing what's inside. And you can give them descriptive names so you can tell what kind of thing they're supposed to hold. Note: They don't start with a number, and they can't have spaces.

CONDITIONALS These let the computer make decisions by comparing things, usually variables. Here's an example:

```
if (X > 10) {

// Do something.

} else {

// Do something else.

}
```

In plain English, this reads "If the value of variable X is greater than 10, then do whatever is in the first block of code. Otherwise, do the second block of code." Conditionals sometimes use borrowed and improvised logical symbols, like != for "not equal to" or >= for "greater than or equal to."

LOOPS Use a loop to make computers do the same thing over and over. They're like conditionals with something extra going on:

```
for (x=0; x < 10; x=x+1) {

// Do something.

}
```

In plain English: "Set X to zero. If X is less than 10, do the block of code. When the block is complete, add one to X. If X is still less than 10, do the block of code..." etc., adding one to X each time through. When X is no longer less than 10, the loop stops and the computer moves on.

FUNCTIONS If you have a bit of superuseful code, you can split it into a function that you can reuse without copying every time. Here's an example in JavaScript:

```
// A small function to return the cube of a number.

function cube(num){

var output = num * num * num;

return output;

}

alert("The cube of 12 is " + cube(12)); // 12 cubed is 1728

alert("The cube of 42 is " + cube(42)); // 42 cubed is 74088
```

Here, we send a number (num) to the function, which cubes the number, returns the answer (output) to where it came from, and displays it on-screen. A basic JavaScript program that combines these concepts is easy to find online.

015 Get to Know Microcontrollers

For makers and robotics geeks everywhere, the advent of the cheap, power-efficient microcontroller has been a godsend. With a microcontroller, some patience, and some basic coding, you can make anything from a blinking LED flashlight to Twitter-enabled kitchen appliances. Consider the following points when deciding which microcontroller is right for you and your project.

READ & WRITE Most microcontrollers marketed to hobbyists feature rewritable and erasable memory, but not all. If you need it, make sure yours has it.

EXPANSION If your project is a complex one, you might choose a microcontroller with lots of memory and/or expansion ports for external memory.

EASE OF USE If you're new to the game, pick a microcontroller that has a large board with widely spaced pins (for easy manipulation) and that uses a familiar programming language.

The gamut of consumer-grade microcontrollers runs from the bare-bones Arduino Uno, with its 16 MHz processor and three kilobytes of memory, to the Raspberry Pi 1 Model B+, a bona fide computer the size of a credit card.

• The Arduino Uno, and its successor the Due, are favorites among makers, hackers, and hobbyists, due to their simplicity, low cost, and low power consumption. They run a custom programming language that is similar to the ubiquitous C language that powers Unix.

• In contrast, the Raspberry Pi and Beaglebone lines of single-board computers are full-fledged computers that run a variant of Linux and provide a wide range of input and output, including video, Ethernet, and USB. They will compile or interpret nearly any programming language that runs on Linux.

• A few microcontrollers, including the Arduino Yun and the Intel Galileo, combine the simplicity of a low-end Arduino with the power of a single-board computer. If you think your project might expand beyond your original goals, one of these might be right for you.

016 Program an Arduino

The Arduino is a great choice for both experienced makers and the uninitiated. Here's how to use one.

STEP 1 Download and install the Arduino software, including the integrated development environment (IDE), on your computer. Connect the board's programming port to the USB port on your computer.

STEP 3 Different Linux, Mac, and Windows computers require different procedures for determining the correct serial port for your specific board. Every board has its own unique port ID. Use the documentation online to

follow the instructions for your operating system.

STEP 4 Launch the Arduino application on your computer. Open an example program, called a sketch.

STEP 5 Click the Upload button in your Arduino application. Your board should soon display the behavior that the program dictates. For instance, if you uploaded the Blink sketch to your Arduino, you should soon see the LEDs on your board start to flash in alternation.

STEP 6 Seek out other sketches online to see how they function on your board. Modify them slightly to get a feel for the Arduino programming language.

017 Get Familiar with CNC Software

So you want to get into laser-cutting, 3D printing, plasma-cutting, or another supercool preprogrammed manufacturing method. First things first: Take a primer in the software that controls these machines and allows you to design and create whatever you dream up.

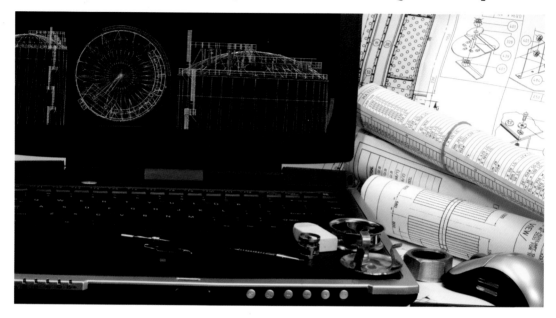

The CNC (Computer Numerical Control) software tool chain consists of three distinct "layers" between your draft idea and the finished, gleaming end product. Today, these functions are increasingly being integrated together in all-in-one programs, but it's still very helpful to understand what's going on under the hood.

CAD (COMPUTER-AIDED DESIGN) These programs are used to draw the part you want to make in two or three dimensions. Depending on your software, your CAD file may be as simple as a raster image showing a picture you want to laser-etch on a part's surface, or it may be as complex as a 3D model with multiple materials and specific instructions and parameters that change how it would be assembled depending on what tool is used to create it. CAD software, especially for 3D objects, used to be very expensive, but no more—nowadays many free

programs are available online, even websites with full-featured CAD packages that run right in your browser window.

CAM (COMPUTER-AIDED MANUFACTURING) This type of software analyzes your digital model and adapts it to construction on some particular CNC tool. The CAM software figures out the exact sequence of movements, cuts, and other operations required to produce the shape contained in your CAD file. Very often these operations are represented in more-or-less standard industry formats called G-code or M-code.

CLIENT This program actually controls the tool's operation in real time. It provides basic but essential functions like start and stop, as well as various alignment, adjustment, and setting options. Depending on your particular setup, it may run on your PC or on the tool's built-in electronics.

018 Meet the Lasercutter

It doesn't really get much cooler than drafting and lasercutting your own designs.

The same technology that powers your Blu-Ray player, drives your cats insane, and nails you for speeding on the highway also serves as the maker's best friend: the laser. While it's not easy to obtain your own laser cutter (price tags on low-end versions run well into the five digits), you can probably find one at your local makerspace or technical college.

WHAT CAN YOU CUT WITH LASERS? You can't cut everything with a laser cutter, but you can cut a lot. Materials that are reflective or noxious when heated are out, and you'll want to check with the operator of

the workshop to get a list of approved materials. And expect to take a short course on best practices before you're allowed to work a machine.

PLASTICS Acrylic, a maker mainstay, is compatible with laser cutting and comes off the bed cool and clean-cut. Alternatively, closed-cell urethane and polyethylene foams yield perfectly finished edges.

NATURAL MATERIALS Cloth, leather, paper, and wood are popular laser-cutting media. Cloth, paper, and wood are somewhat susceptible to charring, although that's not always a negative. Leather etchings have their charm, but burning leather is not a pleasant aroma.

RUBBER Some forms of rubber are acceptable to lasercut onto; others are not. Consult with your workshop's supervisor and remember that the thicker the rubber, the rougher the cut.

ANODIZED ALUMINUM Laser cutting is a superior alternative to traditional etching or engraving if detail and contrast are a priority.

019 Start Lasercutting

Try your hand at cutting designs of your own making—with lasers.

STEP 1 Download or create a vector graphics file. Vector graphic formats include Adobe Illustrator (.ai), CorelDraw (.cdr), Portable Document (.pdf), Encapsulated PostScript (.eps), and Scalable Vector Graphics (.svg). Be aware that different models of laser cutter may accept different file formats.

STEP 2 Use the laser cutter's software and a connected computer to import your vector graphics file. Be aware: Different laser cutters use proprietary software, so be prepared for a steep learning curve if you switch platforms.

STEP 3 Establish "home" by telling your laser cutter where to begin.

STEP 4 Instruct the laser cutter to begin cutting or etching. Avoid looking directly at the point of contact between the laser and the material.

STEP 5 Show off your laser-cut or -etched material to your friends.

020 Discover the World of 3D Printing

A 3D printer is a manufacturing robot designed to fabricate objects, layer by layer, from digital files.

It might sound like science fiction, but 3D printers have been around for more than 30 years, mostly used by engineers, industrial designers, and architects for rapid prototyping. In fact, the term is a broad label for an entire category of machines. Each type suits a particular range of materials, precision of resolution, and means of burning, melting, fusing, pressing, gluing, or stacking horizontal layers.

As you get to know the nature of the available materials and how you can push the machines to produce what you need, you'll find a 3D printer handy on any project. You can print rare replacement parts for a classic car, for instance; build a working prototype of a mechanical device; conceptualize complex artwork; or even develop affordable prosthetics. You're limited only by your imagination—and the amount of time you have to tune and mod your printer and printer files.

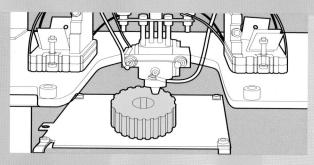

FUSED-FILAMENT FABRICATION (FFF)

This is the most common type of desktop 3D-printing technology, also known by its trademarked name Fused Deposition Modeling (FDM). FFF machines create objects by "drawing" them in melted plastic, extruded through the nozzle of a guided toolhead. For each layer, the nozzle traces an object's outer shell and then follows an infill pattern to fill in the interior of the part at a user-selected density. By depositing layer after layer, each new slab fusing to the one underneath, the FFF machine creates a complete physical object.

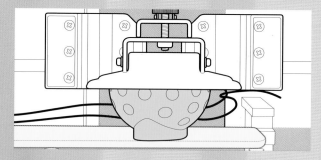

STEREOLITHOGRAPHY (SLA)

Unlike the FFF process, where a toolhead travels across the build platform, squirting out the object in melted plastic, SLA machines use a mirror to selectively cure the surface of a photoreactive resin. After every laser pass, the object is slowly pulled up out of the vat of resin. Recently, a number of new desktop SLA printers have come to market, offering finer-resolution printing but with the tradeoff of longer print times, fragile parts, and expensive and sometimes toxic printing materials.

PREPARE TO PRINT A 3D MODEL

The first step to printing a 3D model is to prepare the digital file, which tells the printer exactly what to print.

STEP 1 Pick an object to print. You'll need a 3D digital model, preferably a stereolithography (.stl) file with solid, watertight geometry. Your design can be created using a mechanically inclined computer-aided design (CAD) software package, a 3D digital art and animation tool, or even captured directly with a 3D scanner. (You may need to clean up a 3D scan before it's ready for printing.) The .stl file format was created decades ago and can be exported from most CAD and computer graphics software packages. There are also a number of online 3D model repositories where designers and artists share their latest work: Thingiverse, YouMagine, GrabCAD, and 3D Warehouse, among others. Browse the sites by object name, category, or designer, and check to see that the object you have selected offers a downloadable model that matches your needs. You can find plans online or develop plans for yourself—from DIY musical instruments to functioning tools, and from a chess set to architectural models and actual bone replacements.

STEP 2 Import the file into computer-aided manufacturing (CAM) software. CAM software helps you translate your digital design into real-world instructions that a 3D printer can follow. Check with the manufacturer of your 3D printer and others who use the same model for recommendations on which package (and preset configurations) best suit your printer model.

STEP 3 Preview your design. When you import the .stl, an image of the model appears in the window that represents the build platform (the area where the printed part will be produced) for your specified printer. You may need to scale down your digital model to match the printed dimensions. (If your model is too small, you might need to convert your digital design from inches to millimeters—scale your model up 25.4 times to convert it.) Other CAM preview features allow you to reposition, rotate, mirror, and duplicate your design until the virtual build platform matches what you intend your printer to produce. Once you move the scaled-down version into the center of the platform and it fits within the bounds of your printer, it's ready for "slicing."

STEP 4 It's time to lean on the core power of your CAM package. Slicing tools (either included in the CAM tool or available as a separate application) are translation utilities that analyze the virtual geometry of your models and create a set of machine-specific instructions your printer will follow to produce the physical object. The term "slicing" refers to dividing the model into horizontal layers first before working out the path the toolhead will follow to deposit each layer of plastic. Before slicing, configure the job-specific print settings that the slicing tools will follow to produce the object.

STEP 5 Look closely at your file to see if there are any challenges for your slicer to overcome—say, the model isn't completely flat on the bottom (a problem for a stable print), or there are no lower features to support the top of the object (referred to as "overhang"). To facilitate this print, activate "raft" and "automatic support" settings in the slicer. A raft is a low, wide pedestal for your design to sit on top of—to provide a stronger base for the bottom of your model. (A similar feature is a brim, which rings the base of the model like a hat brim.) Automatic support options generate breakaway structures to support features higher up in the model that would overhang empty space otherwise. Both rafts and support features are designed to be easy to remove from the original design after the printing process. Most slicer packages offer these options.

STEP 6 Consider other options you may want to adjust from job to job. There's layer height, which determines how thin to slice each layer. Thinner layers mean softer, less blocky curves up the side of your object, but multiply the amount of time necessary to produce the object. Then there's fill density, which determines how tightly to pack the insides of solid objects. Higher density produces stronger, heavier parts but also adds to printing time and amount of material required.

STEP 7 Slicing the file may take a few seconds or a few minutes, depending on the complexity of the job and the slicer you've selected. When it's done, you're ready to print your object! Depending on what specific 3D printer you're using, hitting print varies; refer to its instructions for specifics. Pro tip: Most FFF 3D printers will leave a tiny seam up one side of the model based on where the toolhead moves vertically to create the next layer. After finding where your machine adds a seam, you may want to rotate the design before printing the next time, to ensure that the seam doesn't mar a significant detail on your model (like the face on a 3D portrait).

GEEK TOYS

BUILD IT!

021 Make Your Own Cotton-Candy Machine

COST	$
TIME	☺ ☺ ☺
EASY ● ● ● ○ ○ HARD	

Enjoy a DIY sugar high.

You don't need to wait for a carnival to satisfy your craving for cotton candy. Instead, build this portable, pocket-size machine to turn granulated sugar into an airy treat.

It consists of a small metal container, repurposed lighter parts to provide heat, and a switch-controlled motor to set everything spinning. As you pour granulated sugar into the container, flames from the lighters will melt it. As the motor spins, the liquid sugar flies out through little holes in the container's sides, forming thin strands. A paper cylinder placed around the machine will capture them. Once they've built up, simply swirl a chopstick around the perimeter to gather the candy and taste your sweet success.

MATERIALS

Long-nosed lighter
Torch lighter
Wire
Two-part epoxy
Superglue
Metal standoff with screws, washers, and nuts
DC motor
Pushpin
Small aluminum cosmetic container or metal drink cap

Drill
Soldering iron and solder
AA-battery pack
Small project box
Clay epoxy
Paper
Tape
Rubber band
Sugar
Chopstick

 WARNING
Take care handling lighters and fuel. The sugar is molten when it comes out, so keep your hands out of the way of hot flying white stuff. Also keep hands and paper clear of the open flame.

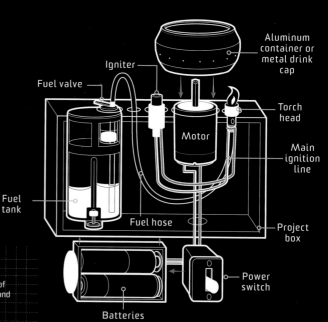

Igniter
Fuel valve
Fuel tank
Fuel hose
Batteries
Motor
Aluminum container or metal drink cap
Torch head
Main ignition line
Project box
Power switch

GEEK TOYS

STEP 1 To build a system for heating the sugar, first open both lighters. Harvest the large fuel tank, igniter, and hose from the long-nosed lighter and the torch head from the torch lighter.

STEP 2 Connect the fuel tank to the torch head with the long fuel hose. For an ignition line, wrap a short length of wire around the metal base of the long-nosed lighter's igniter and seal it with epoxy. Push the igniter's new wire through the torch head, where the torch lighter's wire previously was. This is the main ignition line. Connect the main ignition line to the brass part of the torch head. Seal with superglue.

STEP 3 Next, set up the spinning chamber. Use epoxy to connect the metal standoff to the shaft of

the motor. (When join together with epoxy sides before bondi a stronger bond.)

STEP 4 With th holes all the w the aluminu holes in the the center through i and nut in plac

STE ter sc th prevent

STEP 6 To prepa plan where you will be p fuel valve, igniter, torch head, a spinning chamber. Mark each spot on the project box with a marker,

023 The U Beer

Behold this elaborate home-cr

What if there were a mar machine—and all it did was make you beer? s former PopSci phot he calls "the Dev system that st or pre-fermer

In most ho requires which requ in

canc

022 Turn a Matchstick into a Tiny Rocket

MATERIALS

Paper clips

Sewing pin or needle

Matches

Aluminum foil

STEP 1 Bend a paper clip into a 45-degree angle. Presto! You now have a launch pad.

STEP 2 Lay a pin along a matchstick so that the sharp tip touches the match head. Wrap the head with a piece of aluminum foil, and gently crease the foil around the pin (avoid tears and holes).

STEP 3 Remove the pin. This leaves a hollow channel that will direct gas downward, so it can act as propellant.

STEP 4 Rest the match on the launch pad, hold a small flame under the foil-wrapped match head, and start your countdown.

...ltimate All-in-One
...-Brewing Machine

...deluxe homemade microbrewery: an
...device that boils, ferments, chills, and pours
...afted ale.

...hine—a beautiful, shiny
..., with almost no work from you,
...ouch was the dream that drove
...ographer John Carnett to build what
...ce": a stainless-steel, two-cart brewing
...rts by boiling extract (concentrated wort,
...ted beer) and ends with a chilled pint.

...me-brewing setups, each step in the process
...moving the beer to a new container by hand,
...increases the chance of contamination and
...res lifting. Carnett's machine keeps everything
...the carts' closed system—he only has to swap a few
...CO$_2$-pressurized hoses to move the liquid along.

The delicious brew's journey begins in the boil keg, where concentrated wort extract is heated by a propane burner for 90 minutes. The beer then travels through a heat exchanger—which cools the mix to about 55°F (13°C)—on its way to the fermenting keg. Here, a network of Freon-chilled copper tubes pumps cool water around the keg when the temperature gets too high. After two weeks, the Device pumps the beer into a settling keg, where a CO$_2$ tank adds carbonation. When you pull the tap, the beer travels through the cold plate, so it's chilled on the way to your glass. That's right: The Device is always ready with a cold pour and consumes no power when it's not actively serving or fermenting.

BUILDING A BETTER BREW
The next step? Adding a third cart to make wort from raw grain instead of extract. But, says Carnett, there's a lot of "testing" of the new design to be done first.

Drink Booze from a Melon

Turn basic produce into a hilarious drink dispenser.

MATERIALS

Knife

Medium seedless watermelon

Large spoon

Drill

Ball valve faucet with a handle

Rubber O-ring that fits the faucet

PVC-to-faucet adapter

Alcohol of your choosing

STEP 1 Using a knife, cut off just enough of the bottom of your melon so that it sits flat.

STEP 2 Pick the side of the melon that you want to be the front, then cut a hole in the top, toward the rear. Save the piece you've cut out, as you'll use it later.

STEP 3 Scoop out the fruit with a large spoon.

STEP 4 Drill a hole in the melon's front, near the bottom. Using a knife, widen it so it's big enough for the faucet to fit inside.

STEP 5 Gently screw the faucet into the hole. (It helps to stick your free hand inside the melon and guide the faucet into place from the inside.)

STEP 6 Slide the O-ring onto the back of the faucet inside the melon, then install the adapter. Test for leaks.

STEP 7 Load it up with the elixir of your choosing, put the cut-out top back in place, and get your pour on.

025 Break into Your Beer

STEP 1 Use a metal file to wear down a carabiner's hook end so that it fits under a bottle cap's lip. (Be careful not to file it down too much or the carabiner won't close properly.)

STEP 2 Open the carabiner and place the unmodified end against the beer cap, then tuck the hook end under the cap's lip and use it as a lever to pry open your brew.

STEP 3 Carry your carabiner as a keychain so that you're always ready when beer suddenly, magically happens to you.

026 Install a Shower Beer Caddy

STEP 1 Buy a cup holder at an automotive parts store. (Some have a hook on the back, which you don't need—remove it by gently breaking it off along the seam or cutting it off with a rotary tool.)

STEP 2 Drill a hole into the back of the cup holder that's just wide enough to accommodate the tip of a suction cup.

STEP 3 Insert the suction cup's tip into the hole, press the suction cup to the shower wall, and load your beer of choice into the caddy.

Carabiner

Filed-
down
hook end

1

2

Beer bottle

Beer can

Suction
cup

Cup holder

027 Chill Your Beer Really, Really Fast

STEP 1 Drill a hole into the side of a plastic container. The hole should be just wide enough that you can poke the straw of a container of compressed air through it.

STEP 2 Fill the plastic container with as many beers as you can fit. Cover with the lid.

STEP 3 Tape it shut. (Trust us. Otherwise the injected blast of cool air could blow the lid right off.)

STEP 4 Wearing thick, insulated gloves, turn the can of compressed air upside down and insert the can's straw into the hole, being careful not to touch the cans with it.

STEP 5 Squeeze for up to 1 minute.

STEP 6 Open the container and tap on each can's top for a few seconds to relieve the pressure inside. Then open one up and take a big swig—you've earned it.

028 Disguise Your Brew

STEP 1 Using a can opener, remove the top and bottom of an innocent-looking soda can.

STEP 2 Using scissors, cut off the soda can's bottom lip.

STEP 3 Cut along the soda can's seam.

STEP 4 Using a metal file, sand down the can's edges to avoid cuts and scrapes. Get it as smooth as possible.

STEP 5 Wrap the soda can around your beer and enjoy your incognito beverage.

Soda can

Beer can

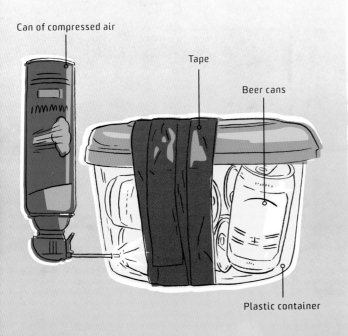

Can of compressed air

Tape

Beer cans

Plastic container

GEEK TOYS

QUICK
HACKS

029 Reuse Those Red Party Cups

Keep the infamous cup in play long after the keg's run dry. (Just rinse out that stale-beer smell first.)

DIY CAMERA LENS HOOD

Fend off glare with an impromptu lens hood. Cut the bottom out of your party cup, and then poke two holes on either side near the bottom. Thread a rubber band through each hole and knot them. Place the cup over your lens, tie the rubber bands around your camera near the viewfinder, and keep rain out of your shots.

MEASURE (MORE) BOOZE

Engineers say that the ridges on party cups are for structural integrity, but people have long used them as measurement lines: the first indentation from the bottom marks 1 ounce (30 ml), the second 5 ounces (147 ml), and the third a full 12 ounces (355 ml).

POOR MAN'S CHANDELIER

Poke holes in the bottoms of about 60 cups. Then glue the cups together along their sides with their open ends facing outward, forming a ball. Insert a bulb from a string of Christmas lights into each hole as you go to make a huge, sparkling plastic orb.

MAKESHIFT BEER INSULATOR

Cut Styrofoam to fit the bottom of your cup and place it inside, then spray a can with nonstick cooking spray. Put the can inside the cup and fill around it with expanding foam. Let the foam dry and trim the excess. Call it a koozie.

030 The Drink-Slinging Droid

This robot tends bar like a pro. And even better, it never needs a tip.

A veteran of the TV show *BattleBots,* Jamie Price has built plenty of destructive machines. But recently he designed a robot with a more mellow calling: offering cold beer and cocktails. The result—a masterpiece of plywood, plastic, aluminum, and electric motors called Bar2D2—serves up everything but the sage advice.

The salesman modeled his machine on the iconic *Star Wars* droid R2-D2, and spent seven months and $2,000 building it. He used a plastic dome from a bird feeder as the head and built the robot's plywood skeleton to match. To make Bar2D2 mobile, Price stripped out the seat, the control system, and a pair of wheels from an electric wheelchair, added a new 12-volt battery, and wired a receiver to the motor so he could control it with an R/C helicopter-type remote.

Price fills each of the robot's six bottles with either liquor or a mixer, and then plugs these ingredients into a software program. The program computes a list of possible drinks, Price picks one, and the software sends pouring instructions to the robot via Bluetooth. A custom circuit board receives the signals and moves actuators that open specific valves just long enough for the robot's air-pressure system to force the right amount of each liquid into a waiting glass.

Bar2D2 has already proven to be a hit among robotics and cocktail fans alike, but Price isn't finished yet. Next he's adding a breathalyzer and an LED-backed projector that displays blood-alcohol content. Give us your keys, Obi-Wan.

BEER ME, BAR2D2

One difficulty was finding a way to move bottles up from the enclosed beer rack to the serving station above. When Price hits a button on his remote, the rod of a motorized caulk gun extends and pushes the beer up from the lower level. He calls it his beer elevator.

031 | Create Powdered Booze at Home

Fluffy like confetti and just as intoxicating as the bottled stuff.

This recipe for powdered booze results in a slightly moist powder, because of the water in the liquor. You can stir the powdered booze into a mixer, to taste, to make a delicious sippable; sprinkle it on food (rum powder is great on desserts); or just lick a little bit of powder off your finger for the novelty.

MATERIALS

Kitchen scale

N-Zorbit

Kitchen whisk

High-proof spirits

Sifter or fine strainer

STEP 1 Weigh out 100 grams of N-Zorbit (a modified starch available from online suppliers) into a mixing bowl. Because the powder is so fluffy and light, this will be a sizable mound.

STEP 2 Whisking steadily, drizzle in 30 grams of high-proof spirit. After you've stirred it in completely, the

powder should be dry, but somewhat chunky. If it's still moist, sprinkle in a little more N-Zorbit.

STEP 3 Sift the dry liquor through a fine sieve to break up the chunks and make a nice powder. (If you're making a larger batch, you can do it in a blender and this step won't be necessary.)

032 | Make Drinks Glow in the Dark

The magic glowing ingredients? Simple riboflavin and quinine, plus a trippy black light.

FOR BLUE DRINKS:

STEP 1 Mix any drink you want.

STEP 2 Add tonic water.

STEP 3 Drink it near a black light.

FOR YELLOW DRINKS:

STEP 1 Crush up a B2 vitamin and put a pinch of the powder in the bottom of your glass.

STEP 2 Pour in a flavored drink, as the vitamin has a faint bitter taste.

STEP 3 Drink it near a black light.

033 Freeze LEGO Ice Cubes

Make a mold of LEGO bricks and enjoy the world's geekiest ice.

MATERIALS

A LEGO base plate and bricks

Petroleum jelly

Mold compound

Craft knife

Food coloring, if desired

STEP 1 Wash and dry the base plate and blocks.

STEP 2 Build a LEGO tray on the base plate: Make four sides three blocks in height, then place single bricks inside the border, spacing them evenly with one or two rows of bumps between each.

STEP 3 Coat the tray in petroleum jelly, then slowly fill the tray with the mold compound and set aside for at least 12 hours. Bang on the table to prevent bubbles.

STEP 4 Peel the mold out of the LEGO tray and trim any random bits off with the craft knife.

STEP 5 Wash the mold and turn it over. Fill the depressions with water (add food coloring, if you roll that way), slide it in the freezer, and await your cubes.

034 Cook a Hot Dog with Electrical Current

An LED display lights up the room and nukes your hot dog, too.

MATERIALS

Wire strippers

Power cord

Soldering iron and solder

Two alligator clips

Hot dog

Nonconductive plate

Two metal forks

Assorted LEDs

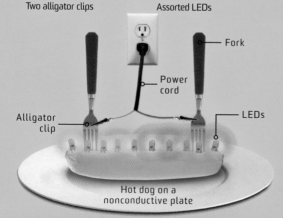

Fork

Power cord

Alligator clip

LEDs

Hot dog on a nonconductive plate

STEP 1 Using wire strippers, cut off the end of the power cord and peel back the outer insulation. Snip back the green ground cord and strip the ends of the remaining two wires.

STEP 2 Solder one small alligator clip to each of the stripped wires (except for the ground).

STEP 3 Put the hot dog on a nonconductive plate (ceramic works nicely). Secure each alligator clip to a fork, and stick the forks into the hot dog.

STEP 4 Stick some LEDs into the hot dog.

STEP 5 Very carefully plug the cord into the wall. Don't touch the hot dog or any of the rest of the contraption while the cord is plugged in.

STEP 6 The hot dog will cook in a minute or two. Not that you're going to eat it, right?

 WARNING
Use this activity to impress your friends with your electrical chops, not your culinary skills. Eating the resulting hot dog is a seriously bad idea. Also, keep water very far away from this science experiment!

035 Mod Your Toaster for Crazy Toast

Because bread tastes a lot better with funny faces on it.

COST	$
TIME	⏱
EASY	● ● ○ ○ ○ HARD

MATERIALS

Toaster	Aluminum flashing
Scissors	Utility knife
Paper	Metal file
Pencil	Bread that needs toasting
Craft knife	
Glue stick	

STEP 1 Unplug your toaster and remove the insert—that's the part that holds bread slices in place. Measure the space between the insert's two prongs.

STEP 2 Cut two pieces of paper to fit between these two prongs. Draw or print a shape that you want to see on your breakfast onto the paper. Include a tab on either side of each shape that you can wrap around the prongs to hold your design in place inside the toaster.

STEP 3 Use a craft knife to cut out the negative spaces around and in your design, creating a stencil.

STEP 4 Glue the paper pieces to aluminum flashing. Use a utility knife to cut the shapes and their tabs out of the flashing, then smooth the edges with a metal file.

STEP 5 Gently and thoroughly wash off the glue and remove all the paper. With the toaster unplugged, use the shapes' tabs to hook them to the toaster insert.

STEP 6 Replace the insert, plug the toaster in, put in some bread, and make some really fun toast.

☠ **WARNING**
Toasters may seem harmless enough, but once they're plugged in they're juiced with powerful voltage. No aluminum flashing or paper bits should come into contact with the toaster's electric heaters.

036 Build a Flameless Hack-o'-Lantern

You can hack a pumpkin and still enjoy the glow of a traditional jack-o'-lantern.

Create a realistic fire effect by wiring up an electronic blinky light. Bonus: It runs off a safe circuit that requires no soldering. It uses six LEDs with a candle-flicker effect, which will shine all night on three AAA batteries. An integrated phototransistor enables the LEDs to automatically turn off at dawn and back on at sunset.

COST $
TIME 🕐
EASY ● ● ● ○ ○ HARD

MATERIALS

Mini breadboard
Jumper wires
Six candle-flicker LEDs (at least 2 red and 2 yellow)
Six 100-ohm resistors
Two NPN transistors
Infrared phototransistor
5k-ohm resistor

Wire cutters
Wire strippers
Three AAA batteries
Battery box
Carved jack-o'-lantern

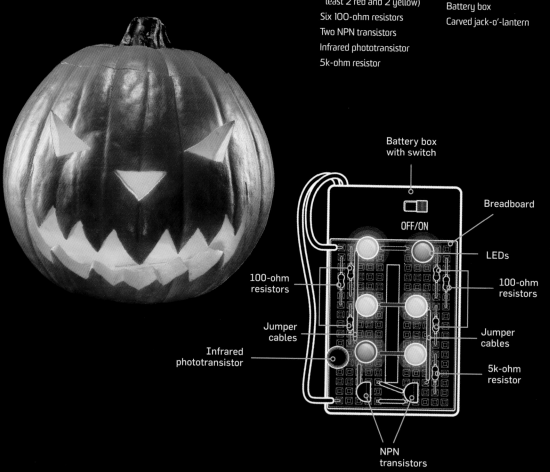

Battery box with switch

OFF/ON

Breadboard

LEDs

100-ohm resistors

100-ohm resistors

Jumper cables

Jumper cables

Infrared phototransistor

5k-ohm resistor

NPN transistors

STEP 1 Assemble the components and jumper wires on the breadboard according to the circuitry diagram you see at left. The LEDs, NPN transistors, and phototransistor (which looks like an LED with a black lens) are polarized, meaning the circuit won't work if you install them backward. For the four LEDs positioned nearest the switch, place their flat sides facing away from the switch. The flat sides of the other LEDs and the phototransistor should face toward it.

STEP 2 Trim the leads and jumper wires with the wire cutters as you go so everything is flush against the breadboard face.

STEP 3 Peel the film off the adhesive on the back of the breadboard and stick it to the battery box, right below the switch.

STEP 4 Connect the red battery-box wire to the breadboard corner nearest and left of the switch, and the black wire to the far left corner.

STEP 5 Load the batteries into the box and turn on the switch. If the LEDs don't come on right away, try covering the phototransistor with your thumb, or moving the breadboard into a dark room. (The sensor responds to sunlight and bright incandescent bulbs, but not to LEDs or fluorescent lights.)

STEP 6 Set the project inside your carved jack-o'-lantern and place it on a porch or windowsill. If your carving is fairly open and admits a lot of natural light into the pumpkin, the phototransistor should easily detect when the sun sets. But if your pumpkin is dark inside, you might need to leave the lid off to prevent the LEDs from turning on early in the day.

STEP 7 You can adjust the circuit's light sensitivity by replacing the 5k-ohm resistor. Swapping it for a stronger resistor (up to 10k-ohms) creates a circuit that turns on only at brighter light levels. A weaker resistor (down to 1k-ohm) makes a circuit that can turn on in dimmer conditions.

037 Blow Safer Smoke Rings

No need to inhale— blow these from a bottle.

You don't have to take up bad habits to blow smoke rings. A balloon, an incense stick, and a plastic bottle can do it for you. The balloon propels puffs of smoke through the bottle's mouth, creating picture-perfect smoke rings.

MATERIALS
Scissors
16-ounce (475-ml) plastic bottle
Balloon
Incense stick
Match or lighter

STEP 1 Use scissors to cut off the bottom of a dry, empty plastic bottle, taking care not to slice your skin on the sharp plastic.

STEP 2 Cut off and discard the narrow mouth of a balloon. Carefully stretch the balloon over the bottom of the bottle until it's taut.

STEP 3 Light an incense stick with a match or lighter, and then blow it out. Hold the smoky end inside the bottle, covering the open mouth of the bottle with your hand.

STEP 4 Once the bottle has filled with smoke, remove the stick. Lightly tap on the balloon end of the bottle to produce a smoke ring.

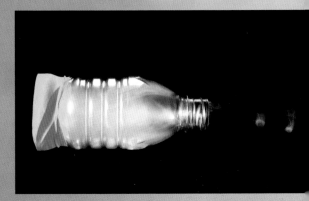

038 Wield a Potato Launcher

Potatoes—they're not just for the dinner table. Build this cannon and see spuds fly.

COST	$$
TIME	☺ ☺ ☺
EASY	● ● ● ○ ○ HARD

MATERIALS

2 feet (60 cm) of 16-gauge insulated wire

Wire strippers

BBQ igniter

Soldering iron and solder

Various PVC parts (see diagram below)

PVC primer

PVC pipe cement

Drill

Two 8-by-2½-inch (20-by-6.35-cm) machine screws

Leather gloves

Electrical tape

Hair spray

Potatoes

STEP 1 Cut the insulated wire in half and strip back a bit of the ends of each piece.

STEP 2 Find the fine wire near the igniter button's lip. Twist this wire's end with one stripped insulated wire; solder them together. Secure with electrical tape.

STEP 3 Locate the igniter's main wire near the base. Cut it, leaving about 2 inches (5 cm) at the plug end. Strip, twist, and solder the end with the other insulated wire.

STEP 4 Prime the adapter, coupler, combustion chamber, and bushing. (Don't get primer on the threads.)

STEP 5 Immediately apply pipe cement to the parts of the adapter, coupler, combustion chamber, and bushing that will fit together. Cement the coupler and bushing to the combustion chamber, and the adapter to the coupler.

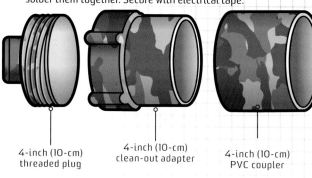

BBQ igniter

Machine screws

10-inch- (25-cm-) long, 4-inch (10-cm) PVC combustion chamber

4-inch (10-cm) threaded plug

4-inch (10-cm) clean-out adapter

4-inch (10-cm) PVC coupler

THE ARTILLERY-GRADE PUMPKIN GUN

YOU BUILT WHAT?!

Gary Arold and John Gill's favorite pastime is sending pumpkins flying. They welded two huge propane tanks onto a platform, connected by a T-shaped steel pipe that extends into a barrel, with an external air compressor that connects the first tank with a rubber hose. Yanking on the lever opens a butterfly valve and pummels the payload with pressurized air, shooting the pumpkin at up to 600 miles per hour (965 km/h).

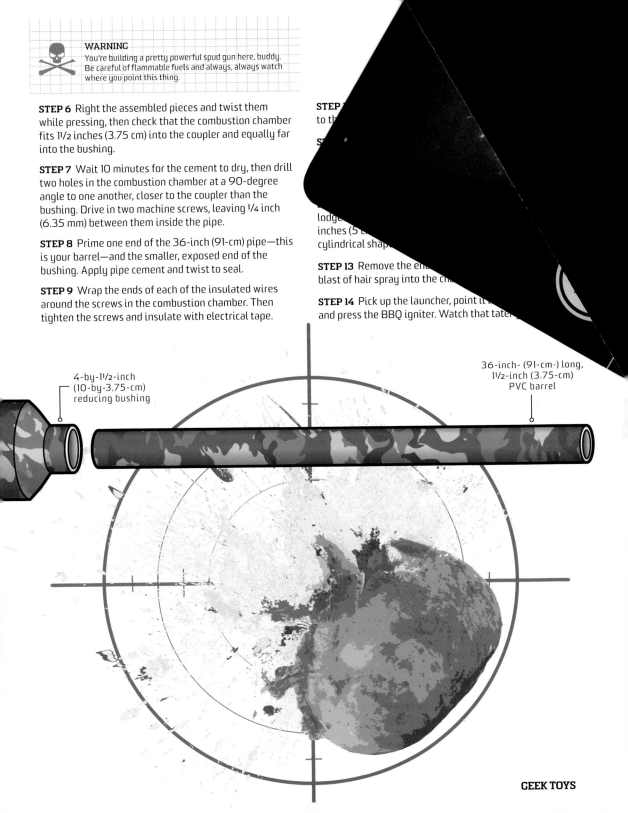

STEP 6 Right the assembled pieces and twist them while pressing, then check that the combustion chamber fits 1½ inches (3.75 cm) into the coupler and equally far into the bushing.

STEP 7 Wait 10 minutes for the cement to dry, then drill two holes in the combustion chamber at a 90-degree angle to one another, closer to the coupler than the bushing. Drive in two machine screws, leaving ¼ inch (6.35 mm) between them inside the pipe.

STEP 8 Prime one end of the 36-inch (91-cm) pipe—this is your barrel—and the smaller, exposed end of the bushing. Apply pipe cement and twist to seal.

STEP 9 Wrap the ends of each of the insulated wires around the screws in the combustion chamber. Then tighten the screws and insulate with electrical tape.

STEP to th

S

lodge inches (5 cylindrical shap

STEP 13 Remove the en blast of hair spray into the ch

STEP 14 Pick up the launcher, point it and press the BBQ igniter. Watch that tater

4-by-1½-inch (10-by-3.75-cm) reducing bushing

36-inch- (91-cm-) long, 1½-inch (3.75-cm) PVC barrel

GEEK TOYS

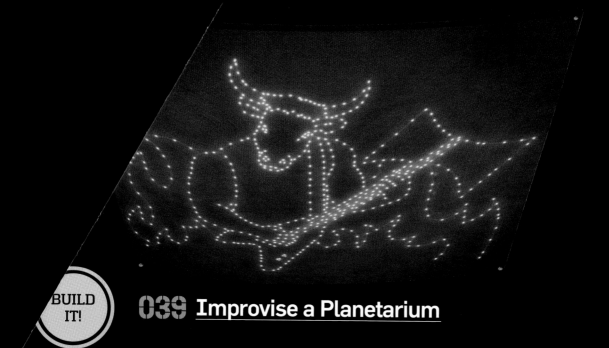

039 <u>Improvise a Planetarium</u>

Gaze at a starfield featuring twinkling constellations of your own devising.

COST	$$
TIME	☺ ☺ ☺
EASY ● ● ● ● ○ HARD	

MATERIALS

LilyPad Arduino

Breakout board

USB cable

Sewing needle and thread

Velcro

Two same-size pieces of black fabric

Conductive thread

Single-stranded wire

Wire strippers

Soldering iron and solder

Six LEDs

Scissors

Fiber optic filament

Electrical tape

3.7-volt polymer lithium ion battery and a mini USB charger for them

Small clear beads

Hot-glue gun

STEP 1 Connect your LilyPad Arduino to your computer using a breakout board and a USB cable. Then load it up with the code at popsci.com/thebigbookofhacks.

STEP 2 Sew Velcro around the edges of the fabric pieces, and sew the LilyPad Arduino near the edge of one fabric piece using conductive thread.

STEP 3 Strip the wire and make small loops. Solder the loops to the six LEDs' connectors, making "buttons."

STEP 4 Create a pattern and print it out in a size to fill your ceiling. Tape it onto the other piece of fabric—not the one you attached the LilyPad Arduino to.

STEP 5 Look at your pattern and decide where you'll need the most fiber-optic bundles. Space the LEDs so the filaments can extend from them to fill the pattern.

STEP 6 Sew the buttons onto the fabric piece that you sewed the LilyPad Arduino to, connecting each LED to one of the LilyPad Arduino terminals with conductive thread. Use terminals 3, 5, 6, 9, 10, and 11.

STEP 7 Cut fiber-optic filaments into varying lengths and gather them into six bundles of 10 to 20 strands. Tape the ends of the filaments in each bundle together.

STEP 8 Attach the battery to the LilyPad Arduino; each LED will light up. Then use electrical tape to secure the filament bundles over the LEDs and to the fabric.

STEP 9 Thread the filaments through the second piece of fabric, following the pattern. It helps to use a small, sharp tool to poke holes for the filaments. When finished, remove the pattern.

STEP 10 Slide a clear bead onto each filament and hot-glue it on the underside of the fabric. Trim the filament.

STEP 11 Use the Velcro to connect the fabric pieces together with the filaments in between them. Hang it up with small nails or hooks, lean back, and admire your new starry, starry night.

040 Put on a Liquid Light Show

Project extreme grooviness with this simple psychedelic setup.

MATERIALS

Scissors

Cardboard sheet

Overhead projector with bottom lighting

Two thin, round glass nesting bowls

White wall or sheet

Water

Water-based dye

Mineral oil

Oil-based dye

Eyedropper

White wall or screen

STEP 1 Measure and cut the cardboard sheet so that it fits over the projector base. Cut a hole in its center that's slightly smaller than the small glass bowl.

STEP 2 Place the cardboard on the projector surface. (It will mask the bowls' edges and keep your hands from blocking the display.)

STEP 3 Position the projector so that the light shining through the cutout completely fills your target screen and the edges aren't visible.

STEP 4 Add just enough water-based dye, such as food coloring, to a glass of water to produce a light tint.

STEP 5 Place the larger glass bowl on the projector surface face up, so it's centered over the cutout. Pour the colored water in it so that its bottom is covered.

STEP 6 Combine mineral oil with oil-based dye in a separate container, and fill an eyedropper with it.

STEP 7 Drop small amounts of colored oil into the water with the eyedropper.

STEP 8 Place the small glass bowl inside the large bowl. The water and oil mixture should just fill the space between the two bowls.

STEP 9 To start the light show, turn on the projector (and some psychedelic tunes), aim it at a white wall or screen, and move the bowls gently. Rotate them to swirl the liquids, or lift and lower them to move the image in and out of focus.

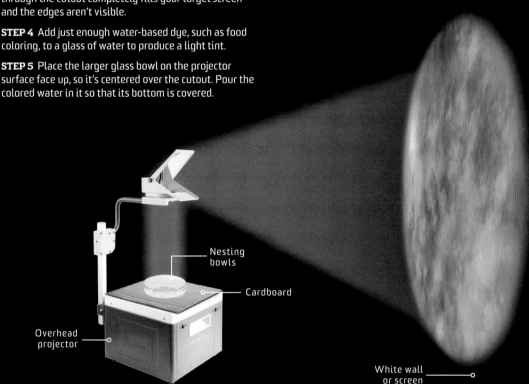

Nesting bowls

Cardboard

Overhead projector

White wall or screen

041 Jam Out to a Sound-Reactive Light Box

Watch beats blink in time with a slick-looking LED display.

COST $$
TIME ☺☺
EASY ● ● ● ○ ○ HARD

MATERIALS

Ruler	Fine sandpaper
Sheet of 3-mm Plexiglas	Six white 5-mm LEDs
Table saw	Hot-glue gun
Drill with a glass bit	TIP31 transistor
Audio cable	Electrical wire
18-volt adapter	Soldering iron and solder

STEP 1 To make the box, measure the Plexiglas into four 6-by-2-inch (15-by-4.7-cm) pieces and two 2-by-2-inch (5-by-5-cm) pieces. Cut them with a table saw outfitted with a plastic-cutting blade.

STEP 2 Drill two holes near a corner in one of the long pieces: one for the audio cable that will go to a stereo and one that's large enough to fit the plug on the adapter cord. Go lightly or the Plexiglas may break.

STEP 3 Using a circular motion, sand both sides of the pieces and the surfaces of the LED bulbs to get a cloudy, frosted look.

STEP 4 Hot-glue three of the rectangular panels together along their long edges, then glue the square pieces to the ends. Sand the joints after the glue dries.

STEP 5 Pull the audio cable through one of the box's holes and peel back the plastic to expose its wires on the inside of the box.

STEP 6 Wire the electronics according to the circuitry diagram. If you want more LEDs, buy an adapter that provides each LED with 3 volts.

STEP 7 Put the circuit in the box. Pull the adapter plug through the hole in the box, then glue it in place.

STEP 8 Glue the last Plexiglas piece onto the box. Plug the audio cable into your stereo's speaker output and plug the adapter into a power outlet.

STEP 9 Pick a song, and see it in lights.

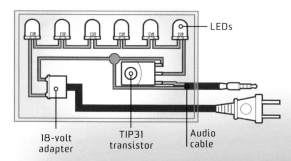

LEDs

18-volt adapter · TIP31 transistor · Audio cable

042 Wave an LED Lighter at a Concert

Power ballads sound even more epic with this lighter mod.

MATERIALS

Dead lighter with absolutely no fluid inside

Pliers

Hacksaw

Soldering iron and solder

3-volt LED

Electrical wire

Two AAA batteries

Aluminum-foil duct tape

Superglue

STEP 1 Check to make sure your lighter is empty. If not, hold down the lever until the lighter fluid evaporates.

STEP 2 Using the pliers, pry off the metal shield at the top of the dead lighter. Carefully remove the striker wheel, fuel lever, spring, and fuel valve inside; set aside.

STEP 3 Cut ¼ inch (6.35 mm) off the bottom of the lighter with the hacksaw. Pry out the plastic divider.

STEP 4 In the middle of the metal shield's underside, create a dent with your pliers—this will be a contact point for the switch.

STEP 5 Solder the LED's negative lead to the shield near the dent and the positive lead to a piece of electrical wire 1 inch (2.5 cm) in length.

STEP 6 Solder a piece of wire 1 inch (2.5 cm) in length to the underside of the metal part of the fuel lever.

STEP 7 Put the spring and fuel lever inside the lighter. Reinsert the metal shield and thread the long wire attached to the LED through the flint tube.

STEP 8 Line the batteries up with opposite polarities next to each other, then tape a piece of stripped wire across them using aluminum-foil duct tape.

STEP 9 Follow the circuitry diagram, connecting the LED and fuel lever's wires to the batteries with aluminum-foil duct tape.

STEP 10 Slide the batteries inside and glue the bottom back on. It's slow-jam time.

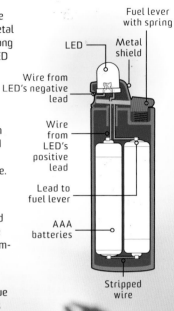

Fuel lever with spring

LED

Metal shield

Wire from LED's negative lead

Wire from LED's positive lead

Lead to fuel lever

AAA batteries

Stripped wire

---

5 MINUTE PROJECT

043 Party with an LED Glow Stick

STEP 1 Using tape, attach a 3-volt LED's longer lead to a coin battery's positive side and its shorter lead to the negative side.

STEP 2 Disassemble the ballpoint pen. Discard everything but the pen tube.

STEP 3 Place the LED into the tube and tape the battery in place. Dance.

044 An LED-Lit Disco Dance Floor

When dance fever hit MIT, students built a computer-controlled, LED-lit disco floor.

A group of undergrads at the Massachusetts Institute of Technology took on a challenge more daunting than classwork: disco. Before a dorm party, Mike Anderson, Grant Elliott, Schuyler Senft-Grupp, and Scott Torborg worked night and day for a week to build a computer-controlled, pixelated dance floor out of 1-by-4-foot (30-by-120-cm) boards, LEDs, tinfoil, paper towels, and old computer parts. The result would make Travolta weep with joy.

Each of the 512 pixels contains three LEDs pointed down at a square of paper towel that sits in a larger piece of foil. The foil reflects the light up through the plastic floor, while the paper towel mutes its glow. (LEDs stay cool, so the towels won't ignite.) A computer controls each pixel individually, and the open-source software generates 25 disco-tastic patterns, enabling DJs to match the light show to the music they're playing—and code-savvy disco fans to add new light patterns. What's more, by varying the intensity of each bulb, the students can blend light from the red, green, and blue LEDs housed in each pixel to produce any color. And should the party get extra wild (and with a dance floor like this, it will), the platform's wooden frame and thick layer of Lexan plastic make it nearly indestructible.

After earning minor fame at MIT (one of the inventors scored dates because of his uncanny soldering skills), the students began upgrading the floor. Their latest model has a prebuilt circuit board and instructions, so anyone can turn a basement into a discotheque.

HOW GEEKS GET DOWN
Everyone who actually worked on the floor and isn't a professional model, raise your hand.

045 Make a Sonic Tunnel of Fire

COST	$$
TIME	🕐 🕐 🕐
EASY ● ● ● ○ ○ HARD	

See your favorite song burst into flame with this classic Rubens' tube.

This may be one of the best bad ideas of all time, and we have physicist Heinrich Rubens to thank for it: He found that if you make a sound at one end of a tube, you get a standing wave equivalent to the sound's wavelength inside the tube—and that the best way to demonstrate this principle is with waves of flame synced with music. Right on, Heinrich.

MATERIALS

4-inch (10-cm) ventilation ducting
Nail
Drill
Duct tape
Latex sheets
Scissors
Two hose splicers

Epoxy putty
Hose T-connector
Propane tank
Teflon tape
Screws for your brackets
Two 4-inch (10-cm) brackets
Scrap wood
Media player and speakers

STEP 1 Leaving 4 inches (10 cm) at either end, mark off every ½ inch (1.25 cm) down the length of your ducting. (Do it on the side without the seam.)

STEP 2 Gently tap a nail at each interval, creating divots that will be easy to drill. Then drill through each resulting depression.

STEP 3 Wrap a strip of duct tape around each end of the tube. Then cut two squares of latex and tape them across both ends of the tube, creating an airtight seal.

STEP 4 Select two spots for fuel entry in the seam, each about one-third of the way across the tube. Tap the locations with a nail to create depressions, then drill two holes large enough to accommodate your hose splicers.

STEP 5 Install the hose splicers, securing the edges around the fuel entry holes with epoxy putty.

STEP 6 Attach the T-connector to the propane nozzle, then the hose splicers to the T-connector. Wrap the ends of the all the components with Teflon tape.

STEP 7 Using screws, attach brackets to scrap wood to make a stand. Then mount the tube onto it.

STEP 8 To use, tape all holes to create a seal. Then pump the tube full of propane for 2 minutes.

STEP 9 Remove the tape and test the tube by lighting one hole. If the flames are 1 inch (2.5 cm) high, it's ready.

STEP 10 Place a speaker as close as possible to one end of the tube (without actually touching the end's latex seal). Hit play, and watch those sound waves ignite.

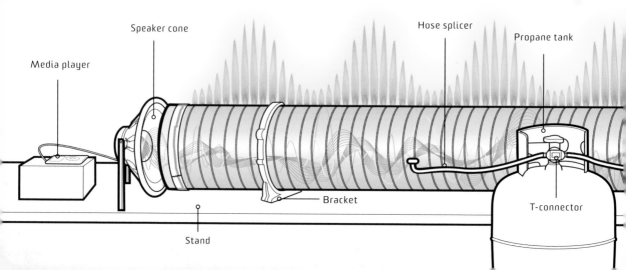

Media player

Speaker cone

Hose splicer

Propane tank

Bracket

T-connector

Stand

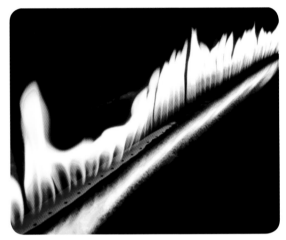

THE RUBENS TUBE IN ACTION
Why just listen to "Light My Fire" when you can listen to it *and* see its sound wave expressed in real flames?

YOU BUILT WHAT?!

SHOOT A PROPANE-POWERED FIREGUN

Fire enthusiasts have long used propane "poofers" to shoot huge fireballs for special effects. But for this particular model, *PopSci* contributor Vin Marshall tried a new approach that incorporates striking visual elements as well as a bit of science. It took 40 crazed hours of near-nonstop parts acquisition, construction, and testing in a friend's partially collapsed warehouse to finish the poofer. Why would someone go to all that trouble just to shoot fireballs over the Philadelphia skyline? The better question is, why not?

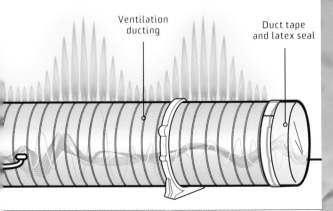

Ventilation ducting

Duct tape and latex seal

046 Turn Your Campfire Green

STEP 1 Pour ¼ inch (6.35 mm) of copper sulfate into a small paper cup. (You can use common tree-root killers, which contain copper sulfate.)

STEP 2 Melt old candle stubs in a double boiler, and pour the wax into the cup over the copper sulfate.

STEP 3 Stir the copper sulfate and wax together until the chemical is coated.

STEP 4 After it cools, peel off the sides of the paper cup.

STEP 5 When you're done cooking at your campsite, throw the copper-sulfate-infused wax into the hottest part of the fire and watch the green flames start licking.

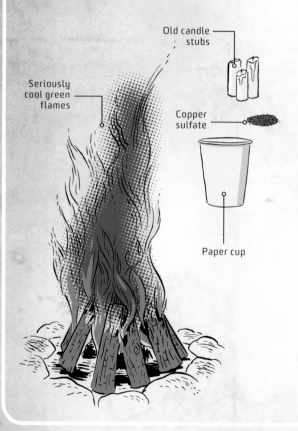

Old candle stubs

Seriously cool green flames

Copper sulfate

Paper cup

047 Hold a Flaming Ball in Your Bare Hand

STEP 1 Use scissors to cut away a 2-by-5-inch (5-by-12.5-cm) strip of cloth from an old T-shirt. Roll the cloth into a ball.

STEP 2 Thread a needle with about 2 feet (60 cm) of sewing thread.

STEP 3 Push the needle all the way through the fabric ball, securing the loose end of the fabric strip.

STEP 4 Wind the thread around the ball many, many times. When you're almost out of thread, pull the needle through an existing loop of thread, then tie it off and remove the needle.

STEP 5 Soak the ball in isopropyl alcohol; squeeze out any excess that may drip onto your hands.

STEP 6 Wash any fluid off your hands, light up your fireball, and let it blaze around in your hand. (The less-adventurous can put on heat-resistant gloves.)

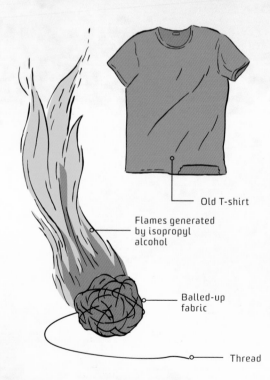

Old T-shirt

Flames generated by isopropyl alcohol

Balled-up fabric

Thread

048 Set Off a Spinning Fire Tornado

STEP 1 In the center of a lazy Susan, mold clay into a base for a fireproof bowl. Press the bowl into the clay, and place pieces of modeling clay along the edges of the lazy Susan.

STEP 2 Measure the lazy Susan's diameter and roll a piece of screen into a 36-inch- (90-cm-) high cylinder of the same diameter. Use straight pins to secure the cylindrical shape.

STEP 3 Pour kerosene onto a rag; place it in the bowl.

STEP 4 With a fire extinguisher nearby, carefully ignite the rag in the small bowl with a long-handled lighter, then place the screen cylinder over the lazy Susan, pressing it into the pieces of modeling clay.

STEP 5 Give the lazy Susan a whirl. Stand back and watch devious, fiery nature at work.

STEP 6 To extinguish, don heat-resistant gloves, wait for the lazy Susan to slow, and remove the screen. Then snuff out the small bowl with a larger fireproof bowl.

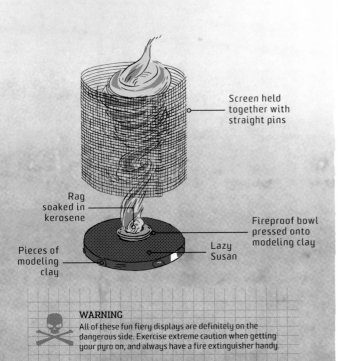

Screen held together with straight pins

Rag soaked in kerosene

Fireproof bowl pressed onto modeling clay

Pieces of modeling clay

Lazy Susan

WARNING
All of these fun fiery displays are definitely on the dangerous side. Exercise extreme caution when getting your pyro on, and always have a fire extinguisher handy.

049 Ignite a Homemade Sparkler

STEP 1 Using a rotary tool, make a small hole into the top of a medicine bottle's lid.

STEP 2 Fill the bottle about one-fourth of the way with water and add 1 teaspoon of salt.

STEP 3 Add 1 tablespoon each of powdered dishwashing detergent and baking soda, and then put the lid on.

STEP 4 Carefully hold the flame of a lighter or match over the hole until the gas you've just created ignites, firing your sparkler. Celebrate.

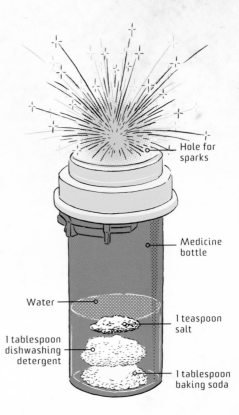

Hole for sparks

Medicine bottle

Water

1 teaspoon salt

1 tablespoon dishwashing detergent

1 tablespoon baking soda

050 Wreak Havoc with a Squirt Gun

Water guns have never been more fun. No, really, we mean it.

This wet weapon is way more than a squirt gun; it's a powerful water cannon that shoots more than 1 quart (950 ml) of water up to 50 feet (15 m) in less than 10 seconds. But don't be a jerk. Keep your H2O gun's spray away from other people's faces.

COST	$$
TIME	☺ ☺
EASY	● ● ○ ○ ○ HARD

MATERIALS

Drill

Various PVC parts (see diagram below)

PVC cement

Waterproof grease

Bucket of water

3/4-inch (2-cm) PVC T-connector

2 feet (60 cm) of 3/4-inch (2-cm) PVC pipe

2-inch (5-cm) PVC cap (piston guide)

2 feet (60 cm) of 2-inch (5-cm) PVC pipe

STEP 1 Use a drill to make a 1/4-inch (6.35-mm) hole in the center of one 2-inch (5-cm) cap and a 1 1/4-inch (3-cm) hole in the center of the second cap. The first is your nozzle; the second is the piston guide.

STEP 2 Glue the T-connector to the small pipe with PVC cement. When gluing, immediately insert the pipe into the fitting and turn it to distribute the solvent evenly. Hold the joint for about 30 seconds to make sure it sets; wipe off excess glue with a rag.

STEP 3 Slide the piston guide over the small pipe with the open end facing away from the T-connector.

STEP 4 Glue the reducer bushing to the small pipe's end, the coupler to the reducer, and the 1 1/4-inch (3-cm) pipe to the coupler with the PVC cement.

STEP 5 Slide the O-ring over the small 1 1/4-inch (3-cm) pipe and glue the 1 1/4-inch (3-cm) PVC cap to the pipe.

STEP 6 Glue the nozzle onto the big pipe. Let the apparatus dry.

STEP 7 Apply a small glob of waterproof grease to the inside of the 2-inch (5-cm) PVC pipe. Insert the piston into the body and push and pull a few times to evenly spread the goop. When it seems sufficiently lubricated, firmly push the piston guide onto the body.

STEP 8 To load, use it like a giant syringe: Compress the handle and stick the huge squirt gun's end into a bucket of water, then pull up on the T-connector to draw water into the pipe.

STEP 9 Super-soak somebody near you.

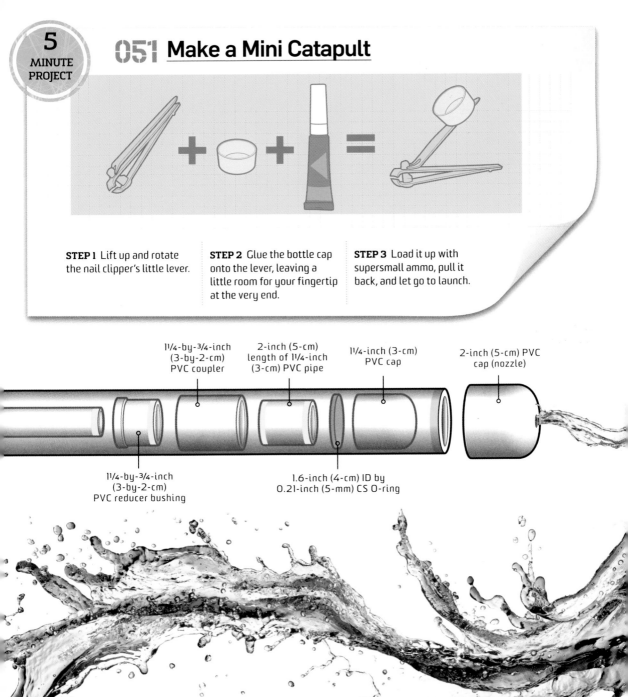

051 Make a Mini Catapult

STEP 1 Lift up and rotate the nail clipper's little lever.

STEP 2 Glue the bottle cap onto the lever, leaving a little room for your fingertip at the very end.

STEP 3 Load it up with supersmall ammo, pull it back, and let go to launch.

1¼-by-¾-inch (3-by-2-cm) PVC coupler

2-inch (5-cm) length of 1¼-inch (3-cm) PVC pipe

1¼-inch (3-cm) PVC cap

2-inch (5-cm) PVC cap (nozzle)

1¼-by-¾-inch (3-by-2-cm) PVC reducer bushing

1.6-inch (4-cm) ID by 0.21-inch (5-mm) CS O-ring

WARNING
This thing can really let loose, so be cautious about spraying it at living creatures. (Zombies, though, you can totally let have it.)

GEEK TOYS

052 Play with a Bike-Part Spirograph

Those mathy whirls of color from your childhood can be yours all over again.

MATERIALS

Bike chain	Superglue
Thin plywood	Paper
Tape	An assortment of chain rings
Pen	Colored pens
Jigsaw	

STEP 1 Arrange a bike chain on the plywood in a perfect circle and tape it down. Faithfully trace around the chain's outer rim, being careful not to move it.

STEP 2 Using a jigsaw, cut out the circle and discard it. Line up the chain so that it fits inside the circular hole.

STEP 3 Use superglue to secure the chain all the way around the inner edge of the hole in the plywood. Let this dry overnight.

STEP 4 Place the plywood frame over paper. Put a chain ring on the paper and insert a colored pen through one of its bolt holes to make contact with the paper.

STEP 5 Keeping your pen in the chain ring's bolt hole, trace around the bike chain to lay down an awesome design. Experiment with chain rings that have different numbers of teeth for patterns of varying complexity.

053 Turn a Rainy Day into Art

Sidewalk art that puts chalk to shame.

MATERIALS

Cardstock
Clear spray paint
Aerosol antiperspirant

STEP 1 Cut a stencil out of cardstock and place it on the sidewalk. Spray with clear paint.

STEP 2 While the clear coat is still wet, mist with the aerosol antiperspirant.

STEP 3 Remove the stencil and let the paint dry for about an hour. Wait for rain to reveal your art—or just use a garden hose to bring it into view.

054 Set Up a Turntable Zoetrope

COST	$$	
TIME	🕐🕐	
EASY	● ● ○ ○ ○	HARD

See LEGOs come to life with this classic animation trick.

The world saw its first modern zoetrope in 1833, and since its invention the device has paved the way to cinema as we know it. This playful update uses a strobe light to interrupt your view of a series of still objects as they go around and around on a record player—causing your eye to perceive them as if they were in motion. It's not 1833 anymore, but the effect is still pretty mind-boggling.

MATERIALS

Protractor	Superglue
A record to sacrifice	Record player
18 LEGO miniature figures	Strobe light

STEP 1 Using the protractor, measure and draw lines every 20 degrees on the sacrificial record. Space out the LEGO figures around the edge of the record according to these marks, and glue them down.

STEP 2 Put the LEGO figures in positions of your choosing—think about creating the look of continuous motion by carefully changing each one's position incrementally from that of the one before it.

STEP 3 Set the record player to 33⅓ RPM.

STEP 4 Adjust your strobe light to flash ten times per second and position it so that it's pointed at the zoetrope at close range.

STEP 5 Turn out the lights, turn on the record player and the strobe, and watch those LEGO figurines start dancing, running, battling, or doing whatever you want them to do.

055 Fold a Paper Robot with an Arduino Brain

Origami, the ancient art of paper folding, also shows up in modern science and engineering—even in robotics projects, like the folded-up 'bot you see here. This one boasts an Arduino brain, which commands the robot to roll over the floor, sticking to dark surfaces, based on the amount of reflected light it detects.

COST	$$
TIME	☺ ☺ ☺
EASY ● ● ● ○ HARD	

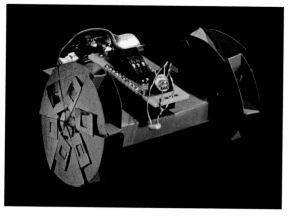

MATERIALS

Custom daughter board

Three sheets 8½-by-11-inch (21.5-by-28-cm) cardstock

Color printer

Craft knife

Straight edge

Two continuous-rotation servos

3.3-volt/8MHz Arduino Pro Mini

30 straight male breakaway headers

6 right-angle male breakaway headers

30 female headers

Switch

Connector for battery

1.8k-ohm resistor

Mini light sensor

White 5mm LED

3.3-volt FTDI Basic Breakout board

3.7-volt, 130mAh IS 25-40C Li-poly battery

Li-poly battery charger

STEP 1 Visit www.popsci.com/bigbookofhacks to download the .grb files for the custom daughter board, the circuit board that will plug into the Arduino. Send these files to a custom-PCB printer.

STEP 2 Download the templates for the 'bot's body and wheels and print them in color onto the cardstock. Cut along the red lines, using a straight edge to guide your craft knife. It helps to cut out the overall shapes first, then cut the details.

STEP 3 Starting with the body, make mountain folds along the blue lines and valley folds along the green ones. Do the same on the wheel cutouts.

STEP 4 To assemble the first wheel, hook the small tab at one end of the long cardstock strip through the slit at the strip's other end, making a loop with six orange-wedge-shaped segments.

STEP 5 Fold one slender connector down so it is flat against the inside of the segment below it, which will bring the segment above immediately next to the first segment. Feed the tabs through the slits on the sides to connect the two segments.

STEP 6 Continue until all the segments are joined, then repeat with the second long cardstock strip to make the second wheel. Slide both arms of the continuous servo into two opposite cutouts at the center of each wheel.

3   4   5   6   7   8

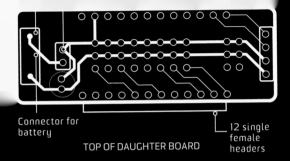

Connector for battery

TOP OF DAUGHTER BOARD

12 single female headers

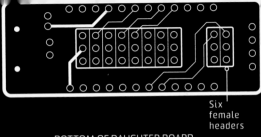

Six female headers

BOTTOM OF DAUGHTER BOARD

STEP 7 To prepare the Arduino, solder six male single pins into the programming header at the board's top. Then solder 12 single male headers along each side on the board's bottom.

STEP 8 To prepare the daughter board, solder battery-connector wires to the positive and negative terminals on the board's top. Then solder three right-angle male headers into rows 9 and 6 on the daughter board's bottom and six female headers into its ANLG holes. (This is where the LED, light sensor, and resistor will go.)

STEP 9 Solder one end of the resistor to the light sensor, then connect the resistor and light sensor to the frontmost three female headers on the daughter board. Connect the LED to two female headers. Solder the switch to the board's bottom. Solder 12 single female headers along each side of the board's top.

STEP 10 Now your electronics are ready to go inside the origami body. Position the body cutout upside down so the valley folds face up, then place the Arduino in the central section of the longer strip, making sure the pins protrude through the holes on the other side. Fold the section shut over the Arduino, pushing the winged tabs through the slits.

STEP 11 Still focusing on the robot's body, rotate the three sections in the longer vertical strip so they are

all flush against the bottom of the longer horizontal strip. Slide the tabs of the two smallest servo paper segments into slots on the Arduino paper segment so all three segments are attached in a row. Place the rectangular parts of the servos into their segments so their shafts stick out through the paper cutouts and fold the segments shut.

STEP 12 Rotate the attached three segments so they overlay the top horizontal strip, again making sure the Arduino's pins protrude through the holes on the back side. Close the paper flap over the three sections and pull the paper tab through the slot.

STEP 13 To attach the wheels to the body, snap the double arms onto the servos. Then tightly attach the daughter board's female connectors to the Arduino's male pins that are piercing through the top piece of cardstock—the switch should be toward the robot's tail. Connect the servo wires to rows 9 and 6 on the daughter board.

STEP 14 Download the sample code at popscsi.com/thebigbookofhacks and upload it to the Arduino using the 3.3-volt FTDIO Basic Breakout board.

STEP 15 Place the battery between the daughter board and the paper, and plug it in. Your paper robot is ready to rock—or, rather, roll.

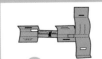

056 The Real Iron Man Suit

This homebuilt superhero suit looks as good as the silver-screen version.

Anthony Le has been a fan of Iron Man since he was a kid. When he heard that the comic-book superhero was hitting the big screen in 2008, he was inspired to build his own Iron Man suit. That version was more of a costume, but his next edition—finished just in time for the movie's sequel—edges much closer to the real thing. With its dent-proof exterior, motorized faceplate, and spinning mock Gatling gun, his take on the movie's War Machine suit could easily frighten a supervillain—not to mention kids in the theater.

To make the suit, Le—who is a fitness consultant by day—studied some concept sketches of the suit posted on the Internet. He focused on the War Machine suit, donned by Stark's buddy Jim Rhodes in *Iron Man 2*, in part because "it just looks more hardcore." He used thin, high-impact urethane for the armor, cutting it into plates and joining them with some 1,500 rivets and washers. He sculpted a clay helmet mold and then used a mix of liquid resin to create the final product. He added a replica of the machine gun on the suit's shoulder made of PVC pipes and other materials. But that was just cosmetic work. He also added a small servo motor that opens the faceplate, as in the movie, and built a gun out of pipes and a motor. LEDs in the eyes and chestplate further add to the illusion.

All the LEDs and the motors that drive the gun and the faceplate have their own batteries hidden within the suit's large frame. Inside the chestplate, Le added a hands-free button that activates the helmet. When the faceplate is open, he just stands up and points his arm forward, causing his chest to press against the button, triggering the servo motors in the helmet to close the mask. This, in turn, switches on the red LEDs set inside the eye openings, which are large enough for him to also see out of. To open the mask up again, he presses another button.

Le wore one of his suits to the Children's Hospital in Aurora, Colorado, to cheer up the kids, and the staff was so pleased they made him his own ID card. The name listed? Iron Man.

HARD TO MISS
The material Le used for the armor is thin but takes stress well. "You can throw it against the wall, and it won't even be damaged," he says. Le has a cult following among fans of the movie featuring Iron Man—he wore the suit to the theater to see *Iron Man 2*.

057 <u>Mix Magnetic Silly Putty</u>

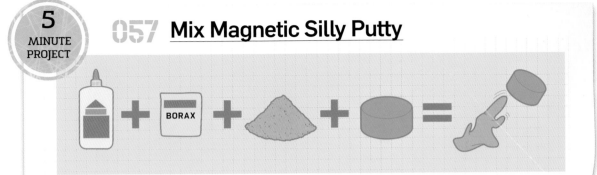

STEP 1 Mix 1 tablespoon of basic craft glue and 1 cup (240 ml) of water in a plastic bag, then add 1 tablespoon of borax. Squeeze to make the putty.

STEP 2 Wearing gloves and a face mask, spread out the putty and sprinkle about 2 tablespoons of iron oxide powder onto it. Work it in for about 5 minutes.

STEP 3 Introduce a magnet to your putty and watch it move and change shape.

058 <u>Cook Up Ferrofluid</u>

Believe it or not, this spiky stuff is a fluid. Put it on a magnet and it goes nuts.

MATERIALS

Syringe	Household ammonia
Ferric chloride solution	Oleic acid
Distilled water	Kerosene
Steel wool	Magnet
Coffee filter	

STEP 1 With a syringe, measure 10 ml of ferric chloride solution and 10 ml of distilled water into a container.

STEP 2 Add a small piece of steel wool. Stir or swirl the solution until it turns bright green, then filter it through a coffee filter.

STEP 3 Add 20 ml more ferric chloride solution to your filtered green solution. While stirring, add 150 ml of ammonia.

STEP 4 In a well-ventilated area, heat the solution to near boiling. While stirring, add 5 ml of oleic acid. Keep heating until the ammonia smell is gone (about an hour).

STEP 5 Let cool, and then add 100 ml of kerosene. Stir until the black color attaches to the kerosene.

STEP 6 Pour off and collect the kerosene layer in a bowl.

STEP 7 Put a magnet under the bowl. See the weird peaks rise

059 Build a Sled for Slinging Snowballs

Whether you make this from scratch or modify an existing sled, winter warfare will never be the same.

COST	$
TIME	☺☺
EASY	● ● ● ○ ○ HARD

Pieces of pine for the deck:
Six deck pieces measuring
1 by 4 by 24 inches
(2.5 by 10 by 60 cm)
Two deck-to-runner attachments
measuring 2 by 2 by 15 inch
(5 by 5 38 cm)

Pieces of pine for two runner/launchers:
Two 1-by-4-by-36-inch
(2.5-by-10-90-cm) runners
Two 1-by-4-by-24-inch
(2.5-by-10-60-cm) posts
Two 1-by-4-by-30-inch
(2.5-by-10-by-75-cm) braces
Two 1-by-4-by-4-inch
(2.5-by-10-by-10-cm) pads

One 1-by-4-by-24-inch
(2.5-by-10-by-60-cm) cross support

2-inch (5-cm) nails or deck screws

Optional: sled

1¼-inch (3.2-cm) nails

Four large screw eyes

7-by-4-inch (18-by-10-cm) piece of
leather or other sturdy material

Hole punch for grommets

Hammer

Mandrel and anvil

Five medium-size metal grommets

10 feet (3 m) latex rubber surgical tubing
(¼-inch/6.35-mm inside diameter,
5/16-inch/8-mm outside diameter,
1/32-inch/0.8-mm wall)

4 feet (1.2 m) rope

Drill

Screwdriver

STEP 1 There are two main parts to this project: the deck assembly and the runner/launcher assembly. It's easiest to build them separately and connect the pieces together at the end. Drawing A shows how the pieces of the deck assembly are arranged. Use 2-inch (5-cm) nails or deck screws to attach the runners to the deck-to-runner attachments and to the brace pads. Use 1¼-inch (3.2-cm) nails everywhere else.

STEP 2 Use Drawing B to build two runner/launchers. Then hold the runner/launchers in an upright

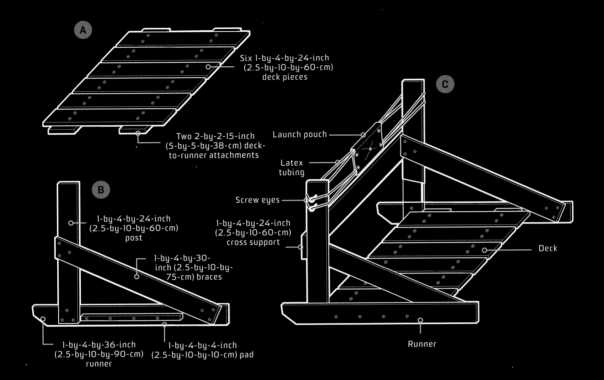

A Six 1-by-4-by-24-inch (2.5-by-10-by-60-cm) deck pieces

Two 2-by-2-15-inch (5-by-5-by-38-cm) deck-to-runner attachments

B 1-by-4-by-24-inch (2.5-by-10-by-60-cm) post

1-by-4-by-30-inch (2.5-by-10-by-75-cm) braces

1-by-4-by-36-inch (2.5-by-10-by-90-cm) runner

1-by-4-by-4-inch (2.5-by-10-by-10-cm) pad

C Launch pouch

Latex tubing

Screw eyes

1-by-4-by-24-inch (2.5-by-10-60-cm) cross support

Deck

Runner

position (having a friend help makes this easier) and nail them securely to the deck, following Drawing C to see how they fit together. Then skip to Step 4.

STEP 3 If you're attaching the launcher to a store-bought sled, you may be able to nail the posts and braces directly to its sides. If not, nail the runners to the sled's deck, one on each side and about 22 inches (56 cm) apart, to create a stable base.

STEP 4 Nail the posts and pads in parallel on each side of the base. The posts should be near the front of the sled, with the pads 18 inches (46 cm) behind. Then nail the braces in place so they connect the tops of the posts to the pads.

STEP 5 Hold the final cross support horizontally so it connects the two

posts, about halfway up each one, and nail in place. At the top of each post, twist two screw eyes into the outside edge in a vertical line, 2 inches (5 cm) apart.

STEP 6 To make a launch pouch out of the leather or fabric, puncture its four corners and the center with the grommet kit's hole punch. Insert the taller grommet half beneath each hole, facing up. Cover it with the other half, facing down. Position the kit's mandrel above the grommet with the anvil below. Then strike sharply with a hammer.

STEP 7 Insert the latex tubing through one of the upper screw eyes, and thread through the grommets on the pouch's upper edge. On the opposite side, run the tubing through the upper screw

eye, then the lower screw eye. Next, thread the tubing through the grommets on the pouch's lower edge and the final screw eye. Adjust the tubing so the tension on both sides is about equal. Tie securely and tape the ends so the knot doesn't loosen.

STEP 8 For a pulling handle, insert about a foot of rope through the central grommet and secure with a knot. The rest of the rope, threaded through a screw eye at the front of the sled, can form a towline.

STEP 9 Now you're ready to do winter battle. Load up the leather pouch with soft snow and let her rip! Note: Your deck will slide easily on icy ground, but less so on powder snow. You can wax the runners to make them slide easier.

060 Set Up a Pinball Game at Home

Because arcades can't stay open all the time, and you're out of quarters, anyway.

COST	$$
TIME	☺ ☺ ☺
EASY ● ● ● ○ ○ HARD	

MATERIALS

Saw
Peg-Board
2x4s
Wood glue
Nails
Hammer
Drill
1/2-inch (1.25-cm) drill bit
5/16-inch- (8-mm-) diameter hex bolt with nut
3/8-inch- (9.5-mm-) diameter spring

Scrap wood
3/4-inch (2-cm) drill bit
1/8-inch (3-mm) drill bit
Wood
Wood pegs
Rubber hose
PVC pipe elbows
Rubber bands
Foam
Bicycle bell
Marble

STEP 1 Use the saw to cut the Peg-Board to your desired size to form the base of the pinball machine.

STEP 2 Measure and cut 2x4s to make a frame. Glue and nail it into place.

STEP 3 Nail a 2x4 under the top of the frame to prop it up at a slight angle.

STEP 4 Drill a hole about 1/2 inch (1.25 cm) in diameter in the bottom frame piece's right corner. Insert the hex bolt and slide the spring over the bolt.

STEP 5 Attach the nut to secure the spring on the bolt. Pull the bolt down to compress the spring—this is the ball launcher. Place a piece of scrap wood alongside the bolt to create a guide for the ball.

061 Play DIY Skee-Ball

Go analog with a good old-fashioned Skee-Ball toss.

MATERIALS

Saw
1-inch (2.5-cm) particleboard
1/2-inch (1.25-cm) particleboard
1/4-inch (6.35-mm) particleboard

Wood glue
Nails
Rubber ball

STEP 5 Stand about 8 feet (2.4 m) away and toss the ball so that it rolls up the ramp—if it goes in the hole, that's one point. Any player who scores may continue until he or she misses; the first to score 15 points wins.

STEP 1 Use the saw to cut pieces of particleboard according to the measurements in the diagram.

STEP 2 On the board that serves as a ramp, trace your ball at one end to create a circular shape. Then add 1/4 inch (6.35 mm) all around this shape, and cut it out.

STEP 3 Build the game using nails and wood glue, making sure that the ramp fits against the back wall and that the opening is large enough for the ball to drop in.

STEP 4 Cut a hole into one side of the box so that you can reach in and grab the ball after scoring tosses.

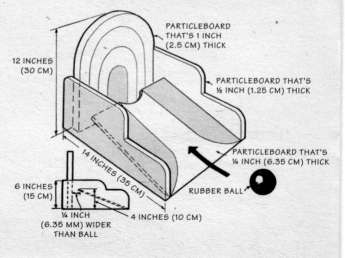

PARTICLEBOARD THAT'S 1 INCH (2.5 CM) THICK
PARTICLEBOARD THAT'S 1/2 INCH (1.25 CM) THICK
PARTICLEBOARD THAT'S 1/4 INCH (6.35 CM) THICK
12 INCHES (30 CM)
14 INCHES (35 CM)
6 INCHES (15 CM)
1/4 INCH (6.35 MM) WIDER THAN BALL
4 INCHES (10 CM)
RUBBER BALL

STEP 6 Toward the bottom of the game, drill through the side boards to create a 3/4-inch (1.9-cm) hole in each. Drill another hole next to the first so that the holes meet, making a long oval hole on each side of the board.

STEP 7 Mark the center of the oval hole on the top of the board, then drill into it from above with a 1/8-inch (3-mm) drill bit. Repeat on the other side.

STEP 8 Cut two pieces of wood into 1/8-inch- (3-mm) thick paddles of your desired length. Sand the edges.

STEP 9 Drill a 1/8-inch (3-mm) hole from the top near the ends of the paddles. Slip the paddles into the holes in the side boards.

STEP 10 Place a nail through the holes in the frame, through the paddles, and into the holes' bottom. Tap it with a hammer to secure them in place. Place a peg on either side of each paddle to restrict its range.

STEP 11 To create tunnels, nail down rubber hoses sliced in half lengthwise and PVC pipe elbows, and for good bumper action, extend rubber bands between pegs or nail scrap wood to the Peg-Board. If you want spinners, try foam X shapes secured loosely with a nail. Don't forget a ramp and bicycle bell.

STEP 12 Load up the launcher with a marble, pull back the bolt, and release it—let the game begin.

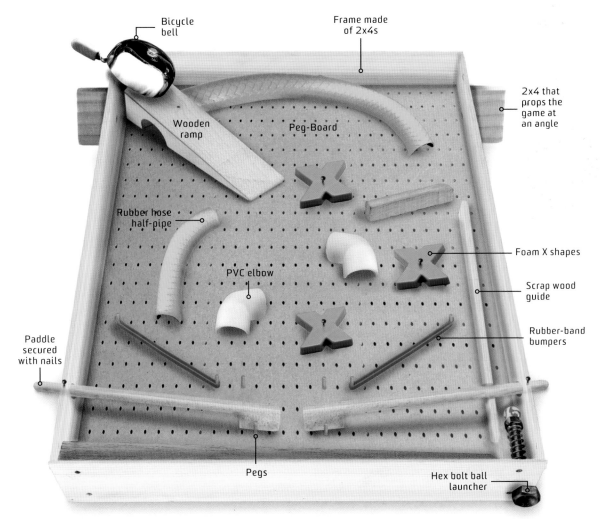

Bicycle bell

Frame made of 2x4s

2x4 that props the game at an angle

Wooden ramp

Peg-Board

Rubber hose half-pipe

Foam X shapes

PVC elbow

Scrap wood guide

Rubber-band bumpers

Paddle secured with nails

Pegs

Hex bolt ball launcher

062 Build a Mint-Tin Racer

STEP 1 Use a drill to make five holes into your tin: two on both of the tin's long sides and one in the top corner of the lid.

STEP 2 Measure and cut two wooden sticks so they are long enough to traverse the width of the mint tin with about ½ inch (1.25 cm) extra on either side.

STEP 3 Slide the axles through the holes in the side of the tin, and attach bottle-cap "wheels" to the sticks with hot glue.

STEP 4 To deck out your racer with a flag, insert a straw into the hole in the tin's top, and tape a triangular flag to the straw's top.

STEP 5 Detail your racer however you like.

063 Shake Up a Martini in a Mint Tin

STEP 1 Drill a hole into one end of the mint tin and insert a plastic nozzle. (You can buy these in bulk online or at home-improvement stores.)

STEP 2 Buy or fill two travel-size bottles: one with gin or vodka, one with vermouth.

STEP 3 Place the booze bottles, a paper cup, and an olive inside the tin.

STEP 4 When you need an emergency drink, remove all the tin's contents and pour the bottles into the tin.

STEP 5 Close the tin and shake it well.

STEP 6 Loosen the nozzle, pour into the cup, and garnish with the olive.

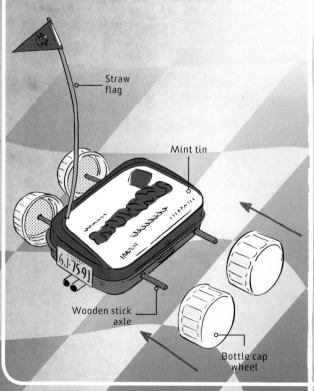

Straw flag

Mint tin

Wooden stick axle

Bottle cap wheel

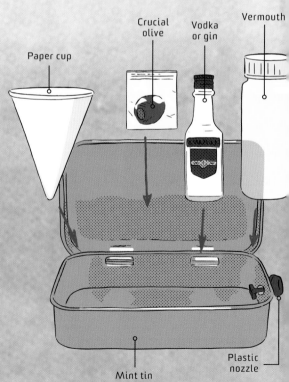

Crucial olive

Vodka or gin

Vermouth

Paper cup

Mint tin

Plastic nozzle

064 Strum a Mint-Tin Guitar

STEP 1 Position the tin so that its label is facing you. Then trace the stacked ends of three rulers onto the far right side to make a rectangle.

STEP 2 Using a drill, make a hole in the rectangle on the box's side, then cut out the rectangle outline with tin snips.

STEP 3 On the other side of the box, just below the lid's lip on the side, make three evenly spaced holes for the guitar strings. Thread the strings through and knot them off inside the box.

STEP 4 Remove the insides of a cheap ballpoint pen and cut the clear tube to about the width of your mint tin. Then cut it in half lengthwise. Make three notches in it for your guitar strings.

STEP 5 Use a hot-glue gun to glue the pen tube facedown onto the tin lid on the side where you've made holes for the strings.

STEP 6 Insert one ruler into the rectangular cutout so that it goes about halfway into the mint tin. Secure it with a hot-glue gun.

STEP 7 Cut a credit card to the ruler's width. Bend one edge up and glue it to the ruler about ½ inch (1.25 cm) from the ruler's end.

STEP 8 Cut the other two rulers down to 1 inch (2.5 cm) shorter than the exposed ruler. Glue them on top of the first ruler.

STEP 9 Drill holes for the eyebolts into the end of the bottom ruler. Insert and secure them with nuts on the ruler's bottom.

STEP 10 String the strings over the pen tube and tie them off around the eyebolts, and start strumming the hits.

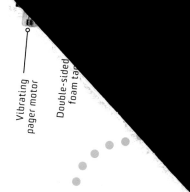

Vibrating pager motor

Double-sided foam ta...

scrap to make pockets in the...

STEP 4 Glue the felt down onto the foam. Trace and cut the pocket shapes out of the foam, too.

STEP 5 Assemble the seven beads into a triangle. Place a piece of copper wire along one side of the triangle; mark its length.

STEP 6 Use this measurement to fold the wire into a triangle shape with sides of equal length.

STEP 7 Cut a small-diameter copper rod to make a pool cue.

STEP 8 Rack 'em go wherever you go.

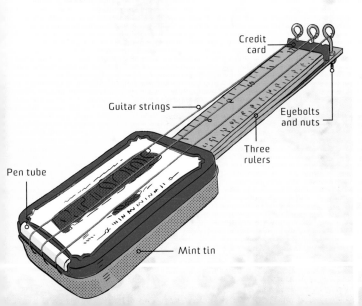

Credit card

Guitar strings

Eyebolts and nuts

Three rulers

Pen tube

Mint tin

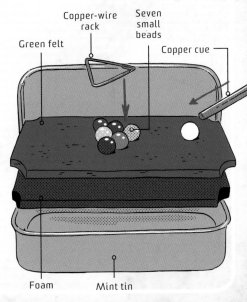

Copper-wire rack

Seven small beads

Green felt

Copper cue

Foam

Mint tin

GEEK TOYS

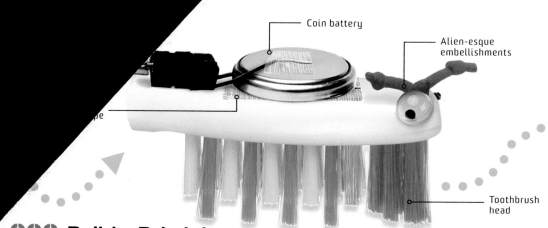

Coin battery

Alien-esque
embellishments

...pe

Toothbrush
head

066 Build a Bristlebot

**All the fun of a hyperactive pet,
minus all the annoying shedding.**

MATERIALS

Rotary tool

Toothbrush with angled bristles

Double-sided foam tape

Pager motor

Coin battery

Electrical tape

Glue

Decorations

STEP 1 Use a rotary tool to cut the head off a toothbrush. Apply double-sided foam tape to the back.

STEP 2 Salvage a pager motor with two wires and connect the wires to a coin battery, positive to positive and negative to negative. Tape the wires in place on the battery with electrical tape.

STEP 3 Glue on decorations, then attach the motor and battery to the foam tape on the toothbrush. Watch the robot merrily frolic.

067 Make a Mini Whirling Motor

**Send current up over a magnetic field
for some head-spinning results.**

MATERIALS

6 feet (2 m) of enameled
copper wire

C battery

Wire strippers

Electrical tape

Two safety pins

AA battery

Magnet

STEP 1 Wrap the wire several times around the C battery, leaving a few inches of excess at each end.

STEP 2 Slide the coil you just made off the battery. Pull one end of the excess wire through the coil, and then wrap it multiple times around the coil to hold it together. Leave about 1 inch (2.5 cm) of excess. Repeat with the other end of the wire.

STEP 3 Strip the bits of wire extending from the coil.

STEP 4 Using electrical tape, secure safety pins to both ends of the AA battery with the hinge ends sticking up.

STEP 5 Stick the coil's stripped ends through the holes in the hinge ends so the coil is centered over the battery.

STEP 6 Place the magnet on top of the battery, then give the coil a push and watch it spin.

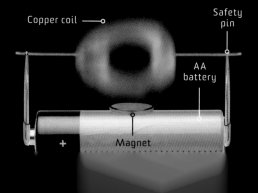

Copper coil

Safety
pin

AA
battery

+

Magnet

COST	$$
TIME	⏱ ⏱
EASY ● ● ○ ○ ○ HARD	

Turn this cruiser loose in your backyard on a sunny day and you'll make even the robotics experts at NASA jealous.

Using a couple of gear motors, solar panels, and leftover LEGOs, you can build a sunshine-powered robot that ambles over rocks and around trees. There is no software or sensors to control the steering, making this project the perfect introduction to solar-powered electronics.

MATERIALS

Assorted LEGO pieces (or the Turbo Quad Kit #31022)

Two gear motors

Two solar panels

Four wheels

Cyanoacrylate glue (found online or in hardware stores)

Hookup wire

Wire cutters

Soldering iron and solder

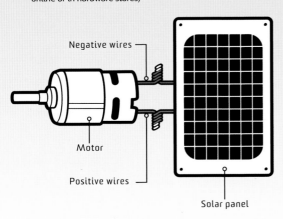

Negative wires

Motor

Positive wires

Solar panel

STEP 1 Use LEGOs to build the all-terrain vehicle of your dreams. The chassis must be able to support the gear motors, solar panels, and four wheels. (Note: Wheels 2 inches/5 cm or more in diameter are best for all-terrain excursions.)

STEP 2 Glue the rover chassis together, but not the wheels—they need to move!

STEP 3 Attach a gear motor to each wheel. You may need to glue the drum of the motor to the inner axis.

STEP 4 Mount the gear motors, one to a side, on the rear of the chassis using hookup wire. Loop wire around each motor, and carefully twist the ends together to secure everything to the rover's chassis.

STEP 5 Join the solar panels together at their edges with glue, or secure them together with a rubber band.

STEP 6 Solder one solar panel to the right rear gear motor. Solder the second solar panel to the left gear motor with the polarity reversed—wire the positive solar panel to the black motor wire, and then the negative solar panel to the red motor wire.

STEP 7 Release the rover into the wild. In bright sunlight, your bot should scoot along at about 2 feet (60 cm) per minute.

069 Make a Mini Hovercraft

According to old Hollywood prophecies, Marty McFly should have hopped out of Doc Brown's DeLorean on October 21, 2015, with his trusty hoverboard in hand. While fans watched the mythic date tick by, you can still channel Marty— just slap together this low-budget hovercraft from a pair of Styrofoam plates and four surplus case fans.

COST	$
TIME	◴
EASY ● ● ● ○ ○ HARD	

MATERIALS

Two 11-inch- (28-cm-) wide, 1-inch- (2.5-cm-) deep foam plates

Four 2-by-4-inch (5-by-10-cm) 5-volt case fans

Drill

Utility knife

9-volt NiMH battery

9-volt battery clip

Hacksaw

Eight ⁵⁄₈-inch (6-mm), 6-32 nylon screws and hex nuts

Wire strippers

Two wire nuts, 22-18 AWG

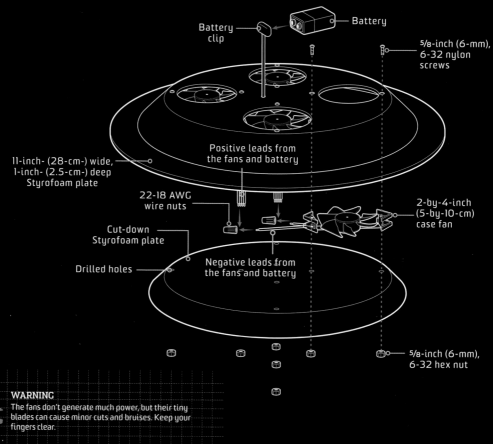

Battery clip

Battery

⁵⁄₈-inch (6-mm), 6-32 nylon screws

11-inch- (28-cm-) wide, 1-inch- (2.5-cm-) deep Styrofoam plate

Positive leads from the fans and battery

22-18 AWG wire nuts

2-by-4-inch (5-by-10-cm) case fan

Cut-down Styrofoam plate

Drilled holes

Negative leads from the fans and battery

⁵⁄₈-inch (6-mm), 6-32 hex nut

WARNING
The fans don't generate much power, but their tiny blades can cause minor cuts and bruises. Keep your fingers clear.

STEP 1 Stack the plates face-up and arrange the fans in a circle on top, with labels up. Point the wired corners toward the center, with the opposite corners close to the rim. Mark the top plate with the locations of each fan's opening and its inner- and outer-corner mounting holes.

STEP 2 Remove the fans and drill eight ⅛-inch (3-mm) mounting holes through both plates. Separate the plates and cut out the four circular fan openings in one of them. This will be the top plate.

STEP 3 Attach the battery to the battery clip, and set it in the center of the top plate. Note the location of the battery clip wires and cut a small triangular slot for them to pass through the plate.

STEP 4 Saw two corners off each fan case, leaving the wired corner and the one opposite attached. Arrange the fans inside the top plate as in Step 1, and pass nylon screws, from below, through the eight mounting holes in both the top plate and the fans. Secure with hex nuts.

STEP 5 Trim the fan wires to reach about 1 inch (2.5 cm) past the center of the plate, and then strip away ½ inch (1.25 cm) of insulation from each.

STEP 6 Thread the battery clip wires through the triangular slot from below and pull the battery and clip up close to the plate. Then trim the wires until they just reach the plate center. Strip ½ inch (1.25 cm) of insulation from each wire and unclip the battery.

STEP 7 Twist all five red leads (four from the fans and one from the battery clip) together with one wire nut, and all five black leads together with the other.

STEP 8 Cut the rim off the bottom plate, about halfway down the side, and discard it. Install the bottom plate inside the top plate, so it fits over the fans and protruding screws, and secure it with eight hex nuts.

STEP 9 Flip your hovercraft over, clip in a freshly charged battery, and set it on a smooth floor.

070 Modify a Magic Mystery Bulb

Transform an old lightbulb into a glowing April Fools' prank.

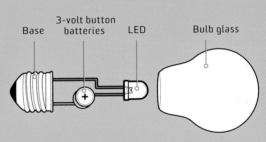

Base 3-volt button batteries LED Bulb glass

MATERIALS

Safety goggles and gloves

Glass lightbulb

Soldering iron and solder

Wire

Zip tie

Two 3-volt button batteries

LED

Electric tape

Hot glue

STEP 1 Wearing thick gloves and safety goggles, carefully twist a glass lightbulb out of its metal base and save both parts. Discard the filament.

STEP 2 Solder a 2-inch (5-cm) wire to the base's inside center and another to the side.

STEP 3 Stack and zip-tie two 3-volt button batteries.

STEP 4 To the short lead of a white LED, solder the center wire. Tape the other wire to the battery pack's negative end.

STEP 5 Tape one end of a third wire to the battery pack's positive terminal. Solder the other end to the LED's long lead.

STEP 6 Coax the LED into the glass, fit the battery pack and wires into the base, and reconnect the bulb's two pieces with hot glue.

STEP 7 Hide a fourth piece of wire in your hand. Grasp the base of the bulb and touch the hidden wire to its side and bottom. To the surprise of your pals, it should light up, even though it doesn't look plugged in!

GEEK TOYS

071 Make a Smartphone-Powered Hologram

Holograms aren't just for dead rappers. Make your own with a piece of transparency paper, a four-sided hologram video, and a smartphone.

COST	$
TIME	☺ ☺ ☺
EASY ● ● ○ ○ ○ HARD	

MATERIALS

Sheet of transparency paper
Compass
Pencil, pen, or marker
Scissors
Ruler
Smartphone or tablet

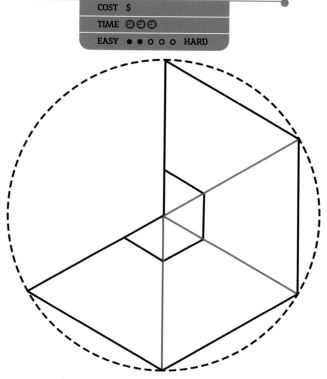

STEP 1 Photocopy this template onto transparency paper. Or draw it yourself: Use a compass to draw a circle with at least a 4-inch (10-cm) radius on transparency paper. Then mark five dots around the circle, each the radius's distance apart, and use a ruler to draw the black and red lines.

STEP 2 Use scissors to cut out the circle. Then cut along the solid black lines, discarding the rounded edges and the leftover third of the circle.

STEP 3 Fold the cutout along the red lines to make four separate equilateral triangles. Cut off their tips 1 inch (2.5 cm) or less from the bottom and tape the two opposite sides together to make a prism.

STEP 4 Load up a four-sided hologram video on your smartphone and place the prism's hole in the video's center. To check out your ghostly illusion, just look through one of the sides of the transparency paper.

Build eyewear that flips your perspective around.

Feel like dancing on the ceiling? All you need are some LEGOS and two prisms. How does it work? The largest facet of a prism acts like a mirror: Light rays enter through the smaller sides and reflect off the big facet's inner surface, flipping an image vertically. Harness that optical trick with one prism for each eye, and soon you'll be walking around in your own upside-down world.

MATERIALS

LEGOs
Two right-angle triangular prisms
String or rubber bands
Hat with a sturdy brim

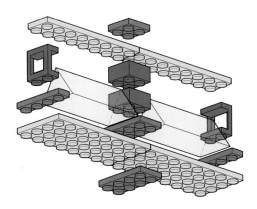

STEP 1 Using LEGOs, build a baseplate for each prism. Place the four-stud baseplate upside down, centering the prism on top.

STEP 2 Build a brace on each side that matches the prism's height—a tight vertical fit will pin the prism in place.

STEP 3 Place a two-stud baseplate upside down on the bottom of each prism, aligned so the right angle of the prism nestles between the two rows.

STEP 4 Place the two prism frames side by side and add another small baseplate to join them together.

STEP 5 Loop the string or rubber bands over the hat brim or crown, positioning each prism in front of an eye.

073 Hack Your Magic 8 Ball

Can you make this fortune-telling gizmo say whatever you want? It is decidedly so.

| COST | $ |
| TIME | ⊙ |
| EASY ● ○ ○ ○ ○ HARD |

MATERIALS

Plexiglas cutter
Magic 8 Ball
Screwdriver
Razor
Sandpaper
Extra-fine permanent marker
Superglue

STEP 1 Use a Plexiglas cutter to cut through the glue at the ball's equatorial seam, then carefully pry it open.

STEP 2 Inside there's a cylinder of blue dye. Remove the screws that hold it in place, and then pour out and reserve the liquid. Fish the answer ball out.

STEP 3 Pat the answer ball dry. Use a razor and sandpaper to scrape off the existing messages.

STEP 4 Write the messages you desire on the ball using an extra-fine permanent marker. Wait for the ink to dry.

STEP 5 Put the answer ball inside the cylinder, and then transfer the blue liquid back into the cylinder, too.

STEP 6 Glue the cap on the cylinder and reinsert it inside the two halves of the Magic 8 Ball.

STEP 7 Glue the ball back together, let it dry, and enjoy rewriting the future.

YOU MUST BE SUFFERING FROM VULCAN MIND-MELD

074 Go Anywhere with Virtual-Reality Glasses

. . . anywhere that Google Street View goes, that is.

MATERIALS

Safety goggles	Craft knife
Large piece of cardboard	Tape
Pencil	Smartphone

STEP 1 Lay the safety goggles on the cardboard so that they're facing forward. Trace around the shape, adding at least 2 inches (5 cm) in front.

STEP 2 Roll the goggles up so that they're resting on an end. Trace around that side, adding extra space again.

STEP 3 Using the craft knife, cut out your tracing as one piece, then fold it so you have a four-sided rectangular tube that fits perfectly around your goggles. Secure it with tape and slide the goggles just inside.

STEP 4 On a separate piece of cardboard, trace the cardboard box's front, leaving 1-inch (2.5-cm) tabs on either side. Cut it out, then trace your smartphone onto its center. Cut out the shape of your phone, making

a window, and insert this cardboard piece into the rectangular tube opposite the goggles.

STEP 5 Dial up Google Street View and locate a place you've always wanted to go. Then tape your phone over the window.

STEP 6 Don your virtual-reality glasses, and take a walk someplace far, far away.

075 File-Share with a USB Dead Drop

Camouflage a USB flash drive so that you can swap files on the sly.

MATERIALS

USB flash drive	Cement
Computer	Paint, if desired
Drill with masonry bit	

STEP 1 Stick your USB drive into your computer's port and upload any files you want to share, then remove it.

STEP 2 Scout for a good place to put your dead drop. You may need a drill with a masonry bit to make a hole in concrete, like the one you see here.

STEP 3 Slide your USB inside and use cement to secure it in place. Don't get any cement on the USB itself. If you want extra camouflage, paint a bit around it.

STEP 4 Scram—and let your contacts know where the secret docs are. To retrieve files from a dead drop, just line your laptop's USB port up with the USB drive and slide them together.

GEEK TOYS

076 The Electric Giraffe

It walks, it blinks, it seats six, and it blasts Kraftwerk. Meet one man's enormous pet project.

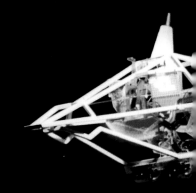

It started with a 7-inch (18-cm) walking toy giraffe and a desire to see Burning Man—the annual art-and-rave party in the desert in Black Rock, Nevada—from a higher vantage point. A year later, Lindsay Lawlor rode into the desert art festival atop Rave Raffe, a 1,700-pound (771-kg) robotic giraffe sporting 40 strobes, 400 LEDs, and bone-shaking speakers.

Lawlor wanted his Burning Man ride to be a true walking vehicle, so he copied the small toy's locomotion system on a massive scale. The front and back legs opposite each other step ahead at the same time, propelled by an electric motor. When those legs land, hydraulic brakes lock the wheeled feet, and the other two legs take a step. Canting from side to side, Raffe lumbers ahead at about 1 mile per hour (1.6 km/h). A 12-horsepower propane engine runs only to recharge the batteries, so the beast is quiet and efficient, while a pneumatic pump raises and lowers the giraffe's massive neck. When Lawlor let Raffe shuffle off alone in the desert, it walked for 8 hours.

Since the giraffe's debut, Lawlor (a part-time laser-light-show designer) has added new features, including computer-controlled flashing giraffe spots, an electroluminescent circulatory system, and a gas grill.

077 Turn Garden Beets into a "Beet Box"

Become a "beet-boxing" DJ in a weekend.

COST $$
TIME 😊 😊 😊
EASY • • • • ○ HARD

People conduct electric charges, and so do vegetables. Introducing the Beet Box: a machine that plays drum-kit sounds at the tap of a beet. The beets conduct body capacitance, or the electrical energy stored inside humans, to a sensor plugged into a Raspberry Pi mini-computer ("Pi" for short). Each touch triggers software to produce one of six percussion sounds. The electronics are hidden inside a wooden enclosure with a lid so that striking the beets emits clashes and snares as if by magic.

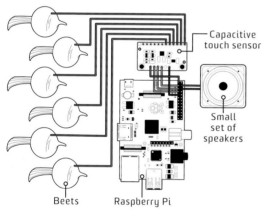

Capacitive touch sensor

Small set of speakers

Beets

Raspberry Pi

MATERIALS

Raspberry Pi

MPR121 capacitive touch sensor

Power cord

Nails

Hammer

Two 4-by-8-inch (10-by-20-cm) pieces of ½-inch- (1.25-cm-) thick wood

Two 12-by-8-inch (30-by-20-cm) pieces of ½-inch- (1.25-cm-) thick wood

Two 8-by-8-inch (30-by-30-cm) pieces of ½-inch- (1.25-cm-) thick wood

Drill

Screwdriver

10-by-10-inch (25-by-25-cm) piece of ½-inch- (1.25-cm-) thick wood

Hole Saw

Six beets

Wire

Wire cutters

Soldering iron and solder

Small set of speakers

STEP 1 To house a Pi, a capacitive sensor, a power supply, and cables, make an 8-inch (20-cm) wooden box. Nail together two 4-inch- (10-cm-) tall sides, two 12-inch- (30-cm-) tall sides, and an 8-inch- (20-cm-) square bottom. Drill a circle of small holes into the lid for a sound port (but don't nail it on). To the 12-inch- (30-cm-) tall sides, add a 10-inch (25-cm) plank that's bored to fit six beets.

STEP 2 Configure a Pi to use I2C communication found here: www.popsci.com/thebigbookofhacks (this will allow it to communicate with the capacitive sensor). Load touch-sensing software found at the same URL onto the Pi so it can interpret the signals.

STEP 3 Solder six wires to individual electrode ports on an MPR121 capacitive touch sensor breakout board. Stick each wire into a separate beet.

STEP 4 Use a wire to connect the SDA port of the breakout board to pin 3 on the computer, and the SCL port to pin 5. Link the board and the Pi's grounds. Connect the board's 3.3-volt line to pin 1 and its IRQ line to pin 7 of the Pi.

STEP 5 Hook up small speakers to the Pi's audio port. Fit the board, Pi, and speakers inside the box. Run a power cord to the Pi, drop the beets into their holes, and then drop some beats.

078 Scratch a Pizza-Box Turntable

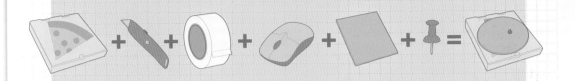

STEP 1 Cut a small hole in your pizza box's lid.

STEP 2 Tape your optical mouse inside the lid so that its eye points up through the hole when you close the box.

STEP 3 Cut a cardboard disc and attach it to the box using a pushpin so that it can spin around over the mouse's eye.

STEP 4 Open your mixing software and scratch away.

079 Pirate a Vinyl Record

If you live in fear of scratching a super-rare record, this silicone mold is for you.

MATERIALS

Nails

Hammer

Four 14¼-inch- (36.5-cm-) square boards

Glass plate

Caulking

Record

Dowel

Silicone rubber designed for mold making

Casting resin

STEP 1 Nail together the boards to make a square wood frame. Place the frame on the glass plate, and seal around the inside edge with caulking.

STEP 2 Put the record you want to copy inside the frame on the glass plate—the side you want to copy should be face up. Fit a dowel into the record's hole.

STEP 3 Prepare the silicone rubber and pour it into the mold. Let it dry overnight.

STEP 4 Peel off the silicone mold, then trim any excess from around its edges.

STEP 5 Mix the casting resin and pour it into the silicone mold. Once it's set, loosen the cast and remove.

STEP 6 Pop your repro record onto your record player and hit play.

GEEK TOYS

080 Craft a Boom Box Duffel Bag

STEP 1 Create a simple image of a boom box, and draw or print it onto contact paper to create a stencil. The boom box's speakers should be more or less the same size as your speakers, which are best if they're of the cheap desktop variety.

STEP 2 Using a craft knife, carefully cut out the stencil.

STEP 3 Lay the duffel bag flat and remove the back of the contact paper. Smooth the contact paper over the fabric.

STEP 4 Squeeze out a line of paint at the top of the stencil, and use a piece of cardboard to spread the paint over it. Repeat until the paint is well distributed. Remove the stencil.

STEP 5 After the paint has dried, cut two holes slightly smaller than your speakers out of the design. These are the holes for the speakers.

STEP 6 Remove the speakers' backs and slide the speakers into the holes from the outside. Reattach the backs with the same screws, sandwiching the fabric.

STEP 7 Plug the speakers into your portable media player, shoulder up the bag, and pump some jams.

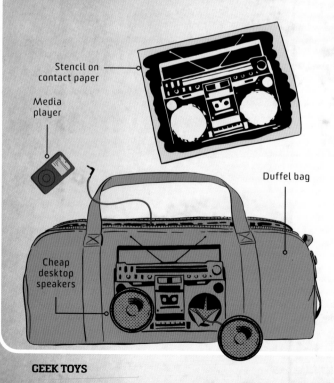

Stencil on contact paper

Media player

Duffel bag

Cheap desktop speakers

081 Make Your Tie Glow in the Dark

STEP 1 Use a needle to poke a hole into the end of a tie where the EL (electroluminescent) wire will enter. It's best to use heavy-duty fabrics and to follow the seams.

STEP 2 Sew a piece of Velcro onto the tie and attach another piece to a battery pack. (We fit ours at the end of the tie.)

STEP 3 Draw a design, lay EL wire over the sketch, and tape it to the tie.

STEP 4 Measure heavy-duty fishing line that's more than twice the length of your EL wire. Thread a sturdy needle with the line and make a knot at its end.

STEP 5 Sew the wire down, securing it every 1/2 inch (1.25 cm). Remove the tape.

STEP 6 Plug the wire into the battery pack and never wear a boring tie again.

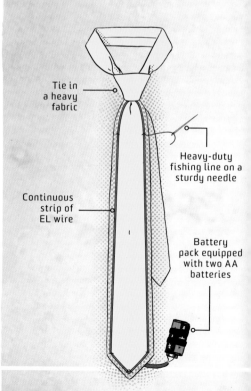

Tie in a heavy fabric

Heavy-duty fishing line on a sturdy needle

Continuous strip of EL wire

Battery pack equipped with two AA batteries

082 Put Head-Phones in Your Hoodie

STEP 1 Use a craft knife to carefully detach the speakers from a headphone band, keeping the ear cushions and speakers (and the wire between them and the one that runs to a media player) intact.

STEP 2 Put on a lined hoodie. Safety-pin the ear cushions in place and test that they fit comfortably.

STEP 3 With a heavy-duty needle, sew four strips of Velcro onto each ear cushion's spot in the hoodie, and four more strips to the back of each ear cushion.

STEP 4 Cut a slit in the lower center of the hood where the speakers' wires will join and enter the lining.

STEP 5 Cut a slit into the lower corner of the hoodie's front where the cord will come out.

STEP 6 Check to make sure your wire is long enough to reach the incision in the jacket's front. If it's not, desolder the cord and solder on a longer one.

STEP 7 Attach the speakers to the Velcro and feed the cord into the hood's lining and out the front.

STEP 8 Pull up your hood and get skulking. To launder, detach the ear cushions and pull out the cord.

Adhesive Velcro

Sew-on Velcro

Ear cushions with intact speakers

Hole for cord entrance

Lined hoodie

Hole for cord exit

Media player

083 Use a Glove on a Touchscreen

STEP 1 Thread a sturdy needle with 1 foot (30 cm) of conductive thread.

STEP 2 On the outside of a glove's pointer finger, sew a few stitches—enough to cover an area of about ¼ inch (6.35 mm) in diameter.

STEP 3 Turn the glove inside out, and sew three to five stitches. Allow some extra thread to dangle—this will ensure that your finger touches the conductive thread, completing a mini circuit and allowing the screen to pick up on your gestures.

STEP 4 Swipe and tap away. If you find that typing with your glove often results in hitting neighboring letters, pull out a few threads from the outside of the fingertip.

Heavy-duty needle

Conductive thread

Smartphone with touchscreen

Standard-issue glove

GEEK TOYS

084 Pump Jams Through a Phonograph

This phonograph probably hasn't played any new music since Stravinsky. Give it new life with this modernizing mod.

COST $$$

TIME ⏲ ⏲ ⏲

EASY ● ● ● ○ HARD

MATERIALS

Wooden box

Drill with a hole bit

Brass horn from an old phonograph

Felt

Miniature mono amplifier with tone control

Transformer for the amplifier

Two potentiometer knobs

3.5-mm stereo socket

Power plug

Power switch

Speaker

Electrical wire

Soldering iron and solder

Hot-glue gun

Media player

STEP 1 Measure and cut two holes in the top of your box: one for the brass horn and a smaller one for the stereo socket.

STEP 2 Measure the box's inside and cut felt to those dimensions, then line the box with felt—it will make for better sound.

STEP 3 Set up the electronics according to the diagram, drilling holes for the power source, potentiometers, and power switch as you go.

STEP 4 Place the horn in its hole and hot-glue it in place. Sand and varnish the box, if you desire.

STEP 5 Close up the box, plug your media device into the stereo socket, and plug the contraption's power cable into an outlet.

STEP 6 Enjoy the sweet, sweet sound of anachronism.

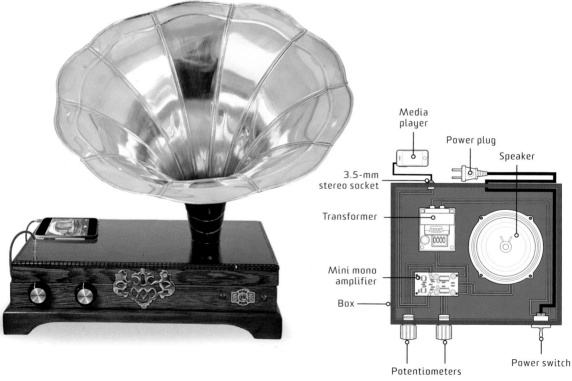

Media player

Power plug

Speaker

3.5-mm stereo socket

Transformer

Mini mono amplifier

Box

Potentiometers

Power switch

Make Speakers with Sticky Notes

You can harness the power of sound using run-of-the-mill office supplies.

Audio cable

Magnet wire

Alligator clip

Rare-earth magnet
beneath Post-it note

MATERIALS

Sandpaper

3 feet (90 cm)
 magnet wire

Tape

Small rare-earth magnet

One sticky note

Audio cable

Wire cutters

Wire strippers

Two alligator clips

STEP 1 Sand the coating off both ends of the magnet wire, starting about 2 inches (5 cm) from each end.

STEP 2 Wind the magnet wire around your finger to form a neat coil. Leave about 3 inches (7.5 cm) on each end. Then slide it off, and secure the coil with tape.

STEP 3 Tape the rare-earth magnet to a flat surface, like a tabletop.

STEP 4 Attach the sticky note next to it so that it forms a flap over the rare-earth magnet.

STEP 5 Tape the coiled wire in the middle of the sticky note.

STEP 6 Cut the female plug end off the audio cable with wire cutters. (The remaining end is the male plug.) Use wire strippers to peel back the outer rubber to expose the two inner wires.

STEP 7 Use an alligator clip to attach each exposed wire to one end of the coiled magnet wire.

STEP 8 Plug the audio cable into your cell phone's audio port, and play some music. Hold your ear over the coil to hear shockingly crisp sound.

QUICK HACKS

086 **Put a New Spin on an Old CD**

In the age of MP3s, most people have a lot of old CDs lying around. Here's what to do with them.

EASY SPINNING TOP

Using a hot-glue gun, secure a large marble to the underside of a compact disc, right under the hole. Glue a plastic bottle cap to the top and give it a whirl.

BEER SPILL BLOCKER

Put a CD over your beer bottle so the bottle's neck sticks up through the CD's hole. Now when you knock the bottle over accidentally, the CD will prevent it from tipping all the way over—and spilling your brew.

ULTIMATE (COMPACT) DISC GOLF

This one's truly easy: Take an old CD and throw it around a disc golf course with some friends. Just don't throw it at your friends.

SUPERSHINY COASTERS

Cover compact discs with felt and use them as coasters. Make sure you cover the side with the artist's information on it—you don't want anyone knowing you once paid actual money for that Third Eye Blind CD, do you?

AIR HOCKEY IN A PINCH

Place a CD on a table about the size of, well, an air hockey table, and mark goal zones with tape. Stand across from your opponent, seize a CD spindle, and use it as an air hockey mallet to swat the CD back and forth.

087 Make Sweet Holiday Music

COST $$
TIME 🕐 🕐
EASY ● ● ● ● ○ HARD

WARNING Don't get milk—or any other liquids—on the circuit or battery.

Jingle all the way with a candy-cane musical instrument.

MATERIALS

Craft knife

Perfboard

TLC555 CP LinCMOS timer, eight-pin DIP

¼-watt resistors, 5 percent (10, 10k, 10m, 270k ohm)

0.1uF, 50-volt 20 percent ceramic disc capacitor

100uF, 35-volt 20 percent radial capacitor

820 pf ceramic disc capacitor

PNP general-purpose amplifier, 2N3906

Wire cutters

Wire stripper

22-AWG hookup wire in red, black, and green

Foam block

2 AAA battery clip

Soldering iron and solder

Mini speaker with wire leads

Double-sided foam tape

2 AAA batteries

Candy cane

Aluminum foil

Electrical tape

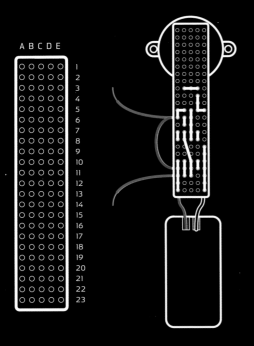

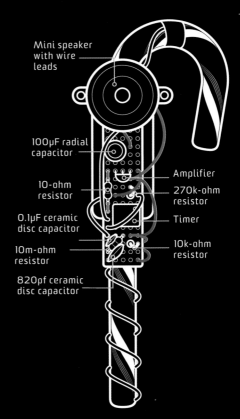

Mini speaker with wire leads

100µF radial capacitor

10-ohm resistor

0.1µF ceramic disc capacitor

10m-ohm resistor

820pf ceramic disc capacitor

Amplifier

270k-ohm resistor

Timer

10k-ohm resistor

STEP 1 Using a craft knife, cut your perfboard into a rectangle with five rows of 23 holes. Insert the TLC-555CP timer with the upper left corner at A16. Bend the timer's legs out underneath the perfboard to keep it in place.

STEP 2 Stick the resistors, capacitors, and amplifier in the perfboard as shown on the circuitry diagram. Use jumper wires to connect A12 to D15, A15 to E19, and A13 to A20. (You can put a foam block beneath the board to hold the pins in place while you work.)

STEP 3 Cut 5 inches (12.7 cm) of green wire, and strip about 2 inches (5 cm) from the other end. Cut 8 inches (20 cm) of green wire, insert one stripped end into B20, and strip 5 inches (12.7 cm) from the other end.

STEP 4 Strip and tin the leads of the battery clip. Insert the negative lead into E20 and the positive into A23, leaving 1 inch (2.5 cm) of wire between the clip and the perfboard. Strip and tin the leads of the speaker, and attach it to the board as shown.

STEP 5 Remove everything from the perfboard except the timer. Solder a jumper between pins 2 and 6. Then insert the other components, except for the speaker, in the same order you did before. Solder their leads together under the perfboard, as shown.

STEP 6 Use double-stick foam tape to attach the speaker to the perfboard. Solder the leads into the circuit.

STEP 7 Test your circuit: Insert batteries and touch the exposed green leads with your hands. The speaker should emit a tone that changes pitch based on the resistance between the green leads. In other words, moving your hands should alter the sounds.

STEP 8 Use double-sided tape to attach the perfboard and battery clip to a candy cane. (If you plan to reuse the circuit to make another instrument, just wind electrical tape around the unit to hold it in place.)

STEP 9 Coil the short green lead up to the hook of the candy cane and the long green lead down its body. Wrap a band of aluminum foil around each lead and tape closed. Now you can make music!

STEP 10 To give it a go, grip the candy cane with one hand, touching the wire, and lick from the top. You can also try dipping the candy cane into a mug of hot chocolate (keeping the circuit dry) and drinking from the mug with a straw. Or stick one finger in some water on a saucer, and make patterns in the liquid while holding the candy cane in your other hand.

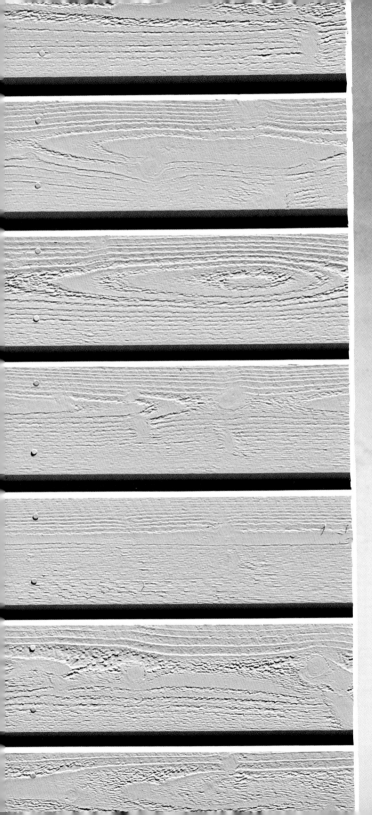

HOME IMPROVEMENTS

If your walls could talk . . .

This device monitors the temperature, humidity, noise, and light level for any room in your home— it can even track the number of people who enter! Within the casing, a collection of sensors sends information to an Arduino, which interprets the input and displays the data on a small screen. Based on the device's readings, you can turn on a dehumidifier, lower the thermostat, or crack open a window—whatever it takes to keep your home environment comfortable.

MATERIALS

3.3-volt/8-MHz Arduino Pro Mini 328
PIR motion sensor
Hookup wire
Soldering iron and solder
Two 1K resistors
Humidity and temperature sensor
5-volt step-up breakout board (NCP1402)
Micro-USB LiPo Charger Basic
Ambient light sensor breakout board
Micro OLED breakout board
MEMS microphone breakout board
1K-mAh polymer lithium-ion battery
Screwdriver
Pi Tin for the Raspberry Pi

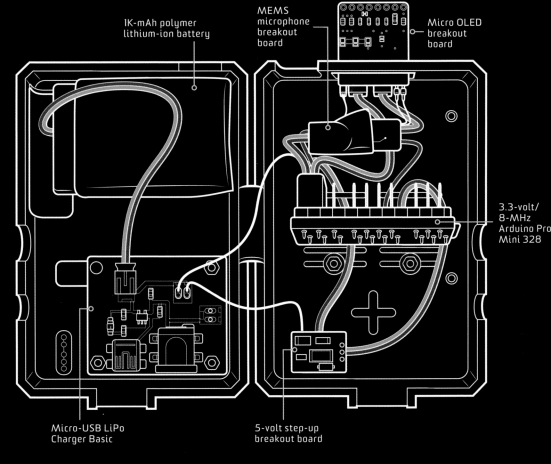

1K-mAh polymer lithium-ion battery

MEMS microphone breakout board

Micro OLED breakout board

3.3-volt/ 8-MHz Arduino Pro Mini 328

Micro-USB LiPo Charger Basic

5-volt step-up breakout board

STEP 1 Program the Arduino with the code found at www.popsci.com/thebigbookofhacks. There's also a helpful hookup guide for the circuit on the site.

STEP 2 Prepare the PIR motion sensor's circuit board by locating and removing the black rectangular three-pad chip (also known as an integrated circuit, or IC) labeled 78L05. On the part of the board where the chip used to sit, identify the now-empty pads 1 and 3. Solder a piece of hookup wire between the pads.

STEP 3 Solder a 1K resistor between pin 2 of the humidity and temperature sensor and the 5-volt pin of the 5-volt step-up breakout board.

STEP 4 Solder the humidity and temperature sensor's power pin to the 5-volt pin of the 5-volt step-up breakout board.

STEP 5 Solder the 3.7-volt pin of the 5-volt step-up breakout board to the output of the LiPo charger.

STEP 6 Solder the Arduino Raw pin and the ambient light sensor VCC pin to the LiPo charger.

STEP 7 Solder the second 1K resistor between the AL pin of the PIR motion sensor and the 3.3-volt pin of the Arduino.

STEP 8 Solder all power pins of the PIR motion sensor, micro OLED, and

MEMS microphone to the 3.3-volt pin of the Arduino.

STEP 9 The key elements of the circuit are complete. Follow the hookup guide to connect the remaining sensor pins to the Arduino (found at www.popsci.com/thebigbookofhacks).

STEP 10 Plug the polymer lithium-ion battery into the LiPo charger, and put all of the electronics into the Pi Tin. Close it up with a screwdriver.

STEP 11 Finally, place the home-health sensor in a room of your choosing. The micro OLED screen will let you keep a finger on your home's pulse at all times of the day, monitoring temperature, lights, and more.

089 Set Up a Laser Security System

Everybody loves a good laser show . . . except maybe the thief caught in one.

COST	$$
TIME	☺ ☺ ☺
EASY	● ● ● ● ○ HARD

MATERIALS

Drill

Two project boxes

9-volt battery

5k-ohm variable resistor

2N3904 transistor

100uF capacitor

Soldering iron and solder

Electrical wire

Hot-glue gun

Photocell

12-volt siren

5-milliwatt red laser

Switch

Wire strippers

3.2-volt AC adapter

Velcro

Small mirrors, if needed

Mounting putty, if needed

STEP 1 Drill two holes in the first project box: one for the siren, and one for the photocell. This will be the receiver.

STEP 2 Follow the circuitry diagram at near right, soldering together the components with electrical wire.

STEP 3 Install the assembled components inside the receiver project box and secure with hot glue. Mount the photocell and the siren on the box's sides and connect it to the interior wiring.

STEP 4 Drill two holes in the second project box: one for the switch, and one for the laser. Mount the laser and switch inside this box with hot glue.

STEP 5 Cut off and strip the ends of the AC adapter wires and run them into the box. Use electrical wire to connect them to the laser and switch, following the circuitry diagram at far right. Then close the box and test the laser.

STEP 6 Line up the laser box with the receiver box. Use the variable resistor to adjust the photocell's sensitivity so it can detect motion during daylight hours. When correctly tuned, the receiver box will not make sound when the laser is shining on it.

STEP 7 Attach Velcro to both project boxes. Mount the laser on the wall at about waist height beside the door you want protected. Plug in the AC adapter.

STEP 8 If you want to protect multiple doors and windows, use mounting putty to attach tiny mirrors to the wall at angles that bounce the laser's beam around the room. You may have to play with the mirrors' positions to get it right.

STEP 9 Once you're done with the mirrors, mount the receiver box so that the photocell lines up directly with the end of the laser beam. When the beam is broken, the alarm will sound.

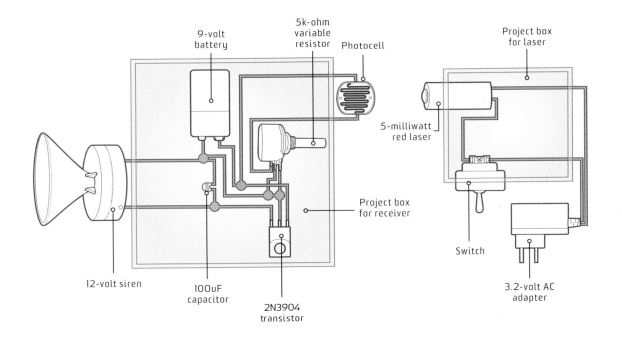

9-volt battery

5k-ohm variable resistor

Photocell

Project box for laser

5-milliwatt red laser

Project box for receiver

12-volt siren

100uF capacitor

2N3904 transistor

Switch

3.2-volt AC adapter

090   Snooper-Proof Your Wallet

Foil RFID thieves with—well, aluminum foil, believe it or not.

MATERIALS

Wallet

Aluminum foil

Lurking inside your wallet's credit cards are radio-frequency identification chips (RFIDs), and lurking outside your wallet are goons who scan that info and make off with your identity.

STEP 1 Tear off a piece of aluminum foil about 6 inches (15 cm) in length.

STEP 2 Fold the aluminum foil to the size of a dollar bill.

STEP 3 Tuck the folded aluminum foil into your wallet's billfold, place your cards inside, and forget about those RFID scammers out there.

091 Install an Electrical-Outlet Wall Safe

Keep small valuables in a place no one would ever look—and hope burglars don't try to plug anything in.

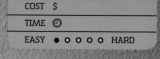

COST	$
TIME	☉
EASY ● ○ ○ ○ ○ HARD	

MATERIALS

Cut-in box
Pencil
Drywall saw
Residential-grade volt receptacle

Roofing nails and washers
Faceplate
Screw
Screwdriver

STEP 1 Place the cut-in box on the wall where you want your safe and trace around it with a pencil. Cut the hole with a drywall saw.

STEP 2 Slide the cut-in box into the hole. Fill it up with small valuables.

STEP 3 The volt receptacle has two holes, one at its top and one at its bottom. Slide the roofing nails through the washers and then through these holes.

STEP 4 Attach the volt receptacle to the cut-in box by sliding the nails into the box's top and bottom holes.

STEP 5 Screw the faceplate onto the receptacle.

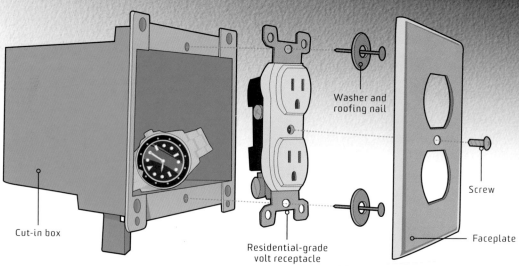

Cut-in box

Washer and roofing nail

Screw

Residential-grade volt receptacle

Faceplate

092 Carry a Film-Roll Keychain

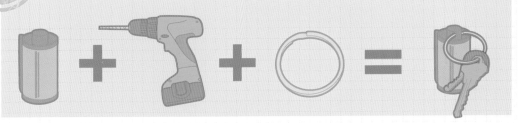

STEP 1 Drill a small hole into the spool hub of a 35mm film roll.

STEP 2 Insert a key-ring loop through the roll's hole.

STEP 3 Thread your keys onto the loop and carry them like an old-school film nut.

093 Make a Musical Stash for Your Cash

Annoy would-be thieves with a safe booby-trapped with bad music.

MATERIALS

Musical greeting card

Double-sided tape

Craft knife

Box

STEP 1 Remove the noisemaker from a musical greeting card by opening the card and tearing off the paper over the noisemaker. Then cut out the speaker and circuit.

STEP 2 The speaker has a paper tab that, when unfolded, plays music. Use double-sided tape to adhere this tab so it straddles your box's hinge, and affix the speaker and circuit inside the box. When the box is opened and the paper tab is unfolded, it will sound the alarm.

STEP 3 Fill your box with treasure and listen for thieves.

Noisemaker speaker and circuit

Noisemaker paper tab

094 Turn Your Roomba into a Sentry

Why? To patrol your home while you're away, capturing pics you can access from any mobile device.

COST	$$$
TIME	☺ ☺
EASY	● ● ● ○ ○ HARD

The Roomba vacuum is an incredibly sophisticated robot, especially for a gadget that costs less than $300. It scoots along at 1 foot (30 cm) per second, while its sensors detect and navigate obstacles. Here we've outfitted one with a webcam so you can keep tabs on your pad from afar.

MATERIALS

Wireless webcam

Video-streaming site account
  or dedicated website for video

Roomba

Strong Velcro

Mobile device for monitoring
  from afar

iPad or tablet, if needed

STEP 1 Get a wireless webcam that comes with its own free website for real-time broadcasting. If you want to use a wireless webcam you already own, set up an account for it on a video-streaming site.

STEP 2 Follow the camera's instructions to configure video capture and have it sent either to the website or to the streaming-video site.

STEP 3 Attach the webcam to your Roomba with Velcro, send it on its way, and head out the door. Any time that you want to check in on your 'bot's findings, load the video feed on your smartphone or a computer.

STEP 4 For extra deterrence, you can attach an iPad or a tablet PC to the Roomba, navigate to the streaming-video page, and display it on the screen. This way, would-be intruders will see what you're seeing in real time—and know they'd better put that Wii system down and scram.

Make a Robotic Artiste

Let your vacuum make a mess for a change—one that's worthy of any 22nd-century gallery.

MATERIALS

Large canvas

Items to use as bumpers

Brushes and rollers

Glue or Velcro

Paint trays

Paint

STEP 1 Lay a large canvas on your floor and—to keep your Roomba from painting areas you'd prefer left undecorated—arrange objects around the periphery to keep the Roomba within bounds. Place your charging station within that boundary.

STEP 2 Attach brushes and rollers with glue or Velcro to the front, back, and sides of the Roomba. For real drips, try repurposing an old chandelier, or cobbling together a paintbrush holder using a colander and kitchen utensils.

STEP 3 Set paint trays near the charging station so it can refuel with color after it recharges.

IT GETS EVEN BETTER
Any Roomba that's rolled off the assembly line since October 24, 2005, has a serial command interface (SCI), which is essentially an open platform for hackers to play with. This software allows your preprogrammed instructions to control your Roomba, making it an ideal ready-made base for any robotics project.

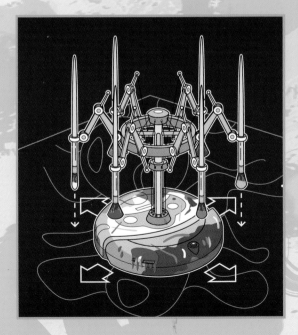

HOME IMPROVEMENTS

For cool mood lighting, combine off-the-shelf parts—and just add mineral oil.

Forget the lava lamp: This modern light source trades in the hippie-dippie vibe for an edgier, more industrial look. And you can make it yourself by filling a glass globe with mineral oil and hooking it up to an air pump for a bubbly effect.

MATERIALS

Craft knife

Clear ¼-inch (6.35-mm) PVC tubing

3-wire 18-awg SJOOW cord

Zip ties

3-prong male plug

Vapor-tight glass globe fixture with a ½-inch (1.25-cm) bulb

Nylon liquid-tight strain relief with flex fitting and threads that match the fixture

Wire strippers

Two 18-awg wire nuts

Rotary tool

Colored, clear 25-watt bulb

Mineral oil

Basic air pump

COST	$$
TIME	⊙ ⊙
EASY ● ● ● ○ ○ HARD	

STEP 1 Measure and cut your clear tubing and electrical cord so that it will reach the power supply from your lamp. Tether them together with zip ties, then wire the male plug to the cord's end.

STEP 2 Remove the vapor-tight fixture's base from the cap.

STEP 3 Screw the strain relief into the threaded opening at the top of the vapor-tight fixture's cap.

STEP 4 Run the air tube and the electrical cord through the strain relief and into the cap. Strip the ends of the electrical cord and connect them to the vapor-tight fixture's leads with the wire nuts.

STEP 5 Use a rotary tool to drill a hole in the bottom of the vapor-tight fixture's base. Feed the clear tube through this hole, leaving about 8 inches (20 cm) below the base.

STEP 6 Screw the base back to the cap. As you do so, ground the fixture by twisting the green ground lead around one of the screws that connects the cap to the base.

STEP 7 Gently tighten the strain relief via its nut—don't overdo it, or you'll constrict the tubing.

STEP 8 Screw the clear, colored bulb into the socket.

STEP 9 Fill the glass globe about one-third full of mineral oil and screw the bulb to the base. Add the vapor-tight fixture's aluminum grill.

STEP 10 Hang your lamp, attach the air tube to the pump, plug in the pump and the light, and presto: bubble light!

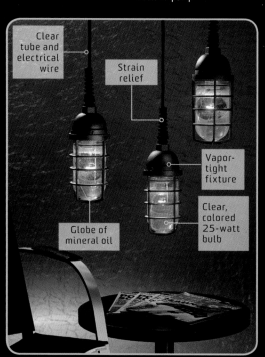

Clear tube and electrical wire

Strain relief

Vapor-tight fixture

Globe of mineral oil

Clear, colored 25-watt bulb

097 Mold a Retro Lamp Base

Use one of those ubiquitous plastic bottles as a mold for a neat lamp base.

MATERIALS

Craft knife

Empty plastic water bottle with a relatively flat top

Drill

Petroleum jelly

Hacksaw

Hollow threaded rod

Hot-glue gun

Empty pill bottle

Small glass

Plaster

Fine-grit sandpaper

Flat washer, lock washer, and nut

Lamp rewiring kit

Lampshade

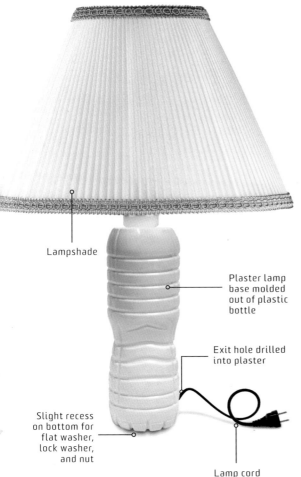

Lampshade

Plaster lamp base molded out of plastic bottle

Exit hole drilled into plaster

Slight recess on bottom for flat washer, lock washer, and nut

Lamp cord

STEP 1 Using a craft knife, cut off the bottom of the plastic bottle. Leave a slight rim so the mold has a rounded edge.

STEP 2 Drill a 1/2-inch (1.25-cm) hole into the center of the water bottle's cap.

STEP 3 Coat the inside of the water bottle and its cap with a thin, even film of petroleum jelly.

STEP 4 Use a hacksaw to cut a 1/2-inch (1.25-cm), hollow, threaded rod to the height of your water bottle, minus about 1/4 inch (6.35 mm).

STEP 5 With the cap screwed onto the bottle, thread the rod from the bottom so that 1/4 inch (6.35 mm) sticks out of the cap. Use a hot-glue gun to seal the area on the outside of the bottle where the threads meet the cap's top.

STEP 6 Find a pill bottle that's 75 percent smaller than your plastic bottle. Remove its lid and drill a 1/2-inch (1.25-cm) hole into the center of its bottom.

STEP 7 Coat the medicine bottle's bottom and halfway up its sides with petroleum jelly.

STEP 8 Holding both bottles with their bottoms facing each other, screw the medicine bottle onto the rod so it fits inside the larger plastic bottle, a bit past flush. (This creates a slight recess in the bottom of your lamp base.)

STEP 9 Place the entire apparatus upside down into a small glass so that the water bottle's cap points down inside the glass.

STEP 10 Mix then pour your plaster into the larger plastic bottle until it fills up to the rim of the larger bottle's bottom. Let set for a half hour or until the plaster sets.

STEP 11 Unscrew the bottle cap and the medicine bottle from the hollow threaded rod. Carefully peel the plastic bottle off the mold with a craft knife.

STEP 12 Once you've removed the bottle, sand the bottom flat and clean up any other rough surface areas.

STEP 13 Attach a flat washer, lock washer, and nut to the rod at the base of the lamp. Don't overtighten.

STEP 14 Drill a 1/4-inch (6.35-mm) hole through the side of the base into the slight recess in the lamp's bottom. Thread the lamp cord through the hole and into the rod.

STEP 15 Wire the socket and attach it to the rod at the top of the lamp base. Top it off with your shade of choice.

098 Make a Modern Mag Rack

Magazines sure can pile up. House 'em in this fiberglass rack.

MATERIALS

Ruler

Grease pencil

1-by-2-foot (30-by-60-cm) polystyrene sheet

Dust mask

Rotary tool with cut-off wheel

Jigsaw

¾-inch- (1.9-cm-) thick wood

Saw blade

Drill

Two wood dowels that are 9 inches (23 cm) in length

Wood glue

Six screws

SLOTS ½ INCH (1.25 CM) WIDE

1 FOOT (30 CM)

1 FOOT (30 CM)

21 INCHES (53 CM)

2 FEET (60 CM)

¾-INCH (1.9-CM) GAPS

STEP 1 With a ruler and a grease pencil, draw the pattern at left onto the polystyrene.

STEP 2 Wearing a dust mask, use a rotary tool with a cut-off wheel to cut out all the ½-inch (1.25-cm) sections.

STEP 3 Use a jigsaw to cut the wood into two strips that are 2 ½ inches (6.35 cm) high and 1 foot (30 cm) long.

STEP 4 Create a groove ¾ inch (1.9 cm) deep in the top of the wood pieces with a saw blade.

STEP 5 Drill two indentations into the inside of each of the wood pieces. Slide the dowels into the holes so that they connect the wood pieces. Secure with wood glue.

STEP 6 Slide the polystyrene into one of the wood pieces' grooves. Secure it with three evenly spaced screws along one of the wood pieces.

STEP 7 Fold the polystyrene into a U shape and slide it into the second wood piece's groove. Secure with screws again.

099 Sew an Easy eBook Reader Case

Protect your slick tablet with a felt case tucked inside an oversize book.

COST	$
TIME	☺ ☺
EASY	● ● ○ ○ ○　HARD

MATERIALS

Box cutter

Book 1 inch (2.5 cm) larger than your tablet on all sides

Ruler

Scissors

Hot-glue gun

Felt

Cardboard

Pencil

3 feet (90 cm) of ½-inch (1.25-cm) braided elastic

Tablet

STEP 1 Using a box cutter, cut out the pages from the book. Glue a strip of felt to the inside of its spine.

STEP 2 Cut two pieces of cardboard to the size of the book's covers. Snip off the cardboard's corners.

STEP 3 Measure and cut two pieces of felt so they're 2 inches (5 cm) larger than the cardboard on all sides. Cut 45-degree-angle slits into the felt pieces' corners.

STEP 4 Position one of the cardboard pieces in the center of a felt piece. Fold the felt over the cardboard's corners and hot-glue it in place. Repeat with the other pieces.

STEP 5 Trace the tablet's outline on the back of one cardboard piece. On both sides of each of the outline's corners, use scissors to punch two holes large enough to fit your elastic. Each hole should be 1 inch (2.5 cm) from the outline's corner.

STEP 6 Cut four 4-inch (10-cm) pieces of braided elastic. Feed one from the back of the cardboard up through one of the holes and then back through the facing hole. Repeat with the other three strips and insert your tablet so that the strips go over the device's corners, holding it in place. If it fits, hot-glue the elastic pieces' ends to the cardboard.

STEP 7 Use scissors to cut two holes into the book's back cover near its outside edge. Thread the remaining elastic through one hole from the outside. Measure how long the elastic needs to be to encircle the book when it's closed with the tablet and cardboard tucked inside, then cut the elastic and glue its ends to the inside back cover.

STEP 8 Line up the felt-wrapped cardboard pieces with the book covers and hot-glue them together (the felt should be facing you, on the inside of the book).

STEP 9 Let the glue dry, slide the tablet under the elastic, and revel in being secretly high tech.

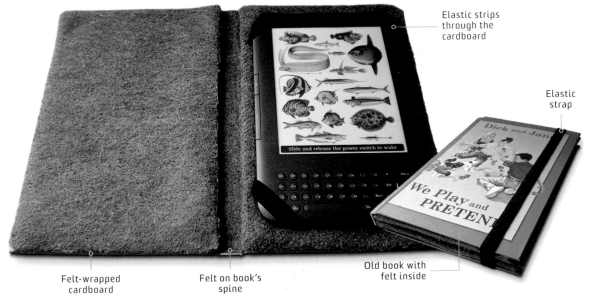

Elastic strips through the cardboard

Elastic strap

Felt-wrapped cardboard

Felt on book's spine

Old book with felt inside

HOME IMPROVEMENTS

100 Make a TV Oscilloscope

STEP 1 Turn off and unplug a black-and-white TV.

STEP 2 Remove the TV's back and find the deflector coil assembly (the large coils looped around the glass tube). There are two pairs of wires on either side of the coil. Follow them to the TV's circuit board and desolder one, then plug the TV back in and turn it on. If the screen shows a horizontal line, you've cut a wire that enables the vertical coil. If the line is vertical, you've cut a wire that enables the horizontal coil. Keep this in mind.

STEP 3 Turn off and unplug the TV. Desolder the coil's remaining three wires, then resolder them so that the two that once plugged into the horizontal coil's input on the circuit board now go to the vertical coil's input.

STEP 4 Peel back an audio cord's end and strip its wires. Twist them with the wires that went to the vertical coil.

STEP 5 Replace the TV's back and plug the audio cord into a media player. Watch your music take shape.

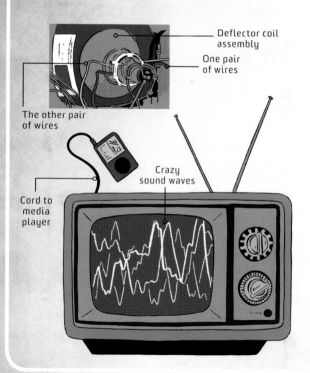

Deflector coil assembly

One pair of wires

The other pair of wires

Cord to media player

Crazy sound waves

101 Hack a TV Console into a Seat

STEP 1 Make sure the TV is off and unplugged, then open up the console's backing. Gingerly remove the electronics, speakers, and television tube inside the TV. Be especially careful with the tube, which could break.

STEP 2 On the front of the console, locate the edges of the TV screen. Draw a line on both sides extending up over the lip and onto the console's top.

STEP 3 Using a jigsaw, cut down along the guides on the console's top until you reach the TV screen's frame. Remove this part of the console's top.

STEP 4 Gently remove the screen and its frame.

STEP 5 Return the console's backing; secure with nails.

STEP 6 Measure and cut two plywood pieces to cover the sides of the cavity. Stain or paint them so they match the rest of the console and nail them in place.

STEP 7 Measure and cut two pieces of foam to serve as bottom and back cushions for the seat. Cover them with material of your choosing. Glue them down inside the console.

STEP 8 Take a seat. You've earned it.

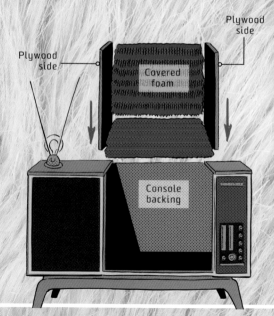

Plywood side

Plywood side

Covered foam

Console backing

102 Install an Aquarium in an Old TV

STEP 1 Unplug the television, remove its back, and carefully pull out the electronics and television tube. Be especially careful with the tube, which is fragile.

STEP 2 Measure the height, depth, and width of the hole in the back of the TV. It should fit your run-of-the-mill 20-gallon (75-l) aquarium, hopefully with a little space left over for the filter, pump, heater, and power strip.

STEP 3 Place supports to hold the aquarium's weight and boost it up so it lines up behind the TV's screen. Leave space above it for a lightbulb.

STEP 4 Use a circular saw to cut off the console's top, then transform it into a lid with two hinges and a handle.

STEP 5 Mount a fluorescent bulb to the underside of the lid with small wood screws.

STEP 6 Place the tank inside the console, along with the power strip, filter, heater, and pump. Run the power strip's wire out of the lid and replace the console's back.

STEP 7 Fill the aquarium slowly. Add fish and accessories.

STEP 8 Plug all the components into the power strip, plug the power strip into the wall, and watch your fishies swim on the big screen.

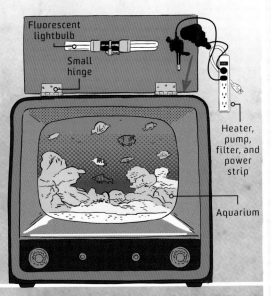

Fluorescent lightbulb

Small hinge

Heater, pump, filter, and power strip

Aquarium

103 Build a Boob Tube Bar

STEP 1 Unplug the television and open up the console's backing. Using caution, take out the electronics, speakers, and glass tube inside the TV, and remove the screen.

STEP 2 Strip out any supports you won't be using on the inside, including unnecessary screws and nails. Sand the interior to remove splinters and old glue globs.

STEP 3 You need two shelves: one for booze that displays behind the TV screen's hole, and one for wine, which should be stored where the speakers used to be. If possible, reserve any plywood bases to use as shelves, or make new ones to fit inside your console and glue them in with wood glue.

STEP 4 Remove the existing grating and grill cloth that cover the speakers. Replace the grill cloth and remount the grating with hinges that allows easy access to the wine.

STEP 5 If you like, sand and paint or stain the outside.

STEP 6 Cut and insert two mirrors: one to fit over the shelf and one to fit on the back wall behind the window. Replace the console's backing.

STEP 7 Stock the bar with your preferred liquor and wine, and host a swanky party.

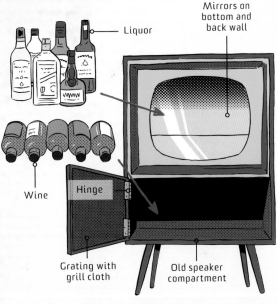

Liquor

Mirrors on bottom and back wall

Wine

Hinge

Grating with grill cloth

Old speaker compartment

HOME IMPROVEMENTS

104 Set Up a DIY Drive-In

Can't find an outdoor movie theater? Set up your own in your backyard.

Seeing a movie outdoors used to be pretty simple. Drive a bit, pay at the entrance gate, find a parking space, and wait for the towering images to flicker into view. But finding a drive-in isn't easy these days. What to do if you yearn to experience the cinema outside? Create it yourself. Here's how to put together a cheap, portable screening for a group of friends.

COST	$$$
TIME	⏱
EASY ● ○ ○ ○ ○ HARD	

Media player

Projector

Cords to power source and FM receiver

MATERIALS

White wall or sheet

Four grommets

Two tent stakes and twine

Battery-powered projector

Media player

Car cigarette lighter adapter

FM receiver

STEP 1 Use a white wall or a bedsheet as your backdrop. If using a sheet, put a grommet in each corner and secure the top grommets to trees or posts and the bottom grommets to the tent stakes using twine.

STEP 2 Hook a battery-powered, presentation-style projector up to your media player (a computer or an iPad).

STEP 3 Plug the projector into your car's cigarette lighter via an adapter to keep it juiced during the feature film.

STEP 4 Connect your media player's audio to an FM receiver. Set the receiver to the frequency of your choice.

STEP 5 Have your friends park within the specified range of the receiver and set their car radios to the same frequency as the receiver.

STEP 6 Hit play on your media player and be sure to pass the popcorn.

WARNING

Before starting this project, visit transition.fcc.gov/lpfm. This page details the FCC's regulations for low-power stations. Don't charge for attendance if you're showing a DVD, and get all proper permits if your DIY drive-in will be in a public place.

THE GRAFFITI LASER

Australian artist Chris Poole was driving around his native Perth when some curbside garbage caught his eye. Unlike the average scavenger, Poole wasn't searching for futons: He had his eye on an old slide viewer—a key component for his next project, a laser-based projector that could display photos (albeit with a green hue) to the entire town.

Thanks to his penchant for collecting, Poole already had the basic materials. To start, he rewired a tiny green laser—the kind used in a pointer—so it could work with a long-running battery pack he had lying around, which he had pulled out of an electric bicycle. Next he nailed an electronics-mounting frame to a wooden board 3 feet (1 m) in length and set the laser at one end, aimed down the frame. He snapped in a lens from a used disposable camera at the other end and set a makeshift slide holder and the scrapped slide viewer's lens in between. The viewer enlarges the beam so it covers the slide, allowing him to project an 8-by-10-foot (2.5-by-3-m) image of former *PopSci* editor-in-chief Mark Jannot from 100 feet (30 m) away.

Everyone's favorite gaming cube gets transformed into clever furniture.

Each drawer swivels to mimic the cube's trademark maneuverability, while the colored patches are magnetized so you can peel them off and arrange them how you like. Cheating never felt so good.

COST	$$
TIME	☺ ☺ ☺ ☺
EASY • • • • ○ HARD	

MATERIALS

Table saw

Straightedge

Three sheets of ½-inch (1.25-cm) plywood

Three sheets of ¼-inch (6.35-mm) plywood

Three pairs of 22-inch (56-cm) full-extension drawer slides with runners

About 60 ½-inch (1.25-cm) flat head screws

Wood glue

Brad nails

Brad nailer

Primer

Orbital sander

White paint

Router with a V-shaped bit

Cordless drill with ⅜-inch (9.5-mm) Forstner bit

54 ¼-by-1¾-inch (0.635-by-3-cm) dowels

Bench saw

Epoxy glue

45 ⅜-inch (3.75-mm) steel washers

Paint in five colors and black

36 ⅜-inch (3.75-mm) rare earth magnets

Two 1-foot (30-cm) lazy Susan bearings

STEP 1 Using a table saw and a straightedge, cut pieces of the ½-inch (1.25-cm) plywood to make the cases (the boxes that hold the drawers). Start by measuring and cutting six 2-by-2-foot (60-by-60-cm) sheets for the tops and bottoms of the cases. Then cut six 24-by-7-inch (60-by-18-cm) sheets for the sides of the cases.

STEP 2 Still working with the ½-inch (1.25-cm) plywood, cut three 24-by-7¾-inch (60-by-19.75-cm) sections for the drawer fronts. Cut six 21-by-6-inch (54-by-15-cm) sections for the drawer sides.

STEP 3 Begin working with the ¼-inch (6.35-mm) plywood. First, measure and cut three 22-by-22-inch (56-by-56-cm) pieces for the drawer bottoms. Then, to make the backs of the drawers, cut three 22-by-6-inch (55-by-15-cm) pieces. For the backs of the cases, cut three 24-by-7¾-inch (60-by-19.75-cm) pieces.

STEP 4 Cut 45 6½-by-6½-inch (16.5-by-16.5-cm) "stickers" from the ¼-inch (6.35-mm) plywood

STEP 5 Attach one of the drawer slides to each of the plywood case side panels with screws, leaving ¼ inch (6.35 mm) at the front edges, and making sure that the slides will be parallel to each other when the drawers are constructed.

STEP 6 Assemble the three cases with wood glue and brad nails, attaching top and bottom panels to side panels with the drawer slides on the inside. Let dry, then sand.

STEP 7 Prime, sand, and paint the drawers white.

STEP 8 Assemble the three drawers to fit inside these cases using the bottom, back, and side panels you cut for the drawers. Let dry and sand.

STEP 9 Attach the drawer runners to the outside of the drawers' side panels and check that they fit smoothly with the slides inside the cases.

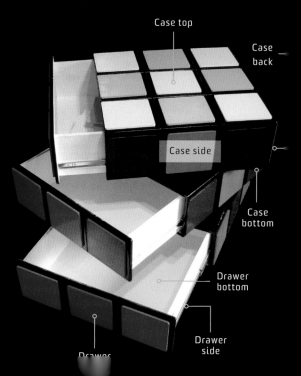

Case top

Case back

Case side

Case bottom

Drawer bottom

Drawer side

Drawer

STEP 10 Attach the faces of the drawers. Let dry and sand.

STEP 11 Use a router with a V-shaped bit and cut grooves in all the exposed faces, creating the look of cubes.

STEP 12 Drill two dowel-sized holes about three-fourths of the way through opposite corners of each of the 45 square "stickers." Using a Forstner bit, drill a shallow hole in the center of each sticker for the washer.

STEP 13 To cut the dowels in half, tape them to a piece of scrap plywood and run them through the bench saw.

STEP 14 Glue the half-dowels into the holes in the stickers, then epoxy the washers into the shallow holes in each sticker's center.

STEP 15 Prime, sand, and paint the stickers using a separate color for each set of nine.

STEP 16 Drill holes in all the exposed faces of the chest for the dowels and washers of the stickers.

STEP 17 Glue the rare-earth magnets into the center holes of the faces with epoxy. These should line up perfectly with the washers in the stickers, with enough clearance for the dowels on either side.

STEP 18 Rout out a thin layer of plywood from the bottom of the top case, the top and bottom of the center case, and the top of the bottom case and screw the lazy Susan bearings into them. Epoxy the bearings into place.

STEP 19 Attach the stickers to the sides and top, sliding the dowels into the holes.

STEP 20 Scramble the stickers or make it look solved, and move them around whenever the whimsy strikes you.

106 Sand Tiny Trim with a Razor

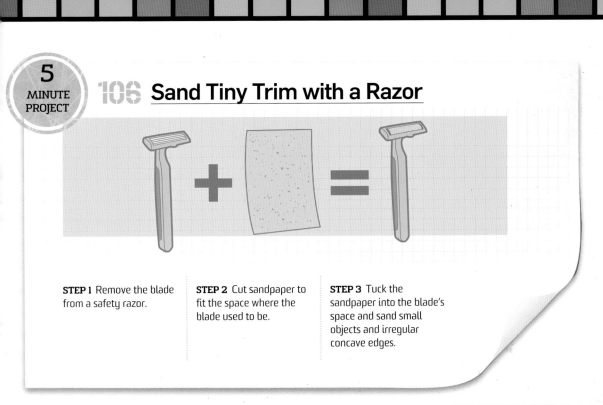

STEP 1 Remove the blade from a safety razor.

STEP 2 Cut sandpaper to fit the space where the blade used to be.

STEP 3 Tuck the sandpaper into the blade's space and sand small objects and irregular concave edges.

Resuscitate a dead electric screwdriver with quick-charging supercapacitors.

COST	$
TIME	☺☺
EASY ● ● ● ○ ○ HARD	

MATERIALS

Phillips screwdriver

3.6-volt cordless rechargeable screwdriver

Soldering iron and solder

Electrical wire

Breakout board for mini USB

Four supercapacitors, 10F and 2.5-volt

Mini B USB cable

It's the do-it-yourselfer's version of Murphy's Law: Every time you need to sink some tough screws, the battery in your cordless screwdriver is dead. So forget those plodding batteries and shorten recharge time to a minute and a half.

STEP 1 Use a standard Phillips head screwdriver to open up the rechargeable screwdriver and remove the battery.

STEP 2 Desolder the barrel-shaped charge connector and the battery connection clip from the screwdriver's circuit board. Solder a red wire from the breakout board's VCC conductor to the positive pad on the circuit board, and a black wire between the ground connections of the boards.

STEP 3 Connect two capacitors in series with the positive lead of one soldered to the negative lead of the other. Repeat with another pair. Then join the two sets together in parallel (positive to positive, negative to negative).

STEP 4 Solder the positive leads from the power pack you just made to the red wires from the switch and the circuit board. Solder the pack's negative leads to the black wires.

STEP 5 Widen the charge port on the screwdriver case large enough to access a mini B USB cable. Fasten the breakout board to the inside of the screwdriver. Line up the port with the opening, and reassemble the case.

STEP 6 Plug the screwdriver into a USB port on your computer. The red LED should glow—when it goes out, in about 90 seconds, the screwdriver is charged.

STEP 7 Enjoy your new quick-charge screwdriver.

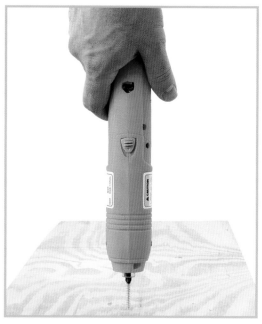

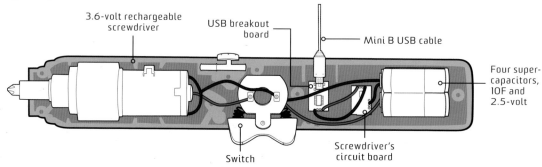

3.6-volt rechargeable screwdriver

USB breakout board

Mini B USB cable

Four super-capacitors, 10F and 2.5-volt

Switch

Screwdriver's circuit board

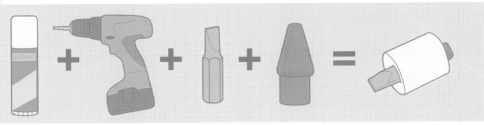

108 Make a Mini Screwdriver

STEP 1 Drill a hole in the top of a glue-stick cap that's slightly smaller than the screwdriver bit.

STEP 2 Wiggle a drill bit through the hole in the cap.

STEP 3 Put a pencil eraser on the back of the drill bit to secure it in place.

STEP 4 Screw away.

109 Remove a Stripped Screw with a Rubber Band

Stripped screws happen. Luckily, you've got that rubber-band ball to use up.

STEP 1 Place a wide rubber band across the head of the screw you want to remove.

STEP 2 Grab a screwdriver that's a size bigger than what the screw is made for.

STEP 3 Through the rubber band, apply hard, slow force to remove the stripped screw.

110 Make Duct Tape Do Double Duty

Ah, duct tape. What can you do with it? A better question may be, what *can't* you do with it?

ROPE IN A PINCH
Cut the length you need, then roll one edge inward for a pretty sturdy rope.

IMPROMPTU HINGE
Lay a small rectangle of duct tape across the gap between a cabinet's lightweight door and its frame, then close the door to fold the tape into a working hinge.

VACUUM HOSE EXTENDER
Sometimes the hose on your vacuum cleaner isn't long enough to get to out-of-reach places—like, say, your ceiling. Just add a length of PVC pipe to the hose and seal the seam with the good stuff.

TEMPORARY ROOF SHINGLE
Roof falling apart? Patch it with an improvised shingle of folded duct tape.

EMERGENCY SUNGLASSES
Fend off glare by folding a length of duct tape in half, cutting a slit in the center, and tying it around your head.

111 Hang a Magnetic Stud Finder

STEP 1 Tie a string to a strong magnet.

STEP 2 Dangle it against a wall, and mark where it clings to nails and screws embedded in the structure.

STEP 3 Look for a pattern in your marks—that's where the studs are, and where you should hang that trippy Magic Eye stereogram you found in your garage.

112 Turn Your Hard Drive into a Tool Grinder

STEP 1 Peel off all the stickers on your hard drive and pry away its top cover, using a Torx screwdriver to remove any screws.

STEP 2 Strip out the fixings inside the hard drive with the Torx screwdriver. Remove the actuator (the magnets), the actuator arm, and the circuit board. Toss these or save them for later projects.

STEP 3 Remove the platter from the spindle and trace it onto the sandpaper. Then cut out the shape with a craft knife.

STEP 4 Glue the sandpaper to the platter and reinstall it onto the drive with the aluminum spindle's bottom under the platter and the spindle's round top over the sandpaper.

STEP 5 Attach a molex connector, plug the molex connector into a power supply, and grind away.

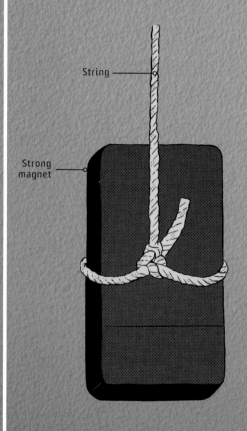

String

Strong magnet

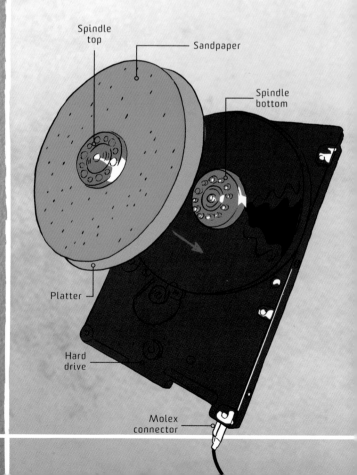

Spindle top

Sandpaper

Spindle bottom

Platter

Hard drive

Molex connector

113 Capture Screws with a Magnetic Wristband

STEP 1 Scrounge up some magnets from your home. You'll need one on the large side and several much smaller round magnets.

STEP 2 Use superglue to attach the smaller magnets to the larger magnet. You'll want to space them pretty evenly. Let dry.

STEP 3 Make a slit in the top of a terry-cloth wristband that's big enough to slide your larger magnet inside.

STEP 4 Slide the larger magnet inside the slit and sew it shut. When you're doing basic woodworking stuff, slip this wristband onto your arm and capture stray metal fasteners with its magnet.

BUILD IT!

Blast away a bucketf

MATERI

Five 18-i
of ½-i
sta

STEP 4 Tilt the
your Picasso.

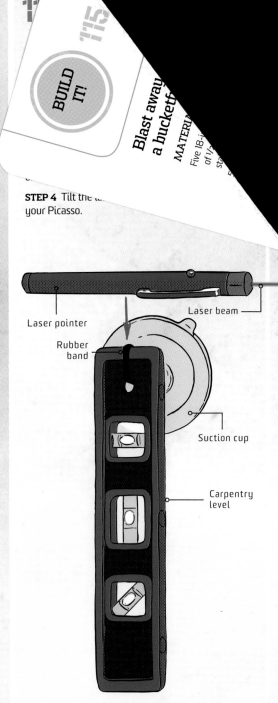

Laser pointer

Laser beam

Rubber band

Suction cup

Carpentry level

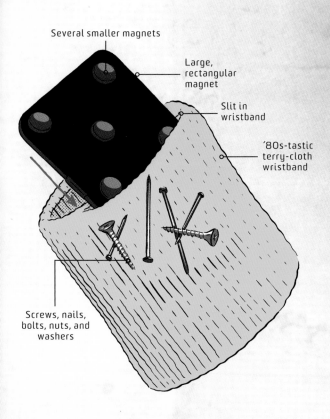

Several smaller magnets

Large, rectangular magnet

Slit in wristband

'80s-tastic terry-cloth wristband

Screws, nails, bolts, nuts, and washers

Remove Rust with Electricity

...resistant rust with
...ul of electrodes.

COST	$
TIME	◑◑
EASY ● ● ● ○ ○ HARD	

...LS

...nch (45-cm) sections
...-inch (1.25-cm) non-
...inless-steel rebar

...-gallon (19-l) plastic bucket

Drill

5 feet (1.5 m) pliable rust-
resistant wire

Pliers

5 feet (1.5 m) 12-awg insulated
copper wire

Wire strippers

Five wire nuts

Box of washing soda

Water

Small board or other
nonconductive object

Small battery charger

Hammer

Nail

One alligator clip

Rusty object

Wire brush extension mounted
on a rotary tool

Antirust spray

STEP 1 Space the five 18-inch (45-cm) non-stainless-steel rebar sections evenly inside the bucket. Use a drill with a ¼-inch (6.35-mm) bit to make two small holes in the bucket near each piece of rebar: one that's 2 inches (5 cm) down from the bucket's rim, and the second about 4 inches (10 cm) down from that.

STEP 2 To secure the rebar, thread rust-resistant wire through each hole, around the rebar, and back out again. Twist the wire tight and snip off the excess with pliers.

STEP 3 Once all rebar is in place, cut five 1-foot (30-cm) sections of copper wire and strip the ends.

STEP 4 On the outside of the bucket, connect rebar sections together with a piece of copper wire and cover with a wire nut. Leave the first and last rebar pieces unconnected, with the fifth section of copper wire loose.

STEP 5 Add 5 tablespoons of washing soda to the bucket and fill within 2 inches (5 cm) of the rim with clean water.

STEP 6 Secure a board (or any nonconductive object) across the top of the bucket.

STEP 7 With the battery charger turned off, attach its positive end to the rebar wire and nail its negative end to the nonconductive board. Then attach several alligator clips to the negative end and let them hang so that they almost touch or barely dip into the water.

STEP 8 Clean a small piece of your rusty object; attach this point to the alligator clips so that the object hangs inside the bucket. It should not touch the rebar.

STEP 9 Set the battery charger to a low setting (such as 6-volt 1.5 amp) and turn it on.

STEP 10 Bubbles will form and rust will begin to flake off. Leave your object in the water for anywhere from an hour to a couple of days. Then remove it and use a wire brush (and antirust spray, if necessary) to remove the remaining flaky rust.

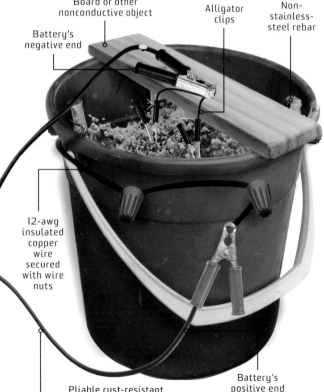

Board or other
nonconductive object

Alligator
clips

Non-
stainless-
steel rebar

Battery's
negative end

12-awg
insulated
copper
wire
secured
with wire
nuts

Pliable rust-resistant
wire to battery charger

Battery's
positive end

WARNING
We're serious about not using stainless-steel rebar for the electrodes. Stainless steel's chrome will leak during the electrolysis and form nasty compounds in your electrolyte.

116 Clean with a Toy-Car Broom

STEP 1 Use a drill and two screws to attach a very small board to the underside of a remote-controlled car.

STEP 2 Attach a disposable sweeper head to the board with a drill and two more screws. Make sure that the sweeper lies flat.

STEP 3 Use your remote to drive the dust away.

117 Rig a Superpowered Scrub Brush

When elbow grease just won't cut it, add mighty power-tool action.

Power saw with mini blade attachment

Bathroom brush with handle

MATERIALS

Scrubber brush	Clamps
Rotary tool	Electrical tape
Power saw with mini saw blade	

STEP 1 Cut a groove into the handle of a bathroom-style scrubber brush with a rotary tool.

STEP 2 Insert the power saw's mini saw blade into the groove and secure it with clamps.

STEP 3 Wrap the brush handle with electrical tape so that the clamps are secured in place.

STEP 4 Reattach the blade to the saw, turn it on, and polish your boat or scrub your tub. Just don't use it on your Benz.

HOME IMPROVEMENTS

118 Construct a Toilet-Powered Zen Fountain

Feel more relaxed with every flush of your commode.

COST	$
TIME	🕐
EASY	● ● ○ ○ ○ HARD

MATERIALS

Drill

Plastic planter

4 feet (1.2 m) plastic tubing

Waterproof silicone

Gravel

Shallow plastic dish

Hot-glue gun

Decorative stones

STEP 1 Drill a hole near the bottom of the planter's side. Insert a piece of tube long enough to reach into the toilet tank, and seal around the tube with waterproof silicone. Let dry for 24 hours and test for leakages. (This tube will direct overflow water.)

STEP 2 Cover the planter's bottom with gravel so that the overflow tube is covered. Nestle a small plastic dish (into which the tiny waterfall will flow) among the gravel pieces, being sure not to obscure the dish.

STEP 3 Stack and hot-glue decorative rocks to create elevation for your tiny waterfall.

STEP 4 On this stack of stones, glue a second piece of tubing, which will act as your intake tube. Glue more stones on top to conceal it (along with any cool decorative stuff you want). Aim the tube toward the plastic dish.

STEP 5 Remove the cover from the basin of your toilet and connect your intake tube to the tube that feeds the water to your toilet (that'd be the one that's connected to the float ball). You may need to prop up the toilet basin cover to prevent crushing the plastic tubing.

STEP 6 Direct the overflow tube back into the toilet basin. Each time you flush, the water travels into your planter and overflows back into the toilet, completing the loop.

119 Double Your Showerhead Action

Make bathtime a splash.

MATERIALS

½-inch (1.25-cm) copper fitting union

Copper-pipe cutter

5-foot (1.5-m) piece of ½-inch (1.25-cm) copper pipe

½-inch (1.25-cm) copper T

Four ½-inch (1.25-cm) 90-degree copper elbows

½-inch (1.25-cm) 45-degree copper elbow

Blowtorch and solder

Two ½-inch (1.25-cm) male adapters

Two new showerheads

Wrench

Plumber's tape

STEP 1 Unscrew your existing showerhead. Screw one half of the ½-inch (1.25-cm) fitting union to the flange.

STEP 2 Using a copper-pipe cutter, cut the pipe into three pieces: one piece 2½ feet (75 cm) long, and two 1¼ feet (38 cm), from which the new showerheads will extend.

STEP 3 Attach the two equal-length pieces of pipe with the copper T to create the T-shaped framework.

STEP 4 Attach this T-shaped framework to the long piece of pipe with a 90-degree elbow and then a 45-degree elbow. Solder all joints.

STEP 5 To the end of the contraption that will connect to the wall, attach a 90-degree elbow and then the remaining half of the fitting union. Solder in place.

STEP 6 To the ends of the T-shaped framework, attach 90-degree copper elbows to point downward. Then attach the male adapters, then the showerheads. Solder in place.

STEP 7 Screw the two halves of the fitting union together to install the double showerhead. Use plumber's tape and a wrench to create a tight seal.

STEP 8 Scrub-a-dub.

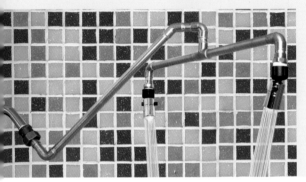

5 MINUTE PROJECT

120 Craft a Toilet-Paper Dispenser

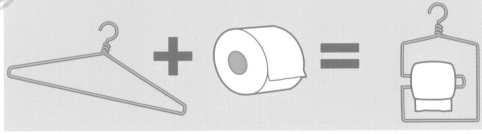

STEP 1 Pull down the corners of a clotheshanger.

STEP 2 Bend one side inward to create a space for the toilet-paper roll. Straighten the bottom of the hanger to make a rectangular shape.

STEP 3 Add toilet paper and hang near the can.

121 Track Your Food's Freshness

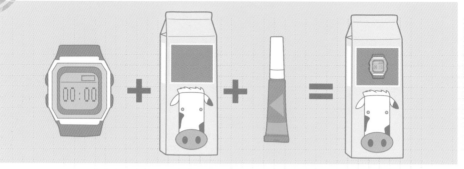

STEP 1 Remove the band from a basic digital watch.

STEP 2 When you open a container of perishable food, set the watch's timer.

STEP 3 Glue the watch face to the food item.

STEP 4 See instantly how many days have passed—no sniffing necessary.

122 Turn a Tea Bag into a Lantern

Just a few quick mods can turn your tea bag into a lantern—and a rocket!

MATERIALS

Scissors

Tea bag

Match or lighter

WARNING
Be careful not to let your homemade lantern come into contact with anything flammable. Whether you perform this experiment indoors or out, keep a fire extinguisher nearby in case of emergencies; be sure to heed local fire codes and fire danger risk levels.

STEP 1 Use scissors to remove the string, tag, and top, crimped edge of a tea bag. Note: This may only work with traditional tea bags, the kind that include the tag and string for steeping.

STEP 2 Discard the contents of the now open tea bag.

STEP 3 Unfold the tea bag. You will note as you unfold it that the tea bag was simply a hollow cylinder, folded over and stapled in order to hold onto the tea leaves.

STEP 4 Use your fingers to gently expand the area inside the former tea bag. Once you open up enough space on the inside, the bag will return to its original shape as a hollow cylinder. Continue expanding the inside of the paper cylinder so that it is round and open on both ends.

STEP 5 Place the hollow paper cylinder upright on a flat surface, so that it stands of its own accord.

STEP 6 Use a match or lighter to ignite the top of the paper cylinder.

STEP 7 Watch as the paper cylinder slowly burns from top to bottom. As the flame reaches the bottom, the hot, burning, lighter-than-air remnants of the paper cylinder will cause your lantern to become buoyant.

STEP 8 Liftoff!

123 Harvest Fridge Magnets from a Hard Drive

Get over that dead hard drive and pry out the superstrong magnets hiding in it.

COST	$
TIME	⏱
EASY ● ○ ○ ○ ○ HARD	

MATERIALS

Computer with a dead hard drive

Torx screwdriver kit

STEP 1 Unplug your computer before you begin working.

STEP 2 Open up your case and locate the hard drive. There'll be a power cord attached to it; unplug that, and undo any screws holding the hard drive in place. Pull the hard drive out of the case.

STEP 3 Using a star-shaped Torx screwdriver kit, start unscrewing the many, many screws on the hard drive's case and remove it. You'll probably need to remove a lot of stickers in the process, too.

STEP 4 Once you're looking at the internal workings of the hard drive, locate the actuator arm (it's the part that protrudes over the disc-like thing, which is called a platter). Behind it is the actuator (aka, one of two big-deal rare-earth magnets that you're after). Unscrew its fasteners with a Torx screwdriver and pry it off.

STEP 5 Once you've got the first magnet off, you'll see a second one beneath it. Pry it out with a screwdriver, too, and use the magnets to spruce up the old fridge.

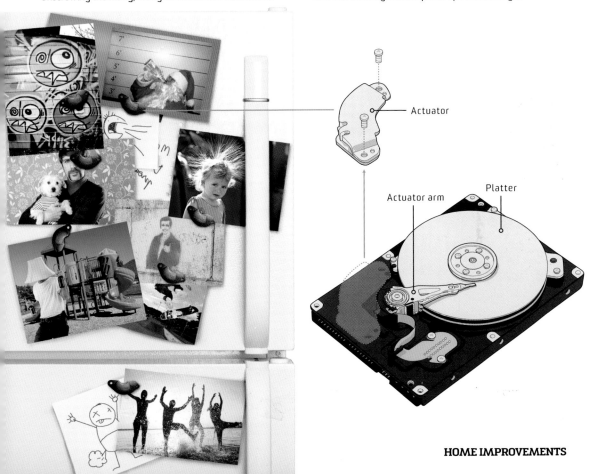

Actuator

Platter

Actuator arm

124 Dinner to Go in a Nitrous-Injected Dining Table

The world's speediest piece of furniture, caught on film.

Why would a man spend a year and $7,000 const
a dining-room table that cruises at 130 miles per h
(210 km/h) and shoots flames up into the air as it s
away? Sheer competitiveness, as it turns out. A rec
the world's fastest furniture existed—92 miles per
(148 km/h) on a sofa—and Perry Watkins wanted

Watkins, a sales director in Wingrave, England, cho
dining table as his furniture type because he thoug
would be easiest to mount onto a small, fast car. H
by buying an old two-seat Reliant Scimitar Sabre \
convertible, ripping off the fiberglass panels, stripp
down to the chassis, and installing an off-the-shelf
oxide injection system for added power.

The resulting vehicle, dubbed Fast Food, smoked tl
record, clocking an average speed of 113.8 miles pe
(180 km/h). But it was the trimmings that really w
onlookers. Watkins bolted dishware to the table, as
variety of authentic-looking foods, including gravy
fiberglass resin and tea kettles that puff flames 10
into the air. The helmeted diner is actually a mann

Watkins is the real man behind the wheel, with his
barely visible underneath a plastic chicken on a pla
chicken is quasi-functional: Before kicking in, the n
system purges excess air through a tube leading to
fowl. "A 6-foot [1.8-m] plume of white smoke come
of the chicken's backside," Watkins says. He figure
probably a world record, too.

RAISE THE ROOF
Where's Watkins? He's in the driver's seat below the table, with his head poking from under a plated chicken.

125 Rig a Coaster that Prevents Mouth Burn

Never burn your mouth on a hot drink again with this ingenious coaster.

COST	$
TIME	◔ ◕
EASY ● ● ● ○ ○ HARD	

MATERIALS

LM324N (low-power operational amplifier)

Thermistor

Empty metal shoe polish container

Electrical tape

Rotary tool

Red LED

Hobby foam

Soldering iron and solder

1k-ohm resistor

10k-ohm resistor

10k-ohm potentiometer

Electrical wire

Wire strippers

3.7-volt battery

Mug

STEP 1 Clip off the unnecessary legs from the operational amplifier, keeping pins 1, 2, 3, 4, and 11.

STEP 2 Attach the thermistor to the inside of the metal container's lid with some electrical tape. Be sure to insulate both of the thermistor leads with tape.

STEP 3 Drill a hole into the side of the metal container for holding the red LED. Insulate the bottom of the container with some scrap paper or hobby foam.

STEP 4 Follow the circuitry diagram to make the circuit.

STEP 5 Fit the components inside the metal container, connect the 3.7-volt battery, and close the metal lid.

STEP 6 Check your LED light by putting your finger on the coaster lid. If it lights up, you're good to start calibrating it. If not, check your wiring.

STEP 7 Place your cup of fresh brew on the smart coaster and use the 10k-ohm potentiometer to adjust the thermistor's sensitivity. Turn the potentiometer until the LED glows and monitor the temperature of your beverage.

STEP 8 When the cup's temp has fallen to your desired drinking level, turn the potentiometer until the LED goes out. Your smart coaster is now calibrated for this mug. Remember, if you change mugs, you will have to recalibrate. Bottoms up.

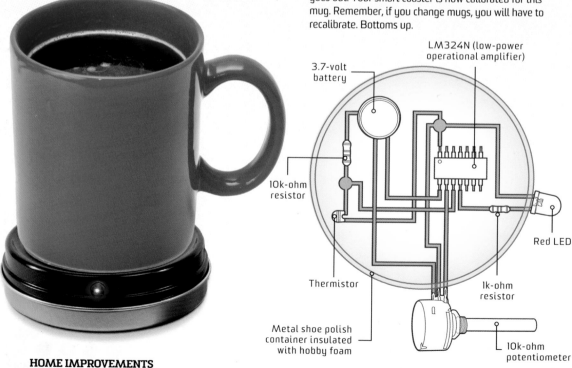

3.7-volt battery

LM324N (low-power operational amplifier)

10k-ohm resistor

Red LED

Thermistor

1k-ohm resistor

Metal shoe polish container insulated with hobby foam

10k-ohm potentiometer

126 <u>Put an Old Coffee Can to Good Use</u>

Long after the caffeine rush has worn off, coffee cans come in handy. Here's some clever stuff to do with your empties.

PIE TINS

LARGE-HUB REEL FOR EXTENSION CORD

DRILL SMALL HOLES

PUNCH HOLE UPWARD FOR COTTON WICK

CRANKCASE OIL

SOLDER WASHER

EMERGENCY FLARE
TO BE ASSEMBLED ON THE ROAD

SMALL PARTS CLEANER
SCREEN HOLDS PARTS, LETS SEDIMENT FALL TO THE BOTTOM OF THE CAN

LINE MARKER
FOR BADMINTON OR TENNIS COURT

COAT-HANGER WIRE

DISPOSABLE PAINT PAIL

FIT WITH WIRE HANDLE FOR WIPING BRUSH

KEROSENE OR SOLVENT

ROLL-BACK TOY
AS CAN IS ROLLED FORWARD, WEIGHT WINDS UP RUBBER BAND, CAUSING CAN TO TURN

PARCHMENT LACED OVER CAN

TOY BANJO
USE GUT OR RUBBER BANDS FOR STRINGS

OUTDOOR COOKER
SAND SATURATED WITH GAS BURNS LONG AND CLEAN

COVER FOR SNUFFER

2 INCHES (5 CM) SAND

127 Improvise a Sous-Vide Cooker

Join the sous-vide craze with this el cheapo home-built model.

The trick to delicious, evenly cooked meat is keeping your water bath at a precise temperature by using a thermocoupler temperature sensor and a proportional-integral-derivative (PID) controller. Once you master this, play with other setups—a pot of water on an electric plate, an electric kettle, or a lightbulb in an insulated chamber.

MATERIALS

Cheap slow cooker or rice cooker with an on/off switch

Water

Thermocoupler temperature sensor

PID controller with auto-tuning feature

Vacuum sealer or zip-top plastic bag and straw

Food

COST	$$
TIME	☺☺
EASY ●●●○○ HARD	

STEP 1 Fill your slow cooker with enough water to cover the food you'll be cooking.

STEP 2 Plug your slow cooker and thermocoupler into your PID controller, and your PID into a power outlet. (If you're feeling ambitious, there are several online tutorials on making your own PID from scratch. The model we use here will run you between $35 and $70—far cheaper than the $1,000 lab-grade immersion cooker on the market.)

STEP 3 Now it's time to vacuum-pack your food. If you don't have a vacuum sealer, try freezing your marinated meat and putting it in a sandwich bag, sticking the thermocoupler into your meat inside the bag, and partially sealing it up. Then suck the remaining air out with a straw and quickly seal it.

STEP 4 Set the desired temperature. The PID controller's LED display will show the thermocoupler's reading. Use the buttons to set how hot you need the cooker to get, based on the required temperature for your meat.

STEP 5 Place your meat in the slow cooker. Cook until the thermocoupler reading indicates that your meat has reached the desired temperature.

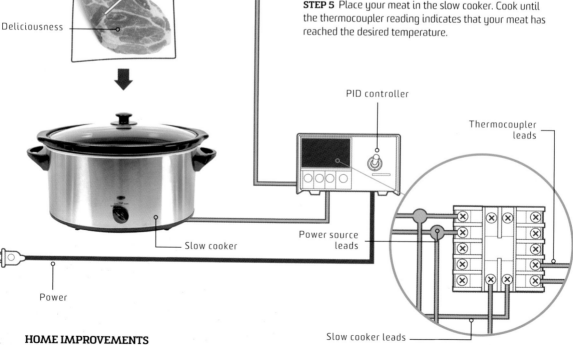

Thermocoupler temperature sensor

Deliciousness

PID controller

Thermocoupler leads

Power source leads

Slow cooker

Power

Slow cooker leads

128 Build a DIY smoker

This clay-pot cooking device gives food a wood-smoked taste.

MATERIALS

Large unglazed clay pot with base

Two bricks or cinder blocks

Hot plate

Drill with masonry bit

Grill thermometer

Stainless steel saucepan without handle

Wood chips

Circular grill grate

STEP 1 Place the pot on two bricks or cinder blocks, then situate the hot plate inside the pot. Run the hot plate's wire through the drainage hole in the pot's bottom.

STEP 2 Attach a masonry bit to a drill and make a hole in the pot's base large enough to fit a grill thermometer.

STEP 3 Place a stainless-steel saucepan on top of the hot plate. (If you have one with a handle, remove it.)

STEP 4 Place wood chips in the pan, and a circular grill grate in the pot above the pan.

STEP 5 Throw some ribs on the grill grate and put the pot's base on the pot as a cover. Then place the pot in an open area, plug in your hot plate, and start cooking.

129 Set Up an Umbrella Solar Cooker

What to do with an umbrella on a sunny day? Fry eggs on it!

MATERIALS

Umbrella with ribs

Hacksaw

Plastic or acrylic mirror sheets, mirror film, or heavy-duty aluminum foil

Newspaper

Pencil

Tape or glue

Soldering iron and solder

Small barbecue grill rack

Metal plant stand

Nonstick aluminum pot or frying pan

STEP 1 Cut the shaft off an umbrella with a hacksaw. Check that its ribs are in good shape, as they'll be supporting the reflective material that cooks your food.

STEP 2 Choose your reflective material, either mirror sheets (which are more durable but more costly and difficult to find) or aluminum foil, which will need to be replaced once you close the umbrella.

STEP 3 Using a piece of newspaper, create a template by tracing one of the triangular areas between the umbrella's ribs. Use this to cut enough reflective triangles to cover all of the umbrella's inside canvas.

STEP 4 Attach the reflective material to the umbrella with tape (or glue, if working with mirror sheets).

STEP 5 Solder the grill rack to a plant stand.

STEP 6 Place the umbrella on the ground in the sun and set the plant stand in the center.

STEP 7 Place an aluminum pot on the grill stand and watch the sun heat up your meal. Rotate the cooker at least twice an hour to keep it in the sun's strongest rays.

130 Do Stuff with Bottle Caps

Next time you pop open a cold beer or soda,
pocket its cap and put it to use.

SOAP-SLIME KILLER
Twist a bottle cap into the bottom of a bar of soap—it prevents sticky crud from building up on your sink or tub surface.

FRIDGE MAGNET
Glue a small circular magnet inside a bottle cap with the nonmagnetic side facing the cap's back, then smack it on the fridge to hold up the number of that take-out joint you like so much.

TINY CANDLES
Place a wick in the cap's bottom, then pour hot wax to fill. You'll be well prepped next time the lights go out.

PLAYING PIECES
If you've got two 12-packs of different brands of beer, you're more than on your way to a good Friday night: You've got a full set of checkers pieces. Now all you need is a checkered tablecloth and a friend to play (and help drink).

MUD-ROOM MAT
Nail caps with their labels facing downward in a grid design onto a piece of wood. Place the mat in front of your door, and never track mud through the house again.

131 Create a Life-Size Cardboard Cutout

STEP 1 Using a digital camera that shoots at least seven megapixels, snap a photo of a hilarious person.

STEP 2 Use photo-editing software to delete the background, turn any negative spaces gray or beige, and enlarge the image to life size.

STEP 3 Print the image out in sections and tape it together, or have a copy shop print out the image full size.

STEP 4 Trim the figure out of its background, leaving about a 2-inch (5-cm) border. Don't cut out the area between the figure's feet—a wide, solid bottom will help support it.

STEP 5 Attach cardboard pieces with spray adhesive to make a single piece that's big enough to fit your image.

STEP 6 Mount the image to the cardboard with the spray adhesive, and trim the cutout with a craft knife.

STEP 7 Cut out two cardboard supports and make slits in the bottom of your cutout. Slide the supports in to make it stand.

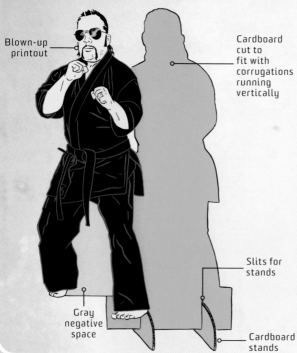

Blown-up printout

Cardboard cut to fit with corrugations running vertically

Slits for stands

Gray negative space

Cardboard stands

132 Lounge in a Cardboard Hammock

STEP 1 Cut cardboard into six strips 4 feet (1.2 m) long and about 1 foot (30 cm) wide, and two pieces 3 feet (90 cm) long and about 2 feet (60 cm) wide.

STEP 2 If you're recycling cardboard, patch holes and reinforce tears and weak spots with duct tape.

STEP 3 Duct-tape three of the six long strips together so their sides touch. Repeat with the other three, then tape the two sections together end to end.

STEP 4 Tape your remaining two pieces of cardboard over the center seam on the top and bottom to reinforce it. Use a lot of tape over each seam.

STEP 5 Make eight holes in the hammock, one at each corner and two near the center along each long edge.

STEP 6 Thread a piece of rope a little longer than the hammock through the holes along one side. Repeat on the other side.

STEP 7 Cut a broom handle in half and thread it through the two holes in the corners of the hammock's short sides. Reinforce with duct tape.

STEP 8 Drill two eyebolts at equal height into two nearby trees. Tie the hammock's rope to the eyebolts. Take it down if there's a chance of rain.

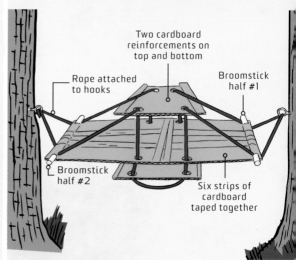

Two cardboard reinforcements on top and bottom

Rope attached to hooks

Broomstick half #1

Broomstick half #2

Six strips of cardboard taped together

133 Chat on a Cardboard Telephone

STEP 1 Take an old phone apart, removing the casing around the electronics.

STEP 2 Cut out pieces of cardboard to fit around the electronics in your phone's handset. This will vary according to your phone—trace its case as a template.

STEP 3 Using a craft knife, cut out spaces in the cardboard handset through which you'll be able to access the keypad. Punch holes in the cardboard that will cover the speaker and the microphone.

STEP 4 Measure your cardboard handset and create a cardboard base that the handset can rest on. It should include a protruding piece of cardboard where the phone's depressor will hit, hanging up the phone.

STEP 5 Tape the electronics inside the cardboard handset and base, lining up all components with the various openings in the cardboard. Make a small opening in the base's bottom for the cord.

STEP 6 Dial someone up.

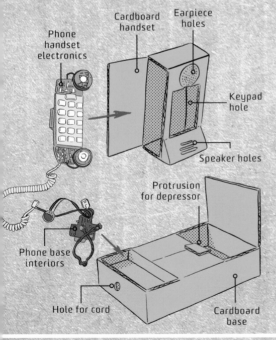

Phone handset electronics

Cardboard handset

Earpiece holes

Keypad hole

Speaker holes

Phone base interiors

Protrusion for depressor

Hole for cord

Cardboard base

134 Hang Up Cardboard Blinds

STEP 1 Measure your window's height and width, then add about 20 inches (50 cm) to the height. Cut your cardboard to these dimensions, with its corrugations running horizontally.

STEP 2 Measure every 5 inches (12 cm) along the cardboard and mark these lines with a ruler. Using the back of a box cutter, score along the marks.

STEP 3 Flip the cardboard over and mark halfway between the scored lines. Score these marks in the opposite direction.

STEP 4 Accordion-fold the cardboard, firmly creasing every other line in the opposite direction.

STEP 5 With the cardboard all folded up, drill a hole through each end of the top all the way through to the bottom.

STEP 6 Thread a needle with twine and pull it through the holes on one side; knot it at the top. Repeat on the other side.

STEP 7 Drill two small eyebolts into the top of the window frame so that they line up with the string. Hang the blinds.

STEP 8 Fasten clothespins to the bottom of the twine lengths. When you want more light, push up the clothespins. For darkness, slide them down and let the cardboard unfold.

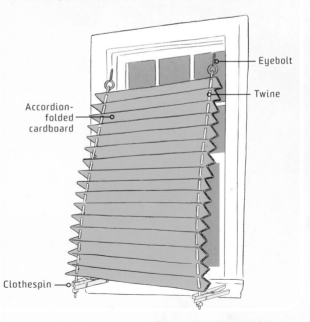

Eyebolt

Twine

Accordion-folded cardboard

Clothespin

135 Put Together a Homemade Wind Mill

Kiss those high energy bills goodbye with a backyard wind turbine.

COST	$$$
TIME	☺ ☺ ☺ ☺
EASY ● ● ● ● ○ HARD	

MATERIALS

Hole saw

Two precut round steel plates 2½ inches (6.35 cm) in diameter

1-inch (2.5-cm) steel tubing

Arc welder

Jigsaw

1-inch- (2.5-cm-) thick plywood

Drill

4-inch (10-cm) PVC pipe

Screws and wingnuts

Aluminum sheeting

Epoxy

¼-inch (6.35-mm) metal rods

Sprockets and chain

Salvaged alternator

Lazy Susan bearing

3-inch (7.5-cm) steel tubing

Charge controller

Four car batteries

DC/AC inverter

Power cord

1-inch (2.5-cm) steel tubing

2-foot (60-cm) disc of 1-inch- (2.5-cm-) thick plywood

2½-inch (6.35-cm) precut metal plate #1

2-foot (60-cm) PVC half-pipe

2-foot (60-cm) aluminum sheeting

¼-inch (6.35-mm) metal rods

2-foot (60-cm) disc of 1-inch- (2.5-cm-) thick plywood

2½-inch (6.35-cm) precut metal plate #2

Sprocket and chain

Salvaged alternator

Lazy Susan bearing

3-inch (7.5-cm) steel tubing

Charge controller

Electrical cord to circuit box in your home

Four car batteries

DC/AC inverter

STEP 1 Using a hole saw, cut holes in the center of the steel plates that fit the 1-inch (2.5-cm) steel tubing.

STEP 2 Cut the steel tubing to 2 feet (60 cm) in length. Use an arc welder to connect it to the small plates, making an axle.

STEP 3 Using a jigsaw, cut the 1-inch- (2.5-cm-) thick plywood into two discs 2 feet (60 cm) in diameter. Drill a hole into their centers for the steel tubing. Slide the wood onto the axle, screwing the discs onto the steel plates.

STEP 4 Measure and cut sections of PVC pipe 2 feet (60 cm) in length; cut them into half-pipes.

STEP 5 Use a jigsaw to cut the aluminum sheeting into three sections 2 feet (60 cm) long and 1 foot (30 cm) wide.

STEP 6 Drill three evenly spaced holes into one edge of each PVC half-pipe and attach the aluminum sheeting with epoxy to form a J shape. Reinforce the J shapes with small screws.

STEP 7 Use epoxy to secure each J shape to the edges of the discs, with the flat face of the sheeting facing the axis.

STEP 8 Drill three holes in the wood discs so you can slide in metal rods at the center point of the half-pipes.

STEP 9 Weld a sprocket around the axle's end and a second sprocket to your alternator's spindle. Hook the two up with the chain.

STEP 10 Fit and weld the lazy Susan bearing to the top of the 3-inch (7.5-cm) steel tubing. Mount the entire assembly onto the lazy Susan bearing so it will swivel when the wind blows.

STEP 11 Hook your alternator to a charge controller, then connect its positive and negative lines to the first car battery. Connect all four car batteries in a row.

STEP 12 Hook the last car battery to DC/AC inverter, and then power your home's circuit box. Check with your local power-supply company for specifics, if needed.

136 Hook Up a Solar Charger

Keep your gadgets powered even when you're off the grid.

MATERIALS

Jigsaw	Soldering iron and solder
Plywood	1/4-inch (6.35-mm) plastic mono plug
Drill	12-volt 12AH rechargeable battery
Hammer	
Nails	4 feet (1.2 m) 18-gauge wire
Two 1-inch (2.5 cm) wood slats	15-amp DC panel meter
5-watt, 12-volt solar panel	Solar DC charger controller
Hinge	Two female terminal disconnects
Cigarette-lighter Y adapter	

STEP 1 Check online to discover your home's latitude. This is the angle at which you'll mount your solar panel.

STEP 2 Cut six pieces of plywood for the box. The lid should be slightly larger than the solar panel. Trim the top edges of the side, front, and back pieces to the appropriate angle. Cut the bottom to fit.

STEP 3 Drill a hole in each side panel for airflow: one in the back panel for the controller and battery cords, and one in the lid for the solar panel's cord. Then nail the wooden slats to the lid and mount the solar panel to it. Assemble the box with a hinge for the lid.

STEP 4 Snip off the cigarette-lighter plug and solder the 1/4-inch (6.35-mm) mono plug onto the Y adapter. Insert the mono plug into the controller's 12-volt output.

STEP 5 Connect all four power leads from the battery and the solar panel to the controller's input terminals. Hook up the 15-amp DC panel meter to the controller's input terminal for the panel.

STEP 6 Test all connections with the meter. Connect the red wire with a female-terminal disconnect to the battery's positive terminal, and connect the black wire to the negative terminal.

STEP 7 Place the station in the sun with the solar panel pointed south (north if you're in the southern hemisphere). Plug something in!

137 Set Up DIY Grow Lights

Create a light system to keep houseplants thriving during winter's short days.

Setting up specialized grow lights that mimic the sun's rays is a good solution, but you can get similar results with LEDs. We connected three inside a clear plastic tube to make a "light spike" that you can stick into a pot for direct exposure, and added a controller that adjusts the brightness.

COST	$$
TIME	🙂 🙂
EASY ● ● ● ○ ○ HARD	

MATERIALS

Drill
Project box
2.1-mm power-connector jack
10-position header
100k-ohm slide potentiometer
Soldering iron and solder
Electrical wire
10k-ohm resistor

White LED design kit
Wire strippers
Five clear plastic tubes with endcaps
Five two-position connectors
15-volt 1A wall-mount power supply

STEP 1 Drill six holes in your project box to accommodate the various components, then assemble the controller by mounting the power-connector jack inside the box and the 10-position header and the 100k-ohm slide potentiometer on the box's sides.

STEP 2 Wire the box according to the circuitry diagram.

STEP 3 Cut the wire inside the LED design kit into five equal lengths. Attach the red wire to the red connector, and the black wire to the black connector, on each LED strip. Slip each strip inside a clear tube, and seal it with the endcaps so that it's watertight.

STEP 4 Add the two-position connectors that will hook up the tubes and the box. Attach each one to the red and black wires from each LED strip.

STEP 5 Press a spike into your plant container. Keep all wiring, electrical connections, and the LED strips away from soil and moisture.

STEP 6 Plug the spikes' two-position connectors into the control box's 10-position header, and connect the power supply to turn the LEDs on.

STEP 7 Adjust the slide potentiometer to control the brightness of the spikes, and watch your garden grow.

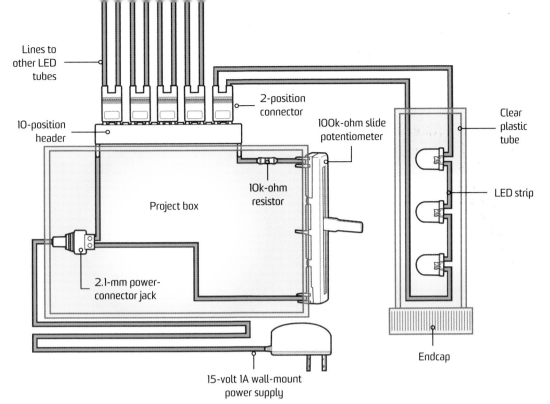

Lines to
other LED
tubes

2-position
connector

10-position
header

100k-ohm slide
potentiometer

Clear
plastic
tube

10k-ohm
resistor

LED strip

Project box

2.1-mm power-
connector jack

Endcap

15-volt 1A wall-mount
power supply

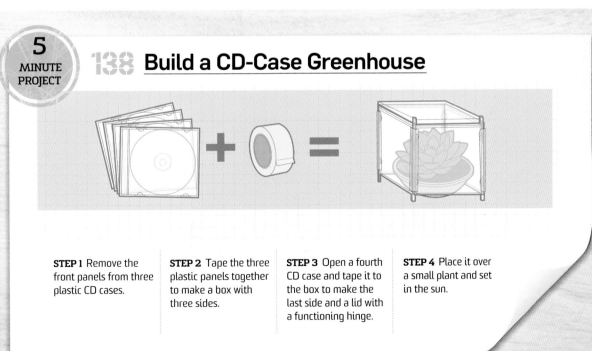

5 MINUTE PROJECT

138 **Build a CD-Case Greenhouse**

STEP 1 Remove the front panels from three plastic CD cases.

STEP 2 Tape the three plastic panels together to make a box with three sides.

STEP 3 Open a fourth CD case and tape it to the box to make the last side and a lid with a functioning hinge.

STEP 4 Place it over a small plant and set in the sun.

Never get caught in a surprise shower again with this umbrella stand, which lights up when the forecast calls for rain. To make it, you can 3D-print the model you see here, or repurpose an old umbrella stand. You can even program your phone to alert you when you've forgotten your umbrella!

COST $$

TIME ☺ ☺ ☺

EASY ● ● ● ● ○ HARD

MATERIALS

3D printer and filament

Four M3 hex nuts

littleBits light wire module

Wire cutters or pliers

Tape or zip ties

Pressure sensor bit

Soldering iron and solder

¼-inch- (6.5-mm-) thick, 3-inch- (7.6-cm-) diameter round stainless steel plate

Four 10mm M3 hex bolts

Allen wrench for M3 bolts

littleBits USB power module

littleBits cloudBit module

littleBits mounting board

USB power cloudBit Light wire

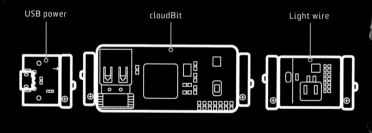

Using littleBits modules and miniature circuit boards that snap together with magnets is the easiest way to handle this hack. The stand connects to an online weather forecast through a service that allows Web applications to talk.

STEP 1 To print your own stand, visit www.popsci.com/thebigbookofhacks and download the 3D design files. Print both the top and bottom STL/OBJ files. Note: You should print the "repaired" version of the top STL.

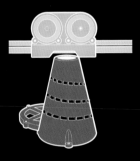

STEP 2 On the bottom piece of the printed stand, pressure-fit the four nuts into the cutouts.

STEP 3 Next, you'll install the light wire into the top part of the stand. The stand prints with support beams around the length of the spiral cutout. (This is to support the printing process.) Before you install the light wire, use a pair of wire cutters or pliers to carefully remove all the support beams. Then snap the EL wire into place, starting from the top. (If you're using a pre-made stand, just wrap the wire around it and fasten with tape or zip ties.) Tie off the excess light wire.

STEP 4 To extend the leads on the pressure sensor, use a soldering iron to carefully desolder the sensor and then insert 1/2-inch (2.5-cm) wires in-line with both leads.

STEP 5 Place the pressure sensor in the center of the round steel plate. Put the plate in the cutout of the bottom of the stand. Then put the top part of the stand on top of the steel plate and the bottom part of the stand. Before inserting the screws, ensure that you can see the pressure sensor centered within the stand cutout when looking down into the stand from above.

STEP 6 Once you're sure it's centered, install the bolts. Be careful not to overtighten them. Once that's done, the hardware is complete.

STEP 7 Snap the littleBits modules onto the mounting board, with USB power feeding into the cloudBit and then the light wire.

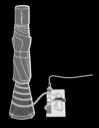

STEP 8 Follow the instructions that came with the cloudBit to connect it to Wi-Fi and register it.

STEP 9 Create an account at IFTTT. com. Add the littleBits channel and make sure your cloudBit shows up.

STEP 10 Create a new "Recipe" on IFTTT. For "This," select the "Weather" channel. Pick "Current Condition Changes To" and select "Rain" to activate the recipe under rainy conditions.

STEP 11 For "That," select the "littleBits" channel. Pick "Set Output Level" for the option. Choose your cloudBit, and set the level to 100 and the duration to "Forever."

STEP 12 Repeat Steps 10 and 11, but choose "Clear" for the weather condition and zero for the output level. This tells the light wire to turn off on a dry day.

140 Set Up a Remote Pet Feeder

COST	$$$
TIME	🙂🙂
EASY ● ● ● ● ○ HARD	

Make sure your fish never goes hungry with this WiFi-activated feeder from littleBits, which you control with your phone or computer.

This hack uses cloudBit, which connects your project to the Internet, and IFTTT (If this, then that), a service that lets you connect to different web apps through simple conditional statements.

When your feeder receives a signal through the cloudBit, the servo (a small device with an output shaft and motor often used in remote-controlled devices) is activated. A food container (with a small hole in its side) is attached to the servo. When the servo turns, a few pieces of food drop out of the container and into a bowl. You can adjust the hole and size of the container to feed a cat or dog, too.

MATERIALS

Laser cutter

¼-inch- (6.5-mm-) thick, 24-by-18-inch (60-by-46-cm) sheet of blue acrylic

¼-inch- (6.5-mm-) thick, 12-by-12-inch (30-by-30-cm) sheet of clear acrylic

⅛-inch- (3-mm-) thick, 12-by-12-inch (30-by-30-cm) sheet of clear acrylic

⅛-inch- (3-mm-) thick, 12-by-12-inch (30-by-30-cm) sheet of white acrylic

No. 33 acrylic glue

Sandpaper

⅜-inch- (9.5-mm-) thick wood dowel

littleBits servo

littleBits cloudBit

littleBits USB power

littleBits microUSB wall adapter

⅜-inch- (9.5-mm-) long acrylic nuts

M3x0.5x8MM nylon hex nut

M3x0.5x8MM nylon screw

Four adhesive shoes

Drill

Round metal tin

High-strength bonding tape

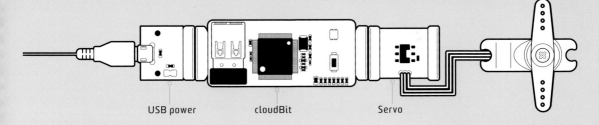

USB power   cloudBit   Servo

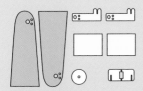

STEP 1 Begin by making the stand for the remote pet feeder. Laser cut all the pieces using the cut template found here: www.popsci.com/thebigbookofhacks.

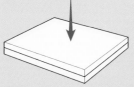

STEP 2 Using the acrylic glue, adhere the two clear rectangles together. (Doubling up the layers here makes for a sturdier base.)

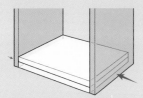

STEP 3 Next, glue the base and two side pieces together.

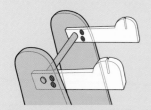

STEP 4 Cut the dowel to 4 inches (10 cm) in length and sand the two ends

to make them smooth. Then assemble the top shelf, securing its arms to the inside of the stand with acrylic nuts.

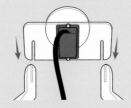

STEP 5 Secure the servo to the servo holder with the small nylon nuts and screws. Then place the servo holder into the slots on the shelf arms.

STEP 6 Build the circuit, following the circuit diagram above. Set up the cloudBit if you haven't already. (Find info about how to do this at www.popsci.com/thebigbookofhacks.)

STEP 7 Stick the circuit to the stand using littleBits adhesive shoes (hook-and-loop strips) to hold the circuit in place.

STEP 8 To make the food container, drill or cut a small hole in the side of the round tin. This is where the food will fall out when the servo turns. Use a high-strength bonding tape to fix the tin to the servo's rotating disc. (If you are using a large container, screw the tin directly to the servo arm for more support.)

STEP 9 Now you can feed your dear pets remotely! You can activate the feeder in a couple of different ways: Use the littleBits button in Cloud Control to send a single pulse to the cloudBit, activating the servo, or set up an automated feeding schedule with an IFTTT channel, like Date & Time, which provides triggers that fire on schedule. Information on both methods is available at www.popsci.com/thebigbookofhacks.

141 Man's Best Friend Gets a High-Tech Home

This dream doghouse comes complete with a solar heating system, LED lights, and a Wi-Fi security camera.

Former *PopSci* photographer John Carnett decided to make this pooch palace for Pearl, his labradoodle, after she dutifully watched him build a new house for three years. A standard model just wouldn't do, though, so he went a little overboard. After creating the design with computer-aided design (CAD) software, he added a solar hot-water radiant-heating system and made a green roof that retains rainwater, creates oxygen, and improves insulation. Then he decked it out with a few other touches, including some colored LED lights to brighten things up and a Web-enabled wireless video camera that lets him keep an eye on Pearl from his computer or phone. That's plenty of features for her, but the doghouse has one extra benefit for Carnett himself: The battery that powers it also powers all the low-voltage exterior lights on his property.

Carnett made a frame of 2-by-4-foot (60-by-120-cm) boards and walls made of insulated wood panels. The south-facing wall has a solar panel, which charges the gel battery mounted inside the house. A solar charge controller, switches, and other parts are inside a waterproof panel mounted on the exterior for easy adjustment. When the photovoltaic panels are exposed to sunlight, a pump circulates glycol fluid through evacuated tubes to a series of copper pipes underneath the floor. The pipes heat a concrete backing board below them, which in turn disperses heat through the hardwood floor into the house.

The porch ceiling contains a waterproof 12-volt LED light, and the two interior lights go on automatically when it gets dark outside. That way, Pearl always has a welcoming light on when she comes home at night.

142 Light Up Your Dog

Keep track of your pooch on those afterdark strolls.

MATERIALS

Dog collar and leash

Electrical tape

EL (electroluminescent) wire with attached battery pack

Tape

Scissors

Needle

Fishing wire

Thimble

Two AA batteries

STEP 1 Fit the collar to your dog so that it's snug. You won't be able to readjust this collar once it's complete, so it's best if Fido is full-grown.

STEP 2 Use electrical tape to attach the EL wire's battery pack to the top of the collar near where the leash attaches.

STEP 3 Bend the EL wire into your desired shape and set it on the outside of the collar. Use tape to hold it in place. Trim any excess wire.

STEP 4 Thread your needle with fishing wire and secure it with a knot at the end. Then sew stitches over the EL wire to secure it more permanently to the collar. The needle may be difficult to get through the collar's thick material, so keep a thimble or a hard surface near by to help you push it through.

STEP 5 Pop a few batteries in your battery pack (how many depends on your exact model; look at the instructions for voltage advice). Now put your dog in his new gear and give the dog park a light show.

143 Build a Cat Door

Have the mewing beasts let themselves out for a change with this DIY cat hatch.

MATERIALS

Pencil

Jigsaw

Continuous hinge

Tin shears

Thin acrylic

Drill

1/4-inch (6.35-mm) bolts and nuts

Metal plate

Magnet

STEP 1 Sketch the opening on your door so it's 9 1/2 inches (24 cm) wide by 8 inches (20 cm) high.

STEP 2 Cut the hole out with a jigsaw. (If your door is hollow, you'll need to secure pieces of thin wood to the top, bottom, and sides of the hole with glue and brads.)

STEP 3 Measure a piece of continuous hinge to the width of your hole and cut it with tin shears.

STEP 4 Measure and cut a piece of lightweight acrylic to fit over the opening. Drill holes into the acrylic that line up with the holes in the hinge, then attach the hinge with 1/4-inch (6.35-mm) bolts and nuts.

STEP 5 Mount the hinge right above the hole on the inside, making sure that it swings freely in both directions.

STEP 6 To keep the door from swinging, mount a metal plate to the hole's bottom ledge. Drill a hole into the acrylic and insert a magnet.

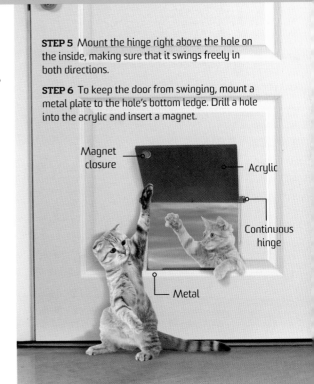

Magnet closure

Acrylic

Continuous hinge

Metal

144 **Make the Lazy Man's Mower**

Mowing the lawn used to suck. Now it kind of rules.

Grass—it'd be great, if you didn't have to cut it. Luckily, you can rig this simple self-propelled lawnmower so it goes in a circle all on its own, doing most of the work for you while you enjoy a brewski on the porch.

COST	$$
TIME	◔ ◔
EASY ● ● ○ ○ ○ HARD	

MATERIALS

Lawnmower	Nails
Drill	2x4
Wooden block	Twine
Hammer	Clamps
Two rebar posts	6-foot (1.8-m) wooden dowel

STEP 1 Locate a good spot in your lawn with equal clearance on all sides so that the mower can go in a circle without running into any permanent fixtures.

STEP 2 Drill two holes into a large wooden block, and pound the rebar into the ground through those holes. Cap it off by nailing a 2x4 on top of the wooden block.

STEP 3 Measure and cut enough twine to reach the outer perimeter of the area you wish to mow, leaving a bit of excess.

STEP 4 Knot one end of the twine to one of the rebar posts in the ground.

STEP 5 Knot the other end to the mower and position it as far away from the posts as possible. The mower will work its way inward as it moves in circles, winding the twine around the posts as it goes.

STEP 6 Place a clamp on the mower's gas lever to keep it moving. Measure and cut a 6-foot (1.8-m) dowel and secure it to the clamp. If the mower gets too close to a structure, the dowel will knock off the clamp, and the engine will shut down.

A GOLF CART POWERED BY THE SPIRIT (AND ENGINE) OF A TRUCK

One day, Bill Rulien decided he'd had enough of people boasting about how they had modified their golf carts with hot-rod paint jobs or monster-truck tires. "I thought, I'm gonna build something that will say, 'Well, top this.'"

Rulien owns several golf-cart sales shops, so he had his choice of bodies. What he needed was a bigger engine. He picked out a cart that he'd been selling for parts and yanked the electric motor, transmission, and drivetrain. Then he bought an old truck for its V8 engine, drivetrain, steering, and transmission, and began cutting up its chassis to fit the tiny cart's body. He shortened the truck's driveshaft as well, but he still had to connect the two vehicles. With steel he had lying around, he fabricated a frame that joins the cart's body with the truck's chassis.

The finished cart clears 120 miles per hour (193 km/h) and can tear up even the deepest sand traps. Rulien is waiting until golf season to really push the vehicle, but it has already made an impression. When a truck driver eyed the beast, he declared, "Jeez, that's overkill!" And thus was she christened.

145 Make a Geodesic Dome Out of PVC Pipe

It's a classic, and with good reason: It looks rad and is child's play to make.

Buckminster Fuller christened this structure in the 1940s, and it's been an icon ever since. You too can build its interlocking system of circles and triangles and know the glee of lightweight, modular housing.

COST	$$
TIME	🕐🕐🕐
EASY ●●●○○ HARD	

MATERIALS

65 2-foot (60-cm) pieces of PVC pipe

Ten four-way pipe connectors

Six five-way pipe connectors

Ten six-way pipe connectors

Drill

130 3-inch (7.5-cm) bolt-and-nut sets

260 washers to fit the bolts

Four T-posts

Parachute

Ten bungee cords

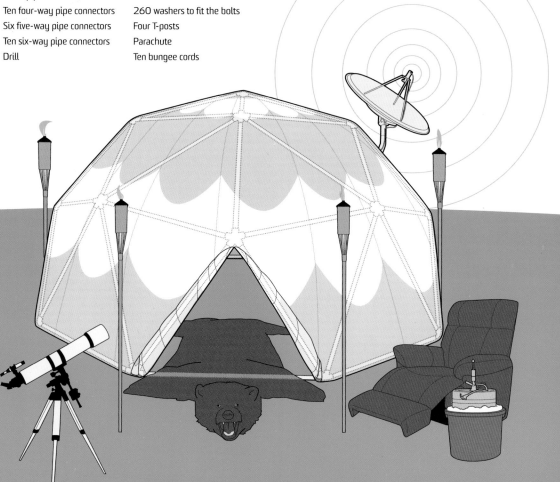

STEP 1 Use ten lengths of pipe and the ten four-way connectors to hook together the circular base.

STEP 2 Fit two lengths of pipe into each four-way connector, pointing up. This should form triangles.

STEP 3 Hook five five-way and five six-way connectors, alternating the two types, to the tops of these triangles all around the first row of the dome.

STEP 4 Fit ten more lengths of PVC between these connectors, horizontally, for the second row of the dome.

STEP 5 Make another row of triangles by fitting 10 lengths of pipe into the upward-pointing openings of these connectors.

STEP 6 Connect five six-way connectors to the tops of these triangles.

STEP 7 Place 10 lengths of pipe horizontally between these connectors.

STEP 8 P[...] connecto[...] of the d[...]

STEP [...] the d[...]

STE [...] an[...] th[...] [...]

S [...] dome s[...] add stability to th[...]

STEP 12 Cover the structure w[...] other piece of fabric, tying it to each o[...] four-way connectors with bungee cords.

STEP 13 Decorate your geo dome and veg out.

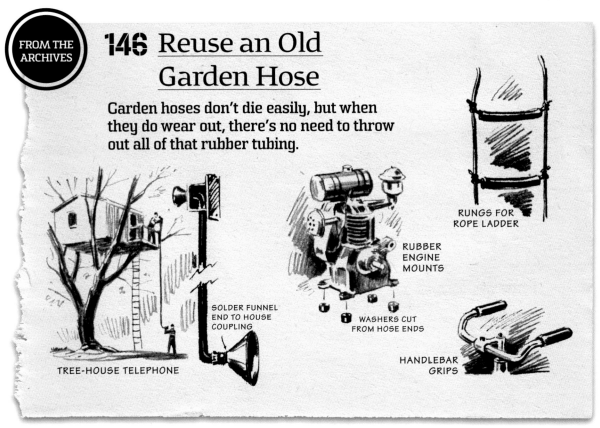

146 Reuse an Old Garden Hose

Garden hoses don't die easily, but when they do wear out, there's no need to throw out all of that rubber tubing.

TREE-HOUSE TELEPHONE

SOLDER FUNNEL END TO HOUSE COUPLING

RUBBER ENGINE MOUNTS

WASHERS CUT FROM HOSE ENDS

RUNGS FOR ROPE LADDER

HANDLEBAR GRIPS

147 The Ultimate Snowblower

Keep your driveway clear of the white stuff with this eight-cylinder blaster.

When Kai Grundt announced he was building a snowblower from a discarded V8 engine, a friend just laughed. So a year later, instead of showing him the finished product, Grundt showed him what it could do. He buried the man's truck under 7 feet (2 m) of snow. From two houses away.

Since Grundt, a metal fabricator in Muskoka, Ontario, started with the huge engine from his old Chevy truck, he knew power wouldn't be a problem. The problem would be making the 800-pound (362-kg) machine easy to handle. He didn't want the snowblower racing away when he revved the blades that suck up the snow—the V8's crankshaft spins them up to 6,200 rpm—so he chose to run its tank-like tracks via a different system. Powered by the 412-horsepower V8, a hydraulic pump feeds a pair of hydraulic motors that each turn one track. This allows him to give the blades a boost while keeping the machine moving at a safe pace.

Moving snow can be a frigid business, so Grundt installed a remote-start system to get the machine warmed up before he steps outside. The blower doubles as a heater, too. He faced the engine's radiator toward the back; an electric fan blows excess heat right at his legs.

And what about noise control? Twin custom-designed pipes ensure that there's no exhaust streaming into the driver's face during operation. Grundt also gave the pipes a series of interior channels that reroute and slow down the expelled air, dampening the noise. Cutting down on the decibel level also keeps the neighbors happy.

THAR SHE BLOWS
Using controls built into the handlebars, Grundt can turn one track forward and the other in reverse, spinning the rig in place. These handlebars are hollow, and the coolant fluid flows through them, keeping his hands toasty.

GADGET UPGRADES

148 Rig a DIY Polygraph Test

If you suspect somebody's putting you on, monitor him with a lie detector test.

COST	$
TIME	⏱
EASY ● ● ● ○ ○ HARD	

MATERIALS

Scissors

Adhesive Velcro

Aluminum foil

Electrical wire

Wire strippers

Arduino UNO

10k-ohm resistor

USB cable

STEP 1 With scissors, cut a strip of Velcro and a strip of aluminum foil so that they are equal in length and long enough to wrap around a finger.

STEP 2 Strip the end of a piece of wire, put it on the foil's center, and place the adhesive Velcro on top to secure it, sandwiching the wire between the foil and the Velcro.

STEP 3 Flip the foil over and adhere a small piece of Velcro to this side, so that you can secure it around a finger with the aluminum foil inside—this is an electrode. Repeat this process so you have two electrodes.

STEP 4 Wire the electrodes to the Arduino UNO according to the circuitry diagram.

STEP 5 Connect the Arduino to your computer using the USB cable. Then download the "Graph" code found at popsci.com/thebigbookofhacks onto the Arduino, and run the processing program on your computer.

STEP 6 Find a person you want answers from. Put the electrodes on one finger of each of the person's hands.

STEP 7 A graph pops up. The more the person sweats, the more conductive his skin becomes, and the higher the line of the graph goes. Skyrocketing right along with it, of course, is the likelihood that he is lying.

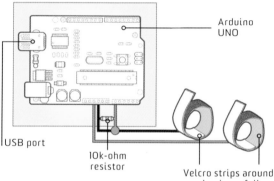

Arduino UNO

USB port

10k-ohm resistor

Velcro strips around aluminum foil

Listen In with a Foxhole Radio

When your radio is dead, this throwback device will do the trick.

Prisoners of war once cobbled together these makeshift radios so they could get the news. Now you can use one to pick up that final radio station that hasn't started online streaming yet.

MATERIALS

Large safety pin	Radiator or metal coat hanger
Toilet-paper tube	Blued or rusty razor blade
Magnet wire	Wood board
Wood pencil stub	Metal thumbtacks
Stripped cat 6 cable for antenna and ground	Earphones

STEP 1 Use a safety pin to poke a hole in the toilet-paper tube, and secure the magnet wire to the tube by tying one end through the hole.

STEP 2 Create a coil by wrapping the magnet wire tightly around the tube 120 times, making sure that the wire is packed closely together as it coils. The number of coils

affects what radio stations you'll pick up, so experiment with their arrangement if you aren't hearing your desired station clearly.

STEP 3 Make a "cat whisker" by poking the safety pin into the graphite of a pencil stub's dull end.

STEP 4 Hang the antenna cable far out the window and attach a ground cable to a metal radiator inside your home. If you don't have a radiator, attach the ground cable to a metal coat hanger and stick it in the ground outside.

STEP 5 Place the toilet-paper tube and a blued razor blade onto the wood board and push in two thumbtacks next to the tube and two next to the razor blade. Wrap the antenna wire around the components according to the diagram, twisting wires together when excess is needed.

STEP 6 Peel back the insulation on your headphones' audio jack. Use stripped wire to connect the safety pin in the pencil to one of the audio jack's wires, and connect the other wire to the ground.

STEP 7 Don your earphones, and touch the pencil lead to the razor blade. Move the pencil until you pick up the smooth tunes you desire.

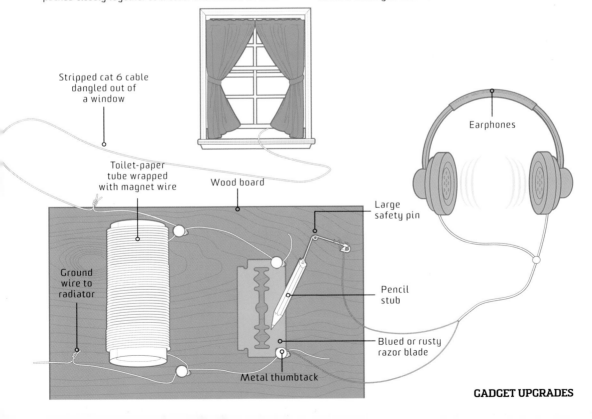

Stripped cat 6 cable dangled out of a window

Earphones

Toilet-paper tube wrapped with magnet wire

Wood board

Large safety pin

Ground wire to radiator

Pencil stub

Blued or rusty razor blade

Metal thumbtack

GADGET UPGRADES

150 Tack Up a Dipole Antenna

STEP 1 Use wire cutters and pliers to snip a coat hanger and stretch it into a length of about 52 inches (132 cm).

STEP 2 Make a small U-shaped loop on each end of the coat hanger's wires. Sand the loops to remove paint or coating.

STEP 3 Cut a piece of plywood to 1 inch (2.5 cm) in width and 1 foot (30 cm) in length. Screw two ½-inch (1.25-cm) sheet-metal screws about ¼ inch (6.35 mm) into the wood.

STEP 4 Hook the U-shaped wire loops around the screws.

STEP 5 Slide the U-shaped tabs of a 75- to 300-ohm matching transformer under the metal screws on the plywood, one per screw. Tighten the screws until the wire ends and the transformer tabs are held together against the wood.

STEP 6 To connect a coaxial cable, screw the cable's F-type connector into the transformer.

STEP 7 Connect the coaxial cable to the FM radio, turn the receiver on, and position the antenna for the best signal.

STEP 8 Use a mounting bracket and screws to mount the antenna where it works the best.

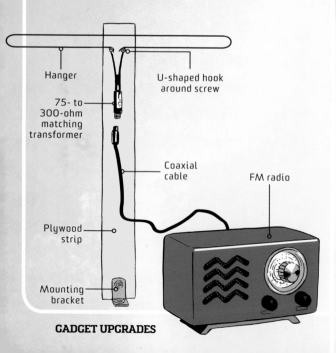

Hanger

U-shaped hook around screw

75- to 300-ohm matching transformer

Coaxial cable

FM radio

Plywood strip

Mounting bracket

GADGET UPGRADES

151 Craft a Cell-Phone "Cantenna"

STEP 1 Use a can opener to remove the bottom of a lidless, empty can that's 4 inches (10 cm) in diameter.

STEP 2 Solder the open end of another lidless, empty can to the first can. The total height should come to 1 foot (30 cm).

STEP 3 Solder a short piece of copper wire to an antenna connector, and drill a hole for it 3¾ inches (9.5 cm) from the closed end of the cylinder. Secure it in place with a nut on the inside.

STEP 4 Screw a passive antenna adapter cord to the antenna connector.

STEP 5 Attach the adapter cord to the back of your phone. (Don't have a smartphone? Try a basic pigtail adapter—choose one that works for your specific phone.)

STEP 6 Enjoy improved reception. Hear what people have to say for a change.

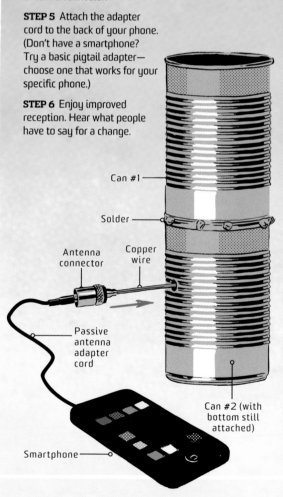

Can #1

Solder

Antenna connector

Copper wire

Passive antenna adapter cord

Can #2 (with bottom still attached)

Smartphone

152 Boost Wi-Fi with a Steamer

STEP 1 Use tin snips to remove the steamer's center post and to make a hole about ½ inch (1.25 cm) long for the USB modem's connector end.

STEP 2 Insert the USB modem into the hole with the connector end facing downward. Superglue it in place and let it dry.

STEP 3 Zip-tie two sets of two of the steamer's leaves together so that all the leaves stay open.

STEP 4 Plug the USB modem's connector end into the USB extension cable, and plug the other end of the extension cable into your laptop's ethernet portal.

STEP 5 Start picking up Wi-Fi signals from far, far away.

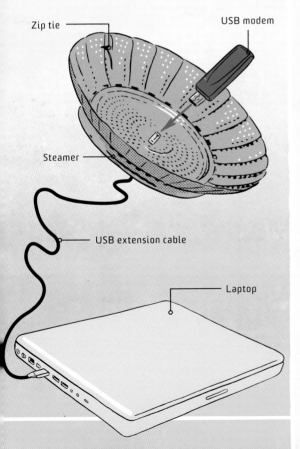

Zip tie

USB modem

Steamer

USB extension cable

Laptop

153 Hang HDTV-Antenna Art

STEP 1 Strip 14-gauge copper wire, then cut and bend it into eight V-shaped pieces. Place these wires onto a picture frame so that the peaks of the V shapes are 5¾ inches (14.5 cm) apart, then drill a small hole on each side of both V ends.

STEP 2 Strip 22-gauge enameled wire, then attach the V shapes to the frame by threading the enameled wire through one of the holes, crossing it over the copper wire, pulling it through the second hole, and twisting it in back.

STEP 3 Cut two lengths of copper wire to 20 inches (50 cm) in length, then bend them as shown. Lay them down the center of the picture frame so that they are 2 inches (5 cm) apart.

STEP 4 Attach the two vertical wires to the V-shaped pieces with more stripped enameled wire. Make a hole on each side of the two vertical wires' ends, then attach them to the frame as you attached the V-shaped pieces.

STEP 5 Wrap stripped enameled wire around the main vertical wires where they are bent so that they nearly touch.

STEP 6 Solder two pieces of stripped enameled wire to the bottom vertical copper wires. Connect these two wires to the matching transformer, and then connect the transformer to your TV using a coaxial cable.

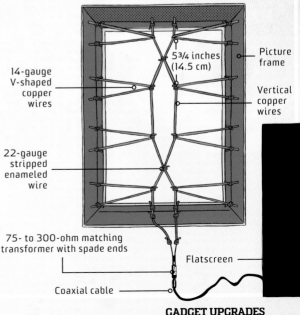

14-gauge V-shaped copper wires

5¾ inches (14.5 cm)

Picture frame

Vertical copper wires

22-gauge stripped enameled wire

75- to 300-ohm matching transformer with spade ends

Flatscreen

Coaxial cable

GADGET UPGRADES

| COST | $ |
| TIME | ☺ ☺ |
| EASY ● ● ● ● ○ HARD |

No orcs or goblins nearby—just an Internet connection.

Bilbo Baggins's sword glows whenever orcs or goblins approach. This hack turns a specific toy sword (which is available online) into a tech tool that glows, too—but in the presence of unsecured Wi-Fi networks instead of otherworldly beasts! When you slash the sword, it jumps on the network and publishes a message: "(Your Wi-Fi network) has been vanquished!"

MATERIALS

Screwdriver

Toy Sting Hobbit Sword

Spark Core Wi-Fi
development kit

Wire cutters

Soldering iron and solder

STEP 1 Disassemble the sword to harvest the electronics in its hilt, which can be accessed by unscrewing a couple of screws. Inside you'll find:

• Two AA batteries to power the electronics. Every AA battery provides 1.5 volts, so when two are connected in series (in which the circuit components are hooked up along the same path, without any branching out), you've got 3 volts. Alternatively, you can use Energizer Ultimate Lithium batteries, which run at 1.7 volts out of the box, giving you 3.4 volts, which is enough to get a bright blue light from the LEDs. (Three volts will still work but the light will be quite dim.)

• Two blue LEDs that are pointed up into the sword to make it glow.

• A button on the front that turns on the sword.

• A vibration switch that detects when the sword is swung. This is basically a spring inside a metal tube; when you swing the sword, the spring bends and hits the tube around it, completing a circuit.

• A tiny sound system that makes one of a few tinny SLASH and CLANG sounds when you swing the sword.

STEP 2 The key to this hack is putting the Spark Core (a tool to create Wi-Fi-connected products) in control of the LEDs and the sound circuit. The Core will also detect the signal from the vibration switch. To do this, cut the wires in the sword's electronics and solder them together according to the circuit diagram. This will hook you into a pre-existing subsystem which actually includes multiple LEDs and a whole system for producing sounds—simply sending voltage to the black box of the circuit will create a SLASH sound.

STEP 3 You will have to reprogram the Core with network-vanquishing firmware. You can download this code at www.popsci.com/thebigbookofhacks. It will scan for unsecured Wi-Fi networks, make sounds, blink the LEDs, and publish messages from the unsecured network.

STEP 4 Reassemble the sword by tucking the Core and attached wires into place where the sword's electronics were. Screw the cover back onto the hilt.

STEP 5 Power up your new sword, and when the sword turns blue, start slashing! If you have a few unsecured networks nearby, it will identify or "vanquish" them one at a time, until they've all been detected, after which the sword will no longer glow blue.

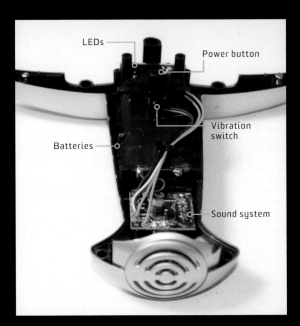

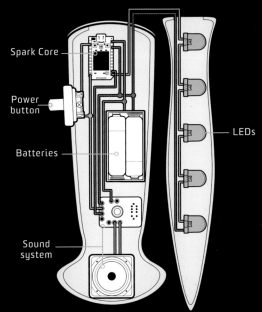

155 Rig a Smartphone Projector

Beam your phone's image onto a wall for an instant big screen.

COST	$$
TIME	⏱
EASY	● ● ○ ○ ○ HARD

MATERIALS

Narrow cardboard box	Speakers
Box cutter	Hot-glue gun
Fresnel lens	Modeling clay
Audio cord	Smartphone

STEP 1 Start with a narrow cardboard box (a shoebox does just fine) and cut a hole that's a little smaller than your Fresnel lens into one of the smaller ends.

STEP 2 Poke a smaller hole into the opposite end of the box that's big enough to allow you to run the audio cord from your phone to the speakers.

STEP 3 Using the hot-glue gun, firmly adhere the Fresnel lens over the larger hole inside the box.

STEP 4 Place modeling clay on the side of your smartphone, then position it on that side inside the box with the screen facing the lens. (The modeling clay helps to stabilize your phone in the box, but you can still adjust its position to get a better picture.)

STEP 5 Select your entertainment of choice, then set your phone's preferences to display in landscape orientation.

STEP 6 Connect your phone to the speakers, threading the audio cord through the smaller hole.

STEP 7 Close up the box, aim the lens at a blank wall, and switch off the lights. Then grab some Milk Duds and kick back with a downloaded movie or the latest episode of *The Daily Show*. Your screen should display at a nice 8½ by 11 inches (22 by 28 cm).

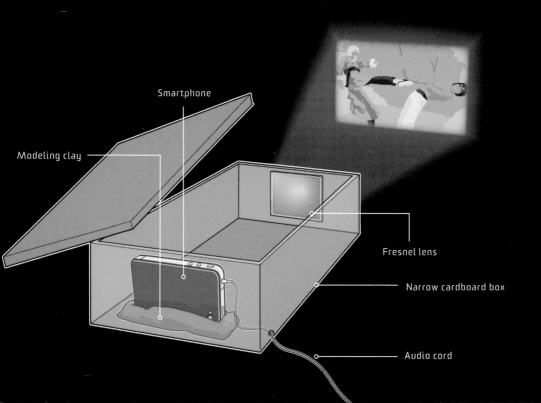

Smartphone

Modeling clay

Fresnel lens

Narrow cardboard box

Audio cord

156 Charge a Phone with Solar Rays

Harness the sun's rays to keep your phone juiced on the go.

MATERIALS

Wire strippers

Two 3-volt, 20-mA mini solar panels

Small heat-shrink tubing

Heat gun

Soldering iron and solder

Cell-phone charger

Large heat-shrink tubing

Double-sided tape

Mint tin

STEP 1 Cut the wires on both mini solar panels to 1 inch (2.5 cm) in length; strip ¼ inch (6.35 mm) of the plastic coating off each wire.

STEP 2 Cut the small heat-shrink tubing into four 1-inch (2.5-cm) pieces. Cover the solar panels' two positive wires with the tubing; shrink with the heat gun.

STEP 3 Solder the negative lead of one solar panel to the positive lead of the other. Cover with a piece of small tubing; shrink with the heat gun.

STEP 4 Cut off 2.5 feet (75 cm) from your charger cord. Strip 2.5 inches (6.35 cm) from the loose end.

STEP 5 Cut ¼ inch (6.35 mm) off the wires inside the cord to make leads. Cover with the large tubing; heat.

STEP 6 Solder the negative leads of the charger cord wires and the solar panels together; repeat with the positive leads. Slide large tubing over them and heat.

STEP 7 Cover the backs of the solar panels with double-sided tape; secure them inside the tin.

STEP 8 Tuck the wires into the tin and close it. To use, open up the tin and let the solar panels juice up.

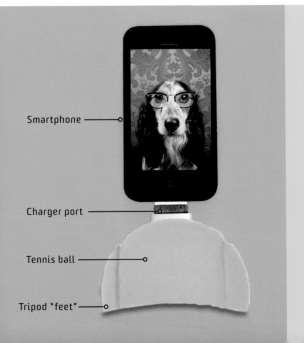

Smartphone

Charger port

Tennis ball

Tripod "feet"

157 Make a Smartphone Tripod

Take steady smartphone shots with a sporty improvised tripod.

STEP 1 Cut a tennis ball in half.

STEP 2 With a pen, mark three "feet" on the bottom. (These will allow the tennis-ball half to balance.) There should be about 2 inches (5 cm) between each foot.

STEP 3 Cut slight arches between the tripod feet.

STEP 4 Make a slit in the top of the tennis ball and insert a charger port.

STEP 5 Plug your phone into the port and snap away.

GADGET UPGRADES

158 Illuminate Sketches with Homemade Conductive Ink

Write it, wire it up, and see it in lights.

MATERIALS

Two pipettes

2.5 ml ammonium hydroxide

Test tube

1 gram silver acetate

Centrifuge

0.2 ml formic acid

Syringe

Syringe filter

Glass vial

Glass to paint on

Thin paintbrush

9-volt battery

LEDs

STEP 1 Use a pipette to measure the ammonium hydroxide into a test tube, then add the silver acetate. Place the tube in the centrifuge; let it mix for 15 seconds.

STEP 2 Using a second pipette, transfer 0.2 ml formic acid into the test tube solution one drop at a time, mixing it in the centrifuge between each drop.

STEP 3 Set the test tube aside for 12 hours.

STEP 4 Pull the plunger out of the back of a syringe and add a filter to the syringe, then decant the solution in the test tube into the syringe.

STEP 5 Open the glass vial and place it under the syringe, then place the plunger back into the syringe and force the liquid through the filter and into the vial.

STEP 6 Using the liquid in the vial, draw or write something on glass with a thin paintbrush, leaving gaps for the leads of the power source and the LEDs.

STEP 7 Heat the glass in an oven set to 200°F (93°C). Wait 15 minutes, then remove it. It should have a conductive silver coating.

STEP 8 Once you've placed the battery and LEDs on the glass, your circuit art will light right up.

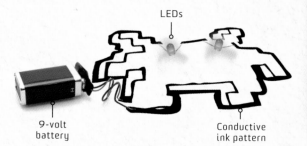

LEDs

9-volt battery

Conductive ink pattern

159 Hack Infrared Goggles

See the world in a whole new light.

MATERIALS

Screwdriver

Welding goggles

Blue gel

Red gel

STEP 1 Unscrew the eyepieces from a pair of welding goggles. Remove the dark green welding lenses, leaving just the clear plastic.

STEP 2 Use a green welding lens as a template to cut out eight circles of blue gel sheet and two circles of red gel sheet.

STEP 3 Add four blue gel sheet pieces to each eyepiece, screw them back onto your goggles, and enjoy the crazy spectrum.

STEP 4 Add a red gel sheet piece for a different effect. Whatever you do, just don't look at the sun.

160 Fashion a DIY Stylus for Your Touchscreen Device

Cobble together a stylus and keep your greasy fingers off that tablet.

MATERIALS

Small scissors

Conductive foam

2-mm drafting lead holder

Plastic ink tube from a ballpoint pen

STEP 1 Use the small scissors to cut a piece of conductive foam to a cube shape about ¼ inch (6.35 mm) in length on all sides.

STEP 2 Trim the conductive foam down further to create a rounded tip.

STEP 3 Drop the piece of foam into the lead holder and use the plastic ink tube from a ballpoint pen to push the foam down until it protrudes just out of the tip of the holder. Discard the ink tube.

STEP 4 Pinch the holder's tip to secure the foam in place. Try it out on a tablet near you.

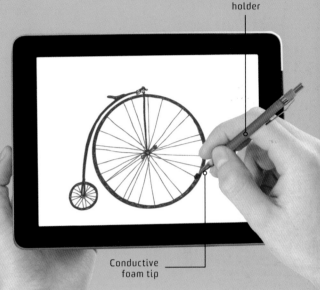

Drafting lead holder

Conductive foam tip

5 MINUTE PROJECT

161 Protect Your Touchscreen with Thin Vinyl

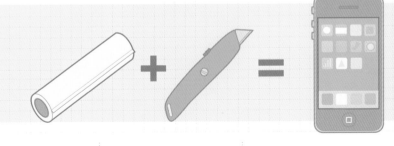

STEP 1 Measure and cut a piece of thin, nonadhesive vinyl sheeting to cover the phone's touchscreen.

STEP 2 Wipe away any dust on the vinyl and on your phone's screen.

STEP 3 Line up the vinyl with the touchscreen and slowly apply it, smoothing out air bubbles as you press it down.

162 Turn Your Laptop into a White Board

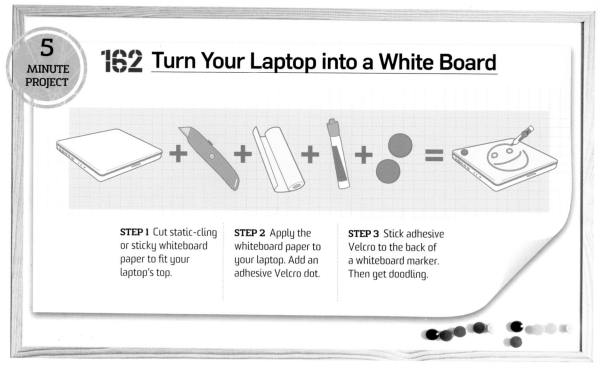

STEP 1 Cut static-cling or sticky whiteboard paper to fit your laptop's top.

STEP 2 Apply the whiteboard paper to your laptop. Add an adhesive Velcro dot.

STEP 3 Stick adhesive Velcro to the back of a whiteboard marker. Then get doodling.

163 Dye Your Laptop

Fight the monotony of boring case colors with a laptop dye job.

MATERIALS

White plastic laptop
Small screwdriver
Sandpaper
Denatured alcohol
Paper towel

Rubber gloves
Deep pan
8 cups (2 L) water
Fabric dye
2 tablespoons table salt

STEP 1 Carefully take apart your laptop. You'll likely need a small screwdriver to remove the screws that hold the case, battery, and other parts in place. Separate the plastic parts (the ones you'll be dyeing) from the metal and electronic parts.

STEP 2 Sand down the plastic pieces to remove the glossy layer, which prevents dye from absorbing quickly and evenly. Leave it if you don't want a matte laptop, but the process takes longer and results in splotchiness.

STEP 3 Clean all the parts with denatured alcohol and a paper towel, then let them dry.

STEP 4 Wearing rubber gloves, fill your deep pan with 8 cups (2 l) of water. Add the dye to the water along with 2 tablespoons of table salt. Stir together.

STEP 5 Place the pan on the stove and heat. When the water starts to boil, submerge the part you wish to dye.

STEP 6 Add water if the liquid boils off, and stir every once in a while. Larger parts require more time.

STEP 7 Once you're satisfied with a part's dye distribution, remove it from the bath, wipe it down, and rinse it with cold water. Dry thoroughly.

STEP 8 Reassemble your laptop. Resume being awesome.

164 Make a Steampunk Laptop Case

Give your high-tech machine an old-school Victorian vibe.

COST	$
TIME	☺ ☺ ☺
EASY ● ● ○ ○ ○ HARD	

MATERIALS

Tracing paper

Laptop

Double-sided heavy-duty adhesive sheet

Wood veneer sheeting

Sandpaper

Masking tape

Craft knife

Hot water

Paint and paintbrushes

Polyurethane

Miscellaneous embellishments

Superglue

STEP 1 Lay tracing paper over the back of your laptop and trace where the wood veneer will go, leaving holes for plugs, fans, and hatches that allow you access to the computer's insides.

STEP 2 Open up your laptop and, using the same method, create patterns for the frame around the screen and the area surrounding the keyboard.

STEP 3 Apply a heavy-duty adhesive sheet to the blank side of the wood veneer sheeting.

STEP 4 Sand the veneer for a smooth look and feel.

STEP 5 Tape the tracing paper onto the wood veneer and cut it out using a craft knife. Cut out the veneer pieces to go around the screen and keyboard, too.

STEP 6 In the corners of the veneer, cut diagonal slits so that you can fold the veneer over the laptop's corners.

STEP 7 Soak the veneer in hot water to make it pliant. Be sure to dry off excess water before applying the veneer to your computer—for extra security, remove the battery before placing the veneer on the laptop.

STEP 8 Use masking tape to secure the wood to the laptop. Let it dry so it can mold nicely to the computer's shape, then remove it and set it aside.

STEP 9 On your laptop, use tape to mask off any areas that the veneer won't cover, including the hinge. Then paint those areas a color of your choosing.

STEP 10 Peel away the veneer's adhesive backing and apply the veneer to the laptop, starting with the inside pieces. Don't press down until you've got it lined up perfectly, then go slowly and press out air bubbles as you apply it. Cut away any excess material.

STEP 11 Mask off areas that aren't covered with veneer, then coat the veneer with polyurethane.

STEP 12 Add any desired embellishments with superglue. Apply another coat of polyurethane to make it for keeps.

Steampunk touches

Painted hinge

Wood veneer sheeting

165 Stash a Flash Drive in a Cassette

STEP 1 Using a small screwdriver, pry off the USB drive's plastic casing.

STEP 2 Decide where you want the flash drive to poke out of the cassette. Then trace the flash drive's connector end onto that spot.

STEP 3 Remove the small screws holding the cassette together with the small screwdriver.

STEP 4 Cut out the traced area with a rotary tool.

STEP 5 Wind the tape so that it's on the spool farther away from the hole for the flash drive.

STEP 6 Tape the flash drive down inside the cassette with electrical tape so that its end sticks out through the hole.

STEP 7 Reassemble the cassette, load up the flash drive with a playlist of songs, then gift it as a throwback "mix tape."

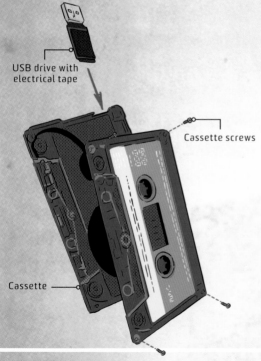

USB drive with electrical tape

Cassette screws

Cassette

166 Make a Pink-Eraser Flash Drive

STEP 1 Remove the flash drive's plastic casing.

STEP 2 Find two erasers of the pink, parallelogram variety. Cut off the end of one, starting where the end begins to slant down. Cut the other to roughly one-third the original length.

STEP 3 Use a craft knife to hollow out both erasers. Test to make sure the flash drive fits nicely.

STEP 4 Stick the drive inside the larger eraser, then cap it off with the smaller one. There you have it: a discreet flash drive that holds your top-secret documents—almost as if they've been "erased."

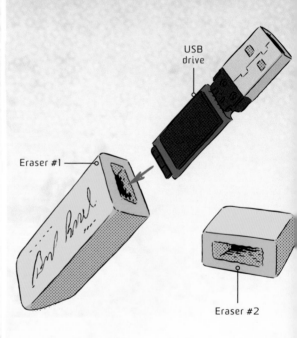

USB drive

Eraser #1

Eraser #2

167 Fake It with a Sawed-Off Flash Drive

STEP 1 Peel off the plastic cover of the USB drive. (It helps to pick a flash drive that's on the smaller side.)

STEP 2 Use a craft knife to make deep cuts in the casing along both sides of the connective end of a USB cord, piercing to the metal shell underneath. Peel off the plastic casing to get at the inner parts.

STEP 3 Use a small screwdriver to pry apart the metal shell. Remove the "lid."

STEP 4 Underneath this lid are a few wires and miscellaneous plastic bits. They're in your way, so go ahead and cut them out with a craft knife.

STEP 5 Grab the flash drive, and protect its back (where there are metal parts that require insulation) with electrical tape.

STEP 6 Apply epoxy to the inside of the opening you've made in the end of the cord, then slide the USB drive inside.

STEP 7 Hack the cord, fray the wires as desired, and plug it into your computer. Await sounds of horror.

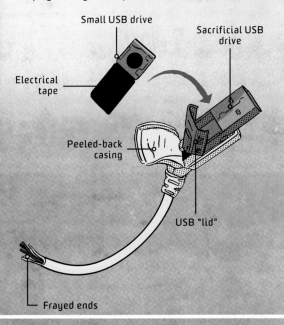

Small USB drive

Sacrificial USB drive

Electrical tape

Peeled-back casing

USB "lid"

Frayed ends

168 House a Flash Drive in a LEGO

STEP 1 Peel off the plastic casing on the flash drive.

STEP 2 Find a LEGO brick large enough to house the drive (a 2x6 one is ideal). Using a rotary tool, scrape out the brick's insides.

STEP 3 Measure the USB connector to get the dimensions that you'll need for the hole in the LEGO. Keep in mind that the hole should fit the USB snugly, allowing the business end to protrude and plug into your computer.

STEP 4 Draw a rectangle of these dimensions against the small end of the brick. Cut the shape out with a rotary tool.

STEP 5 Use the rotary tool to remove the top from a second LEGO of the same size and color.

STEP 6 Tape the flash drive to the top's underside with electrical tape.

STEP 7 Glue the LEGO top to the hollowed-out LEGO, allowing the USB connector to stick out the end.

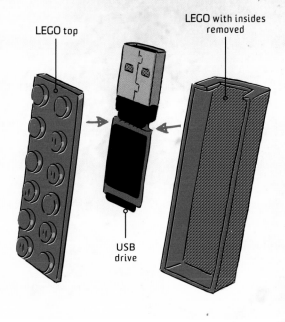

LEGO top

LEGO with insides removed

USB drive

Hack a Foot-Operated Mouse

Take some strain off the old wrist with a funny foot-powered mouse.

COST	$$
TIME	◑ ◷
EASY	● ● ● ○ ○ HARD

MATERIALS

½-inch (1.25-cm) PVC sheet	Metal brackets
Bedroom slippers	Nuts, bolts, and washers
Two roller lever switches	Screws and nails
Optical mouse	Screwdriver
Rotary tool	Metal wire
Small hand file	7 feet (2 m) ¾-inch (1.9-cm)
Soldering iron and solder	clear plastic tubing
Electrical wire	Rubber doorstops

STEP 1 On the PVC sheet, position and trace your slippers the way your feet would rest while you're seated. Mark places for the left- and right-click roller lever switches near the left slipper, where your foot will operate the mouse, then outline the mouse slightly to the left of the right slipper's top.

STEP 2 Using the rotary tool, channel out holes for the roller lever switches and a hole for the mouse. Use the file to smooth the edges of the holes.

STEP 3 Remove the mouse's top cover from the base. Lift out the circuit board and remove the scroll wheel.

STEP 4 On the bottom of the circuit board, locate where the mouse's switches once connected to its buttons. Solder a length of electrical wire to each of the mouse's outboard solder connections.

STEP 5 Put the circuit board back inside the mouse cover. Solder the lead wires from the outboard solder connections to the left and right roller lever switches—the wire from the original left-click switch to the new left switch, and the right to the right.

STEP 6 Secure two metal brackets to the mouse with two nuts, bolts, and washers. Screw the brackets into the underside of the PVC sheet so that the mouse is belly up.

STEP 7 Thread small pieces of metal wire through the mounting holes in each roller lever switch. Bend the ends and use nails to secure the switches under the PVC sheet.

STEP 8 Screw plastic tubing around the edges of the PVC sheet and in between where your feet go to create bumpers that help guide your feet.

STEP 9 Trim four rubber doorstops to work as risers, propping the PVC sheet up off the floor and providing clearance for the mouse. Screw one to each corner of the footboard.

STEP 10 Plug the mouse's USB connector into your computer and scroll with your feet.

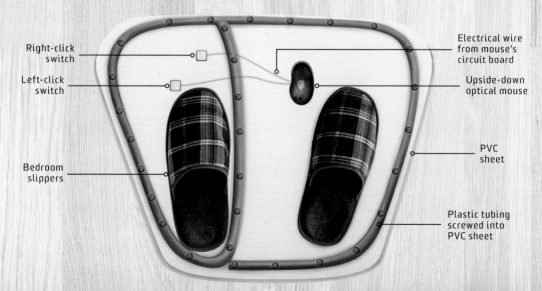

Right-click switch
Left-click switch
Bedroom slippers
Electrical wire from mouse's circuit board
Upside-down optical mouse
PVC sheet
Plastic tubing screwed into PVC sheet

Trick Out Your Computer Tower with Engraving

This is one tower mod that doesn't belong hidden under your desk.

MATERIALS

Paper and pencil or printer	Safety goggles
Screwdriver	Rotary tool
Computer tower	Small engraving bits
Spray paint	Screws and bolts
Plexiglas sheet	Fluorescent strip, if needed
Masking tape	

STEP 1 Draw or print your design on a sheet of paper to fit the tower's side panel.

STEP 2 Unscrew the metal side panel from your computer tower and set it aside for later.

STEP 3 Spray-paint a sheet of Plexiglas with a color to match your case so only the engraved design will be visible later. Let dry.

STEP 4 Tape the drawn or printed design onto your Plexiglas sheet, being sure to tape it over the painted side.

STEP 5 Put on your safety goggles and, using a rotary tool outfitted with an engraving bit, begin engraving. Slowly and carefully follow your design's lines on the paper to etch it on the Plexiglas beneath.

STEP 6 Remove the taped-on template and wipe down the engraved Plexiglas.

STEP 7 Measure and cut a hole slightly smaller than your Plexiglas in the metal panel.

STEP 8 Use your rotary tool to drill four holes into the corners of the Plexiglas and the case. Attach the etched panel to the metal frame with screws small enough that it will fit inside the case.

STEP 9 If your machine lacks a fluorescent strip, install one, either plugging it into the power supply or directly to the circuit board.

STEP 10 Use the original bolts and screws to reattach the metal panel with the Plexiglas inside the tower.

171 Turn on Your Computer with a Magnet Switch

Dupe would-be information thieves with a handy on/off switch mod.

MATERIALS

Screwdriver

Computer tower with plastic front panel

Wire strippers

Reed switch

Electrical tape

Steel or iron nut

Small magnet

STEP 1 Open your computer tower and remove the front panel, exposing the wires attached to the power button. Cut one of the wires, and strip both ends.

STEP 2 Place the reed switch between the two wire ends and twist them together, sandwiching the reed switch.

STEP 3 Tape the reed switch to the inside of the front panel of your computer and tape or glue the steel or iron nut next to it. Close the computer back up.

STEP 4 To turn on your computer, push the power button and stick a magnet to the case where the reed switch is located—the nut should hold the magnet in place. If someone tries to turn your computer on without the magnet, they'll have no luck.

172 Print Secrets with Invisible Ink

Bet the CIA sure wished it had come up with this printer hack.

MATERIALS

Inkjet printer

Syringe

UV invisible ink

UV lamp

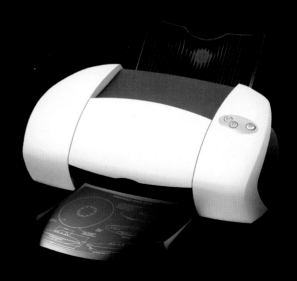

STEP 1 Open up your inkjet printer and extract one of the ink cartridges. Remove its cap and pull out the sponge.

STEP 2 Rinse out the sponge and the inside of the cartridge until the water runs clear, then put the clean sponge back inside the cartridge.

STEP 3 Use a syringe to inject invisible ink into the sponge. Replace the cartridge's cap and put the cartridge back inside the printer.

STEP 4 Adjust your computer's settings to print using only the color that you've replaced with invisible ink.

STEP 5 View the secret info on the documents by holding them up to a UV lamp.

GADGET UPGRADES

173 Fake Out Thieves with a Desktop Hack

Deter computer raiders with a wallpaper that looks just like your desktop—but isn't.

STEP 1 Take a screenshot of your computer's desktop, then set the screenshot as your wallpaper.

STEP 2 Hide the real icons in another folder.

STEP 3 Sit back and watch people try to open your desktop's unclickable folders.

Private

Secrets

Confidential

More secrets

Don't look!

Embarrassing

174 Shield Your Screen from Prying Eyes

Sick of snoops looking at your screen? Improvise your own privacy monitor.

MATERIALS

LCD monitor
Craft knife
Paintbrush
Paint thinner
Paper towels
Piece of plastic
Old glasses
Tape
Superglue

STEP 1 Unplug an old LCD monitor and remove the plastic frame around it.

STEP 2 Use a craft knife to cut around the screen's edge, then peel back both the polarized and the antiglare films. Hang on to the polarized layer and remember its orientation.

STEP 3 Apply paint thinner to loosen the glue on the monitor's screen—don't drip it on the monitor's frame. Then wipe it off with paper towels and scrape off the softened glue with a piece of plastic.

STEP 4 Reassemble your monitor. At this point, when you turn it on, the screen looks white and blank. If you hold up the polarized film, you should see images on the screen.

STEP 5 Pop the lenses out of a pair of old glasses. Tape the lenses to the polarized film and trace around them.

STEP 6 Hold the polarized film lenses up as though you were wearing them, and look at the monitor. If you can see the images on the screen, cut out the lens-shaped film pieces with your craft knife.

STEP 7 Glue the polarized lenses onto your glasses. Put them on, and enjoy the invisible images on your screen.

GADGET UPGRADES

175 Set Up a Laptop Cooling System

Chill down your machine with copper's thermal conductivity.

COST	$$
TIME	☺☺
EASY ● ● ● ● ○ HARD	

MATERIALS

Rotary tool

Paper

Scissors

Sheet of 0.5-mm copper plating

Tin snips

6-mm center-tapped lip and spur drill

Two pieces of 6-mm copper tubing, each 2 inches (5 cm) in length

Solder and soldering iron

Plastic tubing

Rubber tubing

Bilge pump

STEP 1 If necessary, use the rotary tool to cut away at your laptop's plastic casing until the fins of your computer's internal radiator and heat sink are exposed.

STEP 2 Experiment to determine how big the fins of your heat extractor should be. Try inserting strips of paper between the fins of your computer's heat sink, cutting them down until they fit perfectly. For maximum cooling, the fins should fit as deep into the heat sink as possible.

STEP 3 Once you've determined the necessary measurements for your copper heat extractor's fins, clean the copper sheet with soap and water. Using one of your paper fins as a template, trace seven copper fins.

STEP 4 Trace two holes 6-mm in diameter along one of the short edges in each fin, positioning the holes 5/8 inch (16 mm) apart. The 6-mm copper tubing should fit snugly through these holes, once you've drilled them.

STEP 5 Cut out the copper fins with tin snips and use the lip and spur drill to cut out the holes. Set the drill to a slow speed and do your drilling on a flat surface to prevent the copper sheet from warping.

STEP 6 Thread the fins onto the two lengths of copper tubing. You can temporarily place coins between the fins to help space them evenly so that they'll line up with the heat sink's indentations. Solder the tubes and fins together.

STEP 7 Cut a piece of plastic tubing to a length of about 1½ inches (3.75 mm). Heat it until you can bend it to fit over both pieces of copper tubing on one side of the fin-and-tubing contraption. Insert the contraption into your computer's heat sink.

STEP 8 Hook two lengths of rubber tubing to the bare pieces of copper tubing that are plugged into your computer's heat sink. Connect these two lengths of rubber tubing to a bilge pump filled with water. Power it up and the water will circulate, carrying heat from the heat skink and keeping your computer cool.

Line to bilge pump

Copper tubing and fins

Plastic tubing

Heat sink

Laptop that tends to overheat

176 Control Your Mouse from Afar

Direct your mouse with a simple laser pointer.

MATERIALS
Optical mouse
Laser pointer, less than 10 mW

STEP 1 Lean your mouse against your computer monitor so that it's propped upright with its belly facing out.

STEP 2 Identify your mouse's sensor, which looks like a tiny bubble tinted black.

STEP 3 Shine the laser pointer directly at the sensor. Once you get a lock on the sensor, you can move it around in the mouse's vicinity to control your computer's cursor.

5 MINUTE PROJECT

177 Make an External Hard Drive

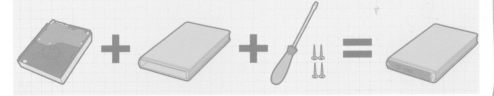

STEP 1 Salvage a working hard drive from a laptop or a computer tower and an empty external hard drive case.

STEP 2 Locate the ports on the hard drive case's baseplate, then attach them to the hard drive.

STEP 3 Line up the holes in the drive and baseplate and screw them together.

STEP 4 Slide these parts inside the case. Screw on the faceplate, lining up its holes with the ports to keep them accessible.

178 Craft Keyboard Thumbtacks

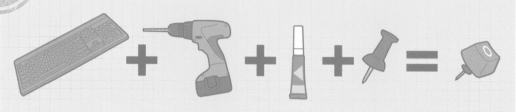

STEP 1 Remove the keys from the keyboard, and cut off the excess plastic on the back of each key with a rotary tool.

STEP 2 Widen the hole in the back of each key using a rotary tool. Put a dab of glue in the hole.

STEP 3 Insert a pushpin into the hole, pointy end facing out. Pin up something important.

179 Rig a Superportable Keyboard

Cut a keyboard to get to the touch-sensitive membrane inside.

MATERIALS

Screwdriver
USB keyboard
Transparent contact paper
Superglue
Adhesive stickers

STEP 1 Use a screwdriver to deconstruct the keyboard. The good stuff is in the middle: It's the three-layer membrane and the attached control board, which feeds the USB wire.

STEP 2 Remove and reserve the membrane's control board and switch pad (the rubber pad that presses the control board's contacts to the membrane).

STEP 3 Using the switch pad, board, and nuts and bolts, reassemble the membrane to the control board. The traces of the membrane should line up with the traces on the control board. (If your keyboard had a socket and ribbon cable, reinsert the cable.)

STEP 4 Cover both sides with transparent contact paper, and apply glue to the edges to keep the three membranes in place.

STEP 5 Apply adhesive stickers for each key, taking care to place the stickers on the keys' contacts. (For instance, the space bar is huge, but the contact is small, so you'll want to be sure that you put the sticker directly on the contact—just not on the key.)

STEP 6 Roll it up and be ready to type anywhere.

GADGET UPGRADES

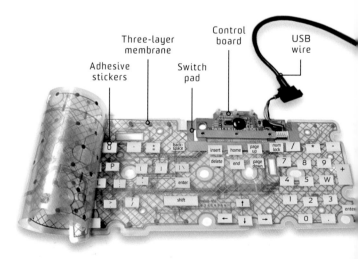

Three-layer membrane

Control board

USB wire

Adhesive stickers

Switch pad

Brighten up your all-night gaming sessions with this LED-lit mousepad.

COST	
TIME	
EASY	

MATERIALS

Safety goggles

Tablesaw with a glass-cutting blade

Plexiglas

Rotary tool with glass-safe bit

Electrical wire

Two small white LED lights

Clear tape

Printed design, if desired

USB connector

STEP 1 Decide what size and shape you'd like your mousepad to be. Then, wearing safety goggles, use a table saw with a glass-cutting blade to cut the Plexiglas to size.

STEP 2 Fit your rotary tool with a glass-safe bit, then use it to round the Plexiglas's edges and wear them down. The more surface area that you make opaque, the more light your mousepad will emit.

STEP 3 Use your rot_____ Plexiglas, starting fro_____ forking into two chan_____

STEP 4 Use the rotary tool to extend the two channels parallel to the glass's top edge, ending 1 inch (2.5 cm) from the Plexiglas's edges.

STEP 5 Attach pieces of electrical wire to the LEDs' leads, then peel back the plastic on your USB cord. Attach the two positive wires and two negative wires on the LEDs to the USB cord's positive and negative wires.

STEP 6 Place the LEDs and wires into the carved channels and secure them with clear tape. Cover the mousepad with a design, if you like.

STEP 7 Plug the USB into your computer, dim the lights, and get your game on.

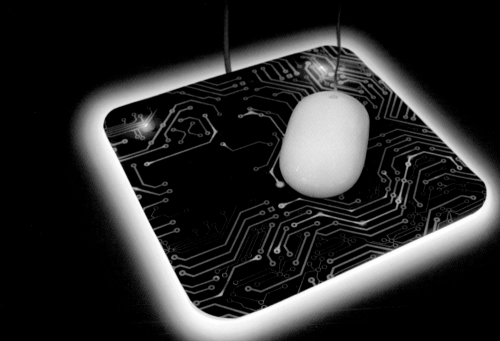

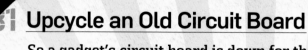

Upcycle an Old Circuit Board

So a gadget's circuit board is down for the count.
There are still countless things you can do with it.

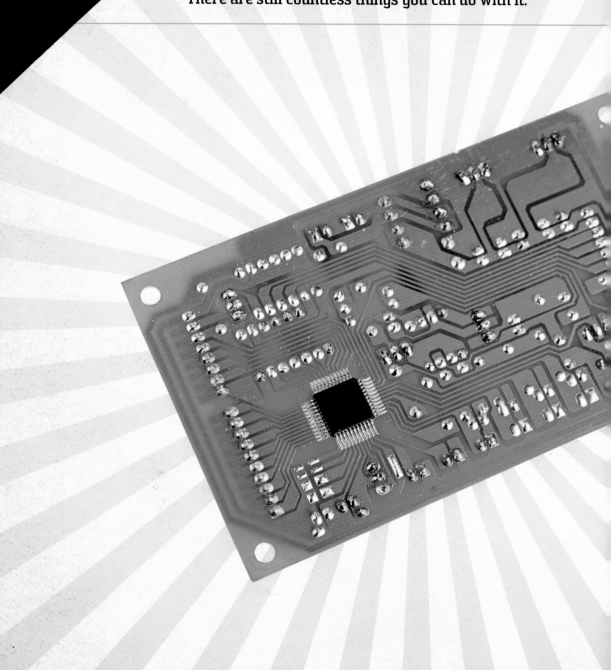

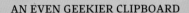

AN EVEN GEEKIER CLIPBOARD

Use a heat gun and pliers to strip off all the solder and bits and bobs, then apply laminate to make it smooth. Swap the clip from an old clipboard onto your new, high-tech version.

NERDTASTIC GUITAR PICK

Use a soldering iron to remove any electrical components on the circuit board, then use a rotary tool to cut out a guitar pick shape. Sand it until it's smooth and start picking.

META MOUSE PAD

Desolder a circuit board so that it's bare and cover both sides with vinyl. Plop your new mousepad on your desk and get your scroll on.

LIGHT UP THE CIRCUIT

Form a box shape with four stripped circuit boards and drill holes in their corners. Fasten them together with zip ties, and hook this box up to a hanging light-socket assembly for some nice spotlight action.

182 Make a Laptop Stand from a Binder

STEP 1 Using a metal saw, cut a piece of aluminum rail so it's the length of a ring binder. Then use a metal file to round the rail's edges so you don't get scraped.

STEP 2 Place double-sided tape on the inner side of the rail.

STEP 3 Drill two sets of two holes big enough for bolts—one set through the rail and one set through the binder.

STEP 4 Line up the holes and attach the rail and binder with the bolts, securing them with a nut on the underside. Cover these bolts with tape to avoid scratches on the laptop.

STEP 5 Measure and cut a strip of no-skid felt to the dimensions of the rail, then adhere it to the inner side of the rail. Measure and cut a larger sheet of felt so that it covers the top of the binder and secure it with adhesive. It will prevent your laptop from sliding around.

STEP 6 Use a rotary tool to cut a hole into the binder's corner for cords to pass through.

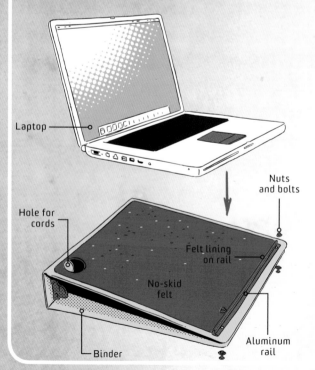

Laptop

Hole for cords

Nuts and bolts

Felt lining on rail

No-skid felt

Binder

Aluminum rail

183 Build a USB Hub into Your Desk

STEP 1 Remove your computer, cords, and other electronics from your work station to protect them from sawdust.

STEP 2 Measure your hub and mark a spot for it on a wood desktop using a pencil and ruler.

STEP 3 Use a jigsaw to cut out the opening, tracing your marked lines. It's better to cut it slightly smaller than your hub (you can always sand it) than too big (you'd have to fill any gaps with caulking).

STEP 4 Remove the plug of wood and insert your USB hub to make sure it fits. Use sandpaper to adjust and smooth the opening.

STEP 5 Use epoxy to attach the USB hub to the inside of the hole; let dry.

STEP 6 Run the input cord from the USB hub up behind your desk to your computer.

STEP 7 Next time you need to plug something in, forget reaching around your monitor. Just plug it into the hub on your desk.

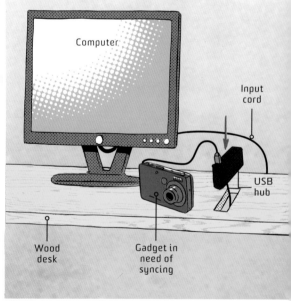

Computer

Input cord

USB hub

Wood desk

Gadget in need of syncing

184 Stash Your Printer in a Drawer

STEP 1 Remove the front panel of a drawer and drill a hole into the back panel for cables. (It's better to do this in a lower drawer so that the weight of your printer doesn't stress the structure.)

STEP 2 Measure and cut two evenly spaced recessed areas for the utility hinges on the front edge of the bottom panel. This way, the bottom and front panels will line up neatly when you reattach the front.

STEP 3 Line up the front and bottom panels and screw on the utility hinges.

STEP 4 With the front panel lowered, screw the support hinges to the drawer's side panels and then to the front panel.

STEP 5 Place your printer in the drawer and feed the cables through the hole in the back to attach it to your computer (or, if it's wireless, to a power source).

185 Mount Stuff Behind Your Monitor

STEP 1 If you have limited desk space, use the back of your monitor for storage. Apply double-sided tape or adhesive Velcro strips to your computer monitor's back, or purchase plastic hooks with suction cups or Velcro backing.

STEP 2 Begin attaching office supplies you need—tape, tissues, notecards, a stapler, or a holder for pens and scissors—and maybe some you don't. (Hey, candy and headphones can make the workday go faster.)

STEP 3 Be sure to use lightweight materials so that your monitor doesn't tip over. Also, keep the fan clear of obstacles. Otherwise, your machine could overheat, which is much more inconvenient than not having any drawers.

Chest of drawers

Support hinge

Utility hinge   Front panel   Printer

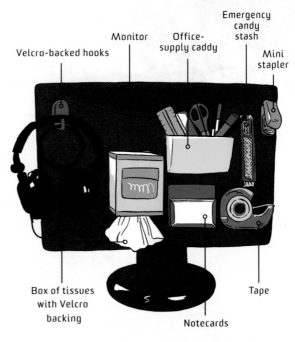

Emergency candy stash

Monitor   Office-supply caddy

Velcro-backed hooks   Mini stapler

Box of tissues with Velcro backing

Tape

Notecards

186 Organize Loose Cables

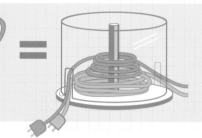

STEP 1 Remove the dome from a CD spool. Cut a slit on the bottom of the dome; cut another slit opposite it.

STEP 2 Wind cables around the spool and run the ends through the slits.

STEP 3 Tug on one end of a cable to adjust how much of it extends outside the dome.

½-inch (1.25-cm) washers and nuts

About 75 CDs on each side

½-inch (1.25-cm) threaded rod

187 Make a Floppy-Disk Box

Solve the double problem of a messy desk and a surplus of useless floppies with one simple DIY craft.

MATERIALS

Five floppy disks	Twelve zip ties
Drill	Scissors

STEP 1 Locate the tiny dimples on the back of each floppy disk. Drill through these dimples, repeating until you have holes in each corner of four of your five disks.

STEP 2 Place two of the four floppies in front of you so that their holes are aligned. Thread a zip tie through the two holes at the bottom, and then another zip tie through the two holes at the top.

STEP 3 Repeat with two more disks, then connect the four floppies into a box shape.

STEP 4 Drill four holes in the fifth floppy, this time slightly above the dimples. This is the box's bottom.

STEP 5 To secure the bottom floppy to the box, line it up with one of the sides at a 90-degree angle. Thread a zip tie through the bottom's holes and the holes in the side.

STEP 6 Close the box and thread zip ties through the remaining holes in the bottom and side pieces. Cut off the ends of the zip ties.

STEP 7 Tighten and trim the zip ties, then stock the box with pens and revel in your newfound tidiness.

188 Get Pumped with a CD Dumbbell

CDs are pretty much obsolete. But having jacked arms never gets old.

MATERIALS

Ruler	Reciprocating saw or hacksaw
Permanent marker	Four 1/2-inch (1.25-cm) washers and nuts
1/2-inch (1.25-cm) solid threaded rod	About 150 CDs
Table vise	1/2-inch (1.25-cm) wrench

STEP 1 Measure and mark 6 inches (15 cm) from one end of the rod. (This is where the first CD stack will end.)

STEP 2 Place one hand on the rod, leaving about 1/2 inch (1.25 cm) of clearance between your hand and the mark. Make a second mark about 1/2 inch (1.25 cm) from the opposite side of your hand.

STEP 3 Measure and make a third mark 6 inches (15 cm) from the second mark for the second CD stack.

STEP 4 Place the rod in a table vise. Saw off any excess at the third mark with a reciprocating saw or a hacksaw.

STEP 5 Thread a nut onto both sides of the rod to the marked lines in the center. Add a washer on both sides.

STEP 6 Put about 75 CDs on each end, and slide on a washer and nut on both ends. Tighten with a wrench.

STEP 7 Pop your new 10-pound (4.5-kg) dumbbell out of the vise and do a few reps—you might not get ripped, but you're well on your way to getting sculpted biceps.

189 Assemble a Cereal-Box Spectrometer

See the rainbow inside everyday light sources with this easy setup.

MATERIALS

Safety glasses	Craft knife
Thick gloves	Cereal box
C-clamp	Tape
CD	Light source

STEP 1 Wearing a pair of safety glasses and thick gloves, clamp a CD down on a surface edge. Score it across the center with the craft knife, then break it in half.

STEP 2 Make a horizontal slit about 1 inch (2.5 cm) in length in one side of a cereal box, near the box's top. It should be about the width of a coin.

STEP 3 In the opposite side of the box, straight across from the first incision, make another slit. Then extend this cut to the front and back of the box, sloping down at a 45-degree angle with your craft knife. It should be deep enough for the CD half to at least partially slide into. Secure the CD in place with tape.

STEP 4 Cut a ½-by-½-inch (1.25-cm-by-1.25-cm) square hole in the box above the CD slice.

STEP 5 Hold the box up with the slit facing your light source. Look through the viewing hole at the top to see the rays of light separated on the CD inside the box.

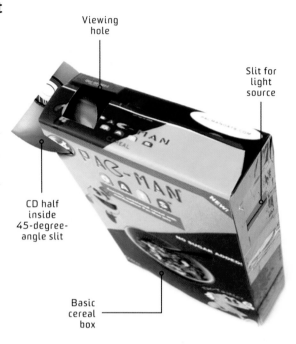

Viewing hole

Slit for light source

CD half inside 45-degree-angle slit

Basic cereal box

YOU BUILT WHAT?!

A PORTABLE X-RAY MACHINE

Late one night, Adam Munich found himself talking with two guys online: one who complained of rolling electricity blackouts and one who had broken his leg in Mexico and said his local hospital couldn't find an X-ray machine. The two situations fused in Munich's mind; he wondered if a cheap, reliable, battery-powered X-ray machine existed. After discovering that the answer was no, he spent two years building one himself out of nixie tubes, old suitcases, chain-saw oil, and electronics from across the globe. It was an incredibly ambitious project for anyone, let alone a 15-year-old.

190 Rig a Supersimple Radiation Detector

Fear fallout no more with a device that tells you when radiation levels are high.

COST $$
TIME ⏱
EASY ● ● ● ○ ○ HARD

Radiation is all around us in small doses, and most of it isn't harmful for you—it's really the ionizing, DNA-scrambling stuff that we have to look out for. Enter this chamber–in-a-can, which lets you see if an object's radiation levels are off the charts.

MATERIALS

Aluminum can
Craft knife
NPN Darlington transistor
Electrical tape
Electrical wire
9-volt battery and snap

4.7k-ohm resistor
Soldering iron and solder
Aluminum foil
Rubber band
Multimeter

STEP 1 Make a hole in the can with a craft knife. Bend the transistor's base leg down into the can and tape it in place.

STEP 2 Use electrical wire to attach the transistor's collector leg to the negative pole of the battery snap. Keep the transistor's leads sticking up, away from the can.

STEP 3 Solder one lead of the resistor to the base of the can, near the edge. Attach the other lead to the positive pole of the battery snap with a piece of wire.

STEP 4 Tape the battery snap to the side of the can and hook the battery up to the snap.

STEP 5 Cover the can's open end with aluminum foil. Pull the foil taut, then secure it with a rubber band.

STEP 6 Attach one probe of the multimeter to the transistor's emitter leg, and the other to the wire between the resistor and the battery.

STEP 7 Turn on the multimeter. Allow the reading to stabilize—avoid touching the can or moving around near it. Once it stabilizes, you'll have the baseline reading for the radiation in the room. Keep the can away from power sources, which could confuse its reading.

STEP 8 To measure the radioactivity of an object relative to the baseline, simply place it beside the can's end and observe the changed reading on your multimeter.

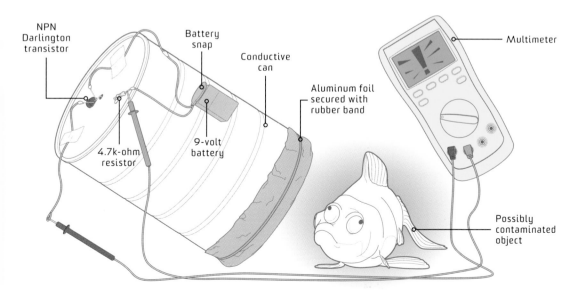

NPN Darlington transistor

Battery snap

Conductive can

Aluminum foil secured with rubber band

Multimeter

4.7k-ohm resistor

9-volt battery

Possibly contaminated object

Watch particles zip through your living room.

COST	$$
TIME	🕐
EASY ● ○ ○ ○ ○ HARD	

Machines designed to reveal subatomic particles operate on huge scales, weigh thousands of tons, and contain millions of sensors. But they don't have to be so complex. In fact, some are small and simple enough to operate in a living room. Take this cloud chamber, which uses evaporated alcohol to make a vapor that's extremely sensitive to passing particles.

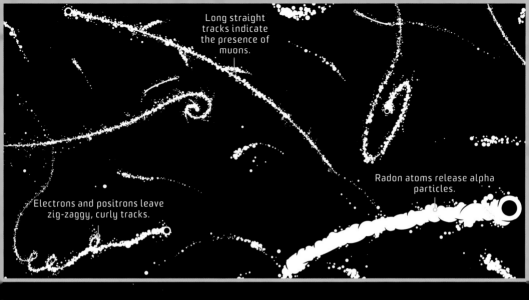

Long straight tracks indicate the presence of muons.

Electrons and positrons leave zig-zaggy, curly tracks.

Radon atoms release alpha particles.

Cosmic rays are constantly crashing into Earth from space, and when they hit the atmosphere, they release a shower of particles. If one of these particles zips through the DIY cloud chamber, it will bump into molecules that make up the air and knock off some of their electrons. This leaves a trail of charged ions, and tiny droplets of airborne alcohol cling to them. The ghostly track that results marks an individual particle's path through the chamber.

MATERIALS

Scissors

Felt

Clear plastic or glass
   fish tank

Superglue

Safety goggles and gloves

Isopropyl alcohol, 90 percent
   concentration or more

Oven mitts

Dry ice

Wide, shallow container
   for the dry ice

Dark metal baking sheet,
   larger than the tank's mouth

Flashlight

STEP 1 Cut the felt to match the fish tank's footprint, and glue it onto the inside bottom of the tank (where the sand and fake treasure chests would normally go).

STEP 2 Put on safety goggles and gloves, and pour enough isopropyl alcohol into the tank to saturate the felt. Drain off any excess.

STEP 3 While wearing oven mitts, place the dry ice in a shallow container. Cover it with the baking sheet.

STEP 4 Flip the tank upside down onto the baking sheet, so that the felt-covered bottom is at the top. You can use extra felt to block the seam between the tank and the baking sheet. Now remove the goggles and mitts

(but put them back on when disassembling the cloud chamber).

STEP 5 Wait about 10 minutes for the alcohol vapor to fill the tank. Then turn off all the lights and shine a flashlight into the tank.

▪ If you see a track inside the tank that looks like the path of a lost tourist in a foreign city, you're looking at an electron or a positron, the electron's antimatter twin. The lightweight particles bounce around when they hit molecules in the air, leaving zigzags and curlicues.

▪ A short, fat track appears when an atmospheric radon atom spits out a bulky, low-energy alpha particle (a clump of two protons and two neu-

trons). Radon is a naturally occurring radioactive element, but its concentration in the air is so low that its airborne presence is less radioactive than peanut butter.

▪ A long, straight track indicates that you've probably got muons, heavier cousins to the electron. Muons are produced when a cosmic ray bumps into a molecule high in the atmosphere. Because they are so massive, muons bludgeon their way through the air and leave clean lines.

▪ If a track suddenly forks, awesome! You just saw a particle decay. Many particles are unstable and will transform into more stable particles. Congratulations—you are watching physics in action

192 DIY a Soldering Stencil

Here's a cheap way to make clean electronics.

Taking an electronics prototype to the next level often means soldering tiny components onto a custom-printed circuit board. Solder paste applied without a stencil, however, can ooze, cause shorts, and end a project in flames. Here's how you can make an inexpensive DIY stencil that will help you lay down consistent amounts of solder with ease.

| COST | $ |
| TIME | 🕐 |
| EASY ● ● ● ○ ○ HARD |

MATERIALS

Scissors
Soda can
Iron
Soft cloths
Acetone
Circuit design software
  of your choosing
Computer
Printer
Thin shelving vinyl
Rubbing alcohol
Sticky notes
Cold water
Permanent marker
Clear tape
Muriatic acid
Hydrogen peroxide
PCB
Solder paste

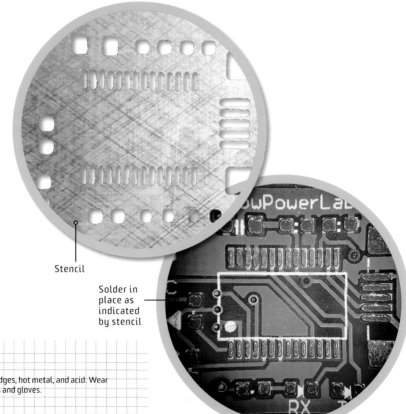

Stencil

Solder in place as indicated by stencil

WARNING
Beware of sharp edges, hot metal, and acid. Wear protective goggles and gloves.

GADGET UPGRADES

STEP 1 Carefully slice the ends off the soda can and cut the cylinder open. Flatten and warm the metal with an iron for a minute, then rub off the interior and exterior coatings with a soft cloth dipped in acetone. This will leave the shiny metal exposed and ready for a toner transfer.

STEP 2 Find a software program for designing and printing your own circuit. Once you've completed your stencil design, print it so it is white on black. Adjust your printer to maximum toner density if it has the option, then laser-print it with toner onto a sheet of thin shelving vinyl.

STEP 3 Trim the vinyl sheeting so that the printed design fits the aluminum sheet. Wipe the metal down with rubbing alcohol to remove any dust.

STEP 4 Working with a pack of sticky notes, lift the top note and place the piece of aluminum underneath it. Then attach the printed design facedown to the aluminum by covering it with the top sticky note. Iron it for a minute, dunk it in cold water to cool, remove the sticky notes, and peel off the vinyl. Your design should have transferred onto the aluminum, creating the stencil.

STEP 5 Fill gaps in the transfer with permanent marker. Cover the aluminum—except for the stencil design—with clear tape, which will repel the acid in the next step.

STEP 6 Soak the stencil in one part muriatic acid and three parts hydrogen peroxide for eight minutes. The acid will etch the stencil's holes in the metal; when they're complete, rinse the stencil in cold water to stop the reaction. Remove the tape and wipe with acetone.

STEP 7 To use, position the stencil over a piece of PCB and squeegee on the solder paste of your choosing.

193 Rig a Cellphone Blocker

Fly under the radar and check out for an hour, a day, or however long you choose. No one can find you if they can't track your phone.

To prevent people from picking up your mobile GPS coordinates, create a type of Faraday cage—an enclosure that blocks electrical fields by distributing incoming and outgoing charges within the conducting material. Traditionally used to protect electrical equipment from lightning strikes, a Faraday cage can also block the radio waves that cellphones need to communicate, which includes Internet connections and GPS tracking signals.

MATERIALS
Aluminum foil

STEP 1 Tightly wrap your cell phone in multiple layers of aluminum foil.

STEP 2 To test your Faraday cage, try calling your phone; if your call goes straight to voicemail, it means that your enclosure works and signals to and from your phone have been successfully blocked.

Turns out panning for gold or ancient artifacts can pay off.

You don't need to be a paleontologist or travel through remote canyons to find exquisite fossils. The teeth, shells, and bones of ancient animals may be buried in a creek, in a quarry, or on a beach near you. This sifter will work best in water, where erosion has done most of the hard work of separating fossils from the soil around them.

COST	$
TIME	🕐
EASY ● ○ ○ ○ ○ HARD	

MATERIALS

Measuring tape
Felt-tip marker
46-by-2-by-1-inch (117-by-5-by-2.5-cm) pine plank
Saw
Drill
Eight 1¼-inch (3.2-cm) wood screws

Hardware cloth, galvanized, with ¼-inch (6.35-mm) holes
Wire snips
Staples
Staple gun
Hammer

STEP 1 Use a measuring tape and felt-tip marker to divide the plank of wood into two 16-inch (40-cm) pieces and two 7-inch (18-cm) ones.

STEP 2 Saw across the markings. The four pieces will comprise the sifter's frame.

STEP 3 Place the short pieces between the ends of the long ones, forming a rectangle. Drive two screws through each corner.

STEP 4 Measure an 8-by-16-inch (20-by-40-cm) rectangle of hardware cloth. Snip it out, being careful to avoid leaving any sharp prongs.

STEP 5 Staple the hardware cloth to the frame. Five staples across each short piece and ten across each longer piece will do. Hammer in any exposed prongs.

STEP 6 Load the sifter with a few scoops of fossil-rich earth. Shake to remove sand, mud, and pebbles. Examine the catch to see if you got lucky.

WARNING
Protect yourself with safety gloves and eyewear. When hunting fossils, don't break the law! Always get permission and permits.

Repurpose a Radio to Listen to Meteor Showers

Listen to the sweet music of meteor trails during the next shower.

Meteors leave streams of gases and vaporized material in their wake. These ionized trails, which form between 262,000 and 330,000 feet (80–100,500 m) up, are visible from Earth as bright shooting stars, but these trails can also reflect radio waves. With your radio tuned to a distant station, all you can hear is static. But when a meteor trail reflects that station's signal, it boosts the power. This jump in signal strength is what your radio, with the help of a good FM antenna, picks up. During a meteor shower, the receiver should detect several meteor spikes per hour, despite cloudy conditions or bright light. Look online to find out when the next meteor shower in your area will occur.

STEP 1 Dust off your old stereo receiver and attach an FM yagi antenna. Then plug in the headphones.

STEP 2 Tune the radio to a frequency without reception, between 88 and 108 mHz, while keeping the antenna in a nearly horizontal orientation. You could attempt to locate a long-distance powerful FM station (operating with a transmission power greater than 30 kw) and use the latitude/longitude coordinates for its transmission tower to guide the orientation of your antenna, but it's more fun to let serendipity guide your search for FM station reflections.

MATERIALS

Stereo receiver

4-element FM yagi antenna

1/4-inch (6.35-mm) plug headphones

Personal computer (PC) or a Mac running a Windows emulator

Male-male 1/4-inch (6.35-mm) audio cable

Optional: USB audio adapter

Radio-SkyPipe II software

STEP 3 Listen closely for a sudden spike in signal reception caused by a meteor passing overhead.

STEP 4 To record, connect the receiver's headphone jack and your computer's line-input jack with an audio cable. (Newer PCs might need a USB audio adapter.)

STEP 5 Download and set up the Radio-SkyPipe II software on your computer, using the online configuration guide (visit www.popsci.com/thebigbookofhacks). Signal boosts should appear as spikes on your radio strip chart.

STEP 6 Adjust the receiver's volume until the audio signal spikes hit just below the maximum threshold of the radio strip chart. You can now "see" meteors in any weather conditions.

196 A 3D Printer that Runs on Sun and Sand

This bizarre-looking contraption turns the desert's resources—a whole lot of sun and sand—into glass.

When design student Markus Kayser wanted to test his sun-powered, sand-fed 3D printer, he knew the gray skies outside his London apartment wouldn't do. So he shipped the 200-pound (90-kg) device to Cairo, Egypt, hoping to find plenty of sun and sand that could, in conjunction with a large lens, produce glassware.

How does this machine work? Two aluminum arms, holding the lens at one end and solar panels at the other, can pivot from straight overhead down to a 45-degree angle to chase the sun. Sensors detect the shadows and feed the data on their position to Kayser's computer, which directs the motorized frame to adjust to properly align the lens. Two photovoltaic panels, one on either side of the machine, keep the printer powered. Since the panels are attached to the same arms as the lens, they also benefit from the sun tracking, ensuring that they always get direct light.

Kayser first designs the object he wants to print in a computer-assisted design (CAD) program. His computer sends instructions to the printer, which works from the bottom up. After a layer has cooled into glass, he adds more sand to the sandbox in the center of the machine and flattens it out, and the printer begins heating the next layer. Kayser's first major piece, a bowl, took about four and a half hours to print.

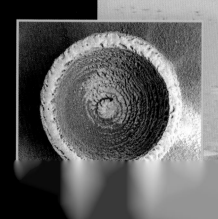

PRINTING A BETTER BOWL
Kayser has printed a glass bowl and several sculptures. He admits they're not perfect; he says he could have used more complicated optics. But, he adds, perfection wasn't the point: "This is about showing the potential."

197 Run a Flashlight on Dead Batteries

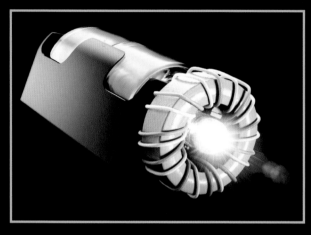

COST	$
TIME	🕐🕐
EASY ● ● ● ○ ○ HARD	

MATERIALS

D-size battery box with leads

Double-sided foam tape

Flashlight push-button switch

Scissors

Wire strippers

Soldering iron and solder

10mm superbright white LED

1-inch (2.5-cm) round protoboard

2N2222 NPN transistor

1k-ohm resistor

24-gauge wire from old network cable

Toroid transformer core, at least ¾-inch (1.9-cm) ID

Battery-shell-adapter set

Dead AAA, AA, C, or D alkaline battery

The dead shall shine again.

Don't throw out that seemingly lifeless battery—it's not dead yet. A brand-new alkaline battery cell has an electric potential of about 1.5 volts, which drops as the juice runs out. The voltage eventually becomes too low to power most devices, but there's still energy trapped inside the battery—as much as 15 percent of the original charge. By wiring a circuit called a "joule thief," you can tap the last of that power to light a white LED.

STEP 1 The D-size battery box has a negative end (with a spring contact and a black wire) and a positive end (with a red wire), plus small holes at all four corners. Route the wires out through the holes nearest the terminals to which they are attached. Loop the black wire across the negative end of the box and back in the opposite corner on the same end. Then run it down the long inside edge and out again on the positive end, opposite the red wire.

STEP 2 Use foam tape to mount the flashlight switch on the negative end of the box. Cut the black wire right underneath the button, strip the ends, and solder them to the switch terminals.

STEP 3 Spread the leads on the LED slightly so that they span three holes on the protoboard. Install the light at the center of the protoboard, passing its leads through the holes.

STEP 4 Turn the protoboard over and bend the LED leads as shown. Solder them under the protoboard.

STEP 5 Refer to the transistor's packaging (or look up the part number online) to identify its collector, base,

and emitter leads. Install it on the protoboard right above the LED, and bend and solder its leads underneath to connect the emitter to the LED's short lead, and the collector to the long lead. Install the resistor on the protoboard right below the LED and solder its leads underneath.

STEP 6 Turn the protoboard over to view the leads. Bend the transistor's base lead down between the LED leads, and solder it to the end of the resistor nearest the black battery wire.

STEP 7 Cut the loose battery wires off about 1¹/₂ inches (3.8 cm) from the positive end of the box, then strip and tin their ends. Thread both of the battery box's wires through the large hole in the protoboard, then install the red wire on the protoboard immediately to the right of the LED, and the black wire to its left.

STEP 8 Bend and solder the battery box's black lead underneath the protoboard to connect with the LED's short lead.

STEP 9 Cut two 20-inch (50-cm) lengths of wire, and strip and tin one end of each. Connect them to the protoboard: one to the red battery lead through the hole immediately below and the other to the transistor collector through the hole immediately to the right. These wires will hold the toroid transformer core to the protoboard. From this point on, we'll call them toroid wires.

STEP 10 Pass the free ends of the wires through the hole in the toroid. Center the toroid over the protoboard, flush against the top, with the LED and other components inside.

STEP 11 Use the toroid wire attached to the transistor collector to "sew" the toroid to the protoboard: Thread the wire through every other hole around the board's edge until you've made a full circle.

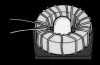

STEP 12 Repeat with the remaining toroid wire, the one attached to the red battery lead: Sew through the holes you skipped in Step 11. Do not cross the wires.

STEP 13 Thread the ends of both toroid wires through the protoboard. The first toroid wire (the one already attached to the transistor collector) should be soldered to the red battery lead, and the second (the one already attached to the red battery lead) should be soldered to the free end of the resistor. Test the circuit by installing a battery in the holder and pushing the button.

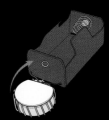

STEP 14 Once you are sure the circuit works, snip off any excess leads, cover the bottom of the board with foam tape, and stick it to the positive end of the battery box. Just pop a dead D battery into the box, or use the battery shell adapter set, which enables the box to accept a dead AAA, AA, or C battery. The joule thief flashlight is now ready to use!

Repurpose Foil for Techie Use

Dig this stuff out of a kitchen cupboard and
make the most of its conductive properties.

DO-IT-YOURSELF CAPACITORS

Cut a 2-foot (60-cm) length of aluminum foil, and three lengths of plastic wrap to match. Cut the foil in half lengthwise and tape a piece of electrical wire to each sheet, then put the pieces of foil on top of each other with plastic wrap in between. Put more plastic wrap on top of and below the foil, then roll it all up and hook the wires to a battery charger. Charge stuff up.

SECURE LOOSE BATTERIES

Sometimes, batteries don't quite connect with the springs inside your devices. So fold up a piece of aluminum foil and slide it between the battery terminals and the springs.

DIY LIGHT REFLECTOR

Wrap a large piece of cardboard in foil to create a quick and cheap light reflector for photography.

199 Improvise a Tripod

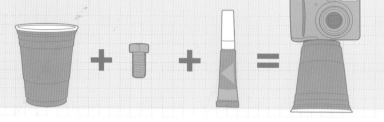

STEP 1 Poke a hole in the center of the bottom of a plastic cup.

STEP 2 Insert a bolt that fits your camera's threaded tripod hole. Glue the bolt in place.

STEP 3 Screw on your camera and start snapping.

200 Mount a Camera to Your Bike

Document your epic rides with a bike-bell mod.

MATERIALS

Bicycle bell

Camera

Bicycle

Screwdriver

STEP 1 Find a bike bell with a central screw that fits the tripod mount on the bottom of your camera. Most tripod mounts measure ¼ inch (6.35 mm).

STEP 2 Attach the bell to the handlebars.

STEP 3 Use a screwdriver to remove the bell's dome.

STEP 4 Screw the camera's tripod mount to the bell's central screw. Orient the camera whichever way you like, and start shooting your photographic travelogue.

Camera

Central screw

Bicycle bell

Build a Time-Lapse Camera Stand

Upgrade your kitchen timer for slick panoramic photos on the cheap.

MATERIALS

Drill

1/4-inch (6.35-mm) 20 set screw

Kitchen timer

3/8-inch (9.5-mm) bolt

3/8-inch (9.5-mm) 20 bushing

Craft knife

Rubber mat

Glue

Tripod

Tripod mount

Camera

Computer with photo-editing software

STEP 1 Drill a 15/64-inch (6-mm) hole into the center of a kitchen timer's dial. Insert a 1/4-inch (6.35-mm) 20 set screw.

STEP 2 In the bottom of the timer, drill a hole 11/32 inches (8.75 mm) in diameter. Screw a 3/8-inch (9.5-mm) bolt into the hole to create threads for a 3/8-inch (9.5-mm) bushing (a threaded insert that will allow you to mount the timer to the tripod).

STEP 3 Measure and cut a piece of rubber mat, leaving a hole for the bushing, and glue it to the bottom of the timer.

STEP 4 Mount the timer on a tripod, attach the tripod mount and camera, and set the timer. Adjust the camera's settings to take pictures at regular intervals, and then transfer the shots to a computer and create a panoramic time-lapse montage with photo software.

202 Rig a Plast[ic]
Bottle Dif[...]

STEP 1 Cut out a small sec[...] plastic water jug.

STEP 2 Cut a hole in[...] the camera's lens t[...]

STEP 3 Place th[...] covers the flas[...]

Tripod

...ic-
...ffuser

...tion of an empty frosted

...the section large enough for
...to fit through.

...e diffuser on the camera so it
...sh. Snap away.

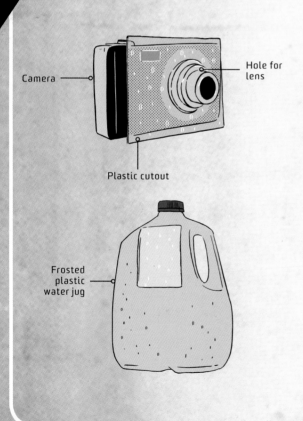

Camera —

Hole for lens —

Plastic cutout

Frosted plastic water jug —

Make Your Camera Waterproof

STEP 1 Cut a piece of toilet-paper tube to match the depth of your camera lens and cover your lens with it.

STEP 2 Stretch an unlubricated condom open. Add a packet of desiccant gel—it will prevent moisture—and slide your camera inside with the tube in place.

STEP 3 Tie the condom slack into a knot and superglue the knot to make it watertight.

STEP 4 Stretch a second condom open and insert the wrapped camera, knot side in. Tie and glue the knot again. Dive in and document.

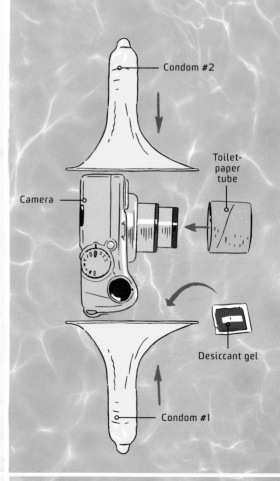

Condom #2 —

Toilet-paper tube

Camera —

Desiccant gel —

Condom #1 —

204 Create a Peephole Fisheye Lens

STEP 1 Turn on your camera and extend the zoom as far as it will go.

STEP 2 Grab a standard peephole from a home-supply store and, making sure the peephole is facing the right way out, pop it over the camera lens.

STEP 3 Hold it in place or attach it to the lens with heavy-duty tape. (Look for tape that doesn't leave a residue, which could make your lens stick.)

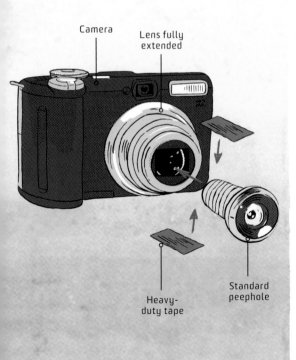

Camera

Lens fully extended

Heavy-duty tape

Standard peephole

205 Adapt a Manual Lens to Your DSLR

STEP 1 Procure a twist-on adapter ring and a compatible manual-focus lens from a vintage film camera. (These options are both way less expensive than the lenses you can buy for a DSLR, and you can even find old macro, fisheye, and ultrazoom lenses relatively inexpensively—just make sure they're compatible with your DSLR before purchasing.)

STEP 2 Insert the lens into the adapter. There is usually a dot or some kind of marking on both the lens and the adapter that makes it easy to see how the two fit together.

STEP 3 Twist the lens while holding the adapter in place, as if you were mounting the lens onto a camera body. The lens should make a click or locking sound when it's secured.

STEP 4 Mount the lens and adapter combination onto your camera like any other lens and get shooting.

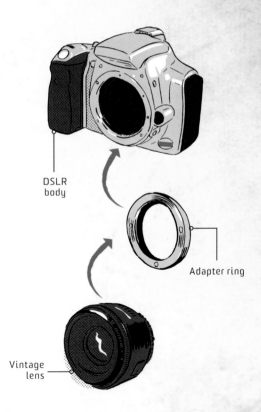

DSLR body

Adapter ring

Vintage lens

206 Turn a Can into a Sun-Tracking Camera

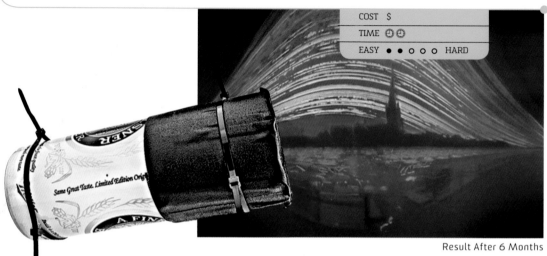

COST	$
TIME	☺ ☺
EASY	● ● ○ ○ ○ HARD

Result After 6 Months

Pinhole photography is hundreds of years old, and you can make these simple cameras out of anything. Using photographic paper, you can build one in a beer can to record the gradual shift in the sun's path over the course of several months.

MATERIALS

Empty 20- or 24-ounce (590- or 710-ml) aluminum can

Can opener

Pin

Scissors

10-by-2¾-inch (25-by-7-cm) black cardstock strip, with ½-inch (1.25-cm) notches on one long side

2½-inch- (6.5-cm-) diameter black cardstock disc

Roll of black gaffer tape

Darkened room with red light

Semimatte photo paper

Zip ties

Hairdryer

Flatbed scanner

Computer with photo-editing software

WARNING
Wear protective gloves when cutting beer cans. Also make sure that strapping up empty cans is not considered littering and illegal in your area.

STEP 1 Remove the can's top with a can opener, and poke the middle of its side with a pin.

STEP 2 Wrap the strip of cardstock around the can's base, and bend the notches inward at a 90-degree angle. Tape the disc on top of the notches to form a removable black lid.

STEP 3 Move everything into a darkened room. Turn on a red light to see, and insert half a sheet of photo paper into the can facing the pinhole. Put gaffer tape over the pinhole.

STEP 4 Remove the lid from the base of the can and secure it over the can's open end with gaffer tape. (Use plenty of tape to ensure the camera is light-tight and waterproof.)

STEP 5 Take the project outside, aim the pinhole toward the southern sky, and vertically fasten the can to a signpost or other stationary object with zip ties. Uncover the pinhole.

STEP 6 Wait a month to a year (the longer the exposure, the more solar tracks appear). After the wait is over, cover your camera's pinhole and take the camera indoors.

STEP 7 Remove the lid and blow-dry the photo. Place it on a flatbed scanner, and make one—and only one—high-resolution scan. (Don't do a preview scan!)

STEP 8 Open the image, enhance its contrast (e.g., via "auto-equalize" or "auto-levels" commands), and invert the colors. Save the image—called a solargraph—to your computer.

207 Grow Your Own Photo

You can use microbes to make black-and-agar still lifes. No joke.

A strain of microbe known as *Escherichia coli* produces black pigment in darkness or, in red light, remains transparent. The result is an organism that behaves like film—which you can harness to "grow" images. In this basic setup, red light shines through a printed transparency that's taped to the bottom of an agar-filled petri dish. Reach out to a biohackerspace for assistance sourcing the ingredients, if needed.

MATERIALS

Six 3¹/₂-inch- (9-cm-) diameter transparencies, sized to fit the petri dishes

100 ml luria broth agar

30 mg S-gal

50 mg iron ammonium sulfate

1 g low-melting-point agarose

Microwave-safe container with lid

Microwave oven

30 μl Voigt's strain of *E. coli*

kanamycin (50 mg per ml of water)

ampicillin (50 mg per ml of water)

chloramphenicol (34 mg per ml of ethanol)

Six 3¹/₂-inch- (9-cm-) diameter petri dishes

Plastic wrap

Razor blade

Clear tape

Red-light source

A bacterial portrait of Edward L. Youmans, founder of *Popular Science*, circa 1886

STEP 1 Come up with six simple, black-and-clear designs to print on your transparencies. Each design cannot exceed 3¹/₂ inches (9 cm) in diameter, as that's the size of your petri dishes. When designing, keep in mind that the dark areas of your transparency will cast shadows on the bacteria, causing them to produce pigment. The recipe here allows for six photographs, so feel free to experiment with different approaches.

STEP 2 Combine the luria broth agar, S-gal, iron ammonium sulfate, and low-melting-point agarose to make an agar mixture. Then transfer 15 ml of the agar mixture to the microwave-safe container and nuke it (about one minute on high). Let cool until it's warm to the touch. This will be the agar mix for your first photo.

STEP 3 Add the Voigt's *E. coli* and the antibiotics kanamycin, ampicillin, and chloramphenicol. (Note: These antibiotics aren't absolutely necessary for the project's success, but we recommend them because they do help prevent contamination.) Mix vigorously, but don't create bubbles.

STEP 4 Pour the mixture into a petri dish and quickly cover with a lid. Let it cool until solid, about 20 minutes.

STEP 5 Remove the lid, cover the petri dish with plastic wrap, and cut three narrow slits in the plastic.

STEP 6 Tape the transparency to the bottom of the petri dish, flip it over, and shine red light down onto the transparency for one to three days. (Make sure the light doesn't melt the agar, as this will kill the bacteria.)

STEP 7 Admire your work. The petri-dish photograph can last for several years in a refrigerator.

208 Snap a Self-Portrait with a DIY Remote Shutter Release

Trigger your camera's shutter from afar with basic household parts.

MATERIALS

Rotary tool

Pill bottle with snap-on lid

Shutter release cable

Craft knife

Rubber tubing that fits snugly over the nozzle of your squeeze bottle

Plastic squeeze bottle

Short piece of plastic tubing that fits snugly into the rubber tubing

Balloon

Thread

Cork that fits into the pill bottle

Talcum powder

STEP 1 Use a rotary tool to drill a hole into the pill bottle's lid big enough to fit the rubber tubing.

STEP 2 Drill a hole in the bottom of the pill bottle for the trigger of your shutter release cable. Insert the trigger.

STEP 3 Use a craft knife to cut the rubber tubing long enough to cover the longest distance that you anticipate being from the camera. Insert the nozzle of your squeeze bottle into one end of the rubber tubing.

STEP 4 Thread the tubing's other end through the hole in the pill bottle's lid and onto the short plastic tubing.

STEP 5 Pull the balloon's opening around the piece of plastic tubing and tie it on securely with thread.

STEP 6 Dust the piece of cork with talcum powder and insert it into the pill bottle. Lower the balloon into the bottle so that it rests against the cork.

STEP 7 Test that everything is airtight, then hook the cable to your camera and get in front of the camera, holding the squeeze bottle. When you're ready, squeeze the bottle, and the balloon will inflate, pushing the cork against the cable's trigger. Say "cheese," anyone?

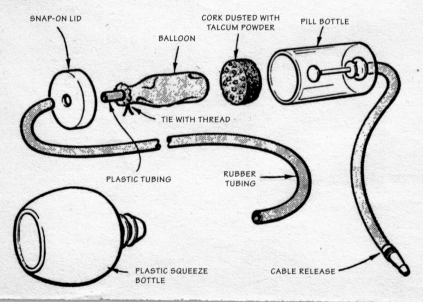

SNAP-ON LID

BALLOON

CORK DUSTED WITH TALCUM POWDER

PILL BOTTLE

TIE WITH THREAD

PLASTIC TUBING

RUBBER TUBING

PLASTIC SQUEEZE BOTTLE

CABLE RELEASE

209   Turn Your Camera into a Photosynthesis Detector

In about an hour, you can hack a camera to display only blue, green, and near-infrared light, which will give you a lovely view of plant life.

This hack converts an obsolete camera into a photosynthesis detector, called the Infragram, a tool you can use to measure plant health. During photosynthesis, leaves soak up blue, green, and red light but reflect invisible near-infrared light. The Infragram blocks red light and—because it's missing a thin glass filter common to digital cameras—can detect near-infrared light. Thus, it sees only blue, green, and near-infrared, and Infragram.org can convert the photos into colored maps of photosynthesis. A farmer who attached the Infragram to a drone, for example, could get a read on a farm field's health after a short flight.

WARNING
Capacitors that power a camera's flash can deliver a dangerous shock even long after batteries are removed. Attempt at your own risk.

MATERIALS

Point-and-shoot camera   Rosco #2007 blue gel
Screwdriver   Blue paper
Tape

STEP 1 Grab an old point-and-shoot that you're OK to donate to the cause—preferably one with custom white balance, which allows you to adjust unrealistic color casts, so that your camera "reads" the color you are shooting without alternative hues. Remove the camera's batteries, memory card, and any screws holding the outer casing together. The rear panel should pry off with little effort.

STEP 2 Push the LCD aside and unscrew the sensor. Move it out of the way too, and shake out the infrared filter. (If the filter is glued on, it's best to try another camera.)

STEP 3 Reassemble the camera, and tape a square of Rosco #2007 blue gel over the lens. (The camera can't accurately measure photosynthesis without this.)

STEP 4 For each new scene, set the white balance with a piece of paper—blue works best. (To do this, place a piece of blue paper alongside your subject so that both objects are in the same light. Fill your frame with the paper, take the shot, and manually select the custom white balance setting from the menu.) Snap photos of plants, visit Infragram.com to convert your image, and admire your otherworldly photography.

210 A Camera that Shoots Huge Photographs

This beast of a camera allows you to capture huge images on X-ray film. Problem is, you'll have to build it first.

Darren Samuelson had just taken his last photo of Manhattan when the police arrived. He and his father had been working from an empty dock across the Hudson River, and the authorities wanted to know what they were doing with a folding contraption that was more than 6 feet (1.8 m) long and 70 pounds (32 kg) pointed at the city. Samuelson pleaded that it was a camera, and that he was just a tourist. They believed him and he got his shot—a photo so detailed that the print could be blown up to half the length of a volleyball court and still remain sharp.

Samuelson specially built this camera for X-ray stock that measures 14 by 36 inches (35 cm by 90 cm) and is cheaper than large-format photo paper. He began by constructing the massive accordionlike bellows required to adjust the camera's focal length manually, spending two weeks on the floor folding, cutting, gluing, and inserting the ribs that would give it form. The camera and bellows unfold and slide out on rails, with a lens at one end and the film holder at the other. To focus, he slides either end in or out. The result is not point-and-shoot, Samuelson admits, and the build wasn't easy (the parts list runs to 186 rows on a spreadsheet). "But when I hold up a print and see the amazing detail," he says, "I think, 'Yeah, this was worth it.'"

MEGA PRINTS
Each print measures 3 feet (90 cm), and while shooting Samuelson drapes an immense black cloak over himself and the camera to block out light.

TRANSPORTATION & FITNESS

211 Light Up Your Bike Wheels

By spending a few hours tinkering with LEDs, you can outfit your dull wheels with hypnotically glowing rings.

Wiring a wheel to display a lighted circle is easy and inexpensive, making this hack an ideal first foray into DIY electronics. You can choose how many LEDs your wheels need. The number should be six or less and ideally a factor of the number of spokes on your wheel.

COST	$
TIME	☺ ☺
EASY ● ● ● ○ ○ HARD	

MATERIALS

3 to 6 LEDs	Electrical tape
3 to 6 resistors	Heat-shrink tubing
Measuring tape	Lighter
Bicycle wheel	9-volt battery
Wire stripper	connector
Insulated wire	9-volt battery
Soldering iron and solder	Black duct tape
	Zip ties

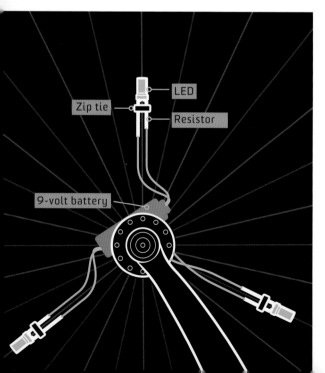

Zip tie
LED
Resistor
9-volt battery

STEP 1 Before choosing resistors, check the LED package for its forward voltage and current. Subtract the voltage from nine, then divide this number by the LED's current in amps. Then choose the nearest standard resistor value that's larger than this number—for blue lights, that's 330 ohm. You'll need one resistor per LED, unless you connect the LEDs in series. (To wire LEDs in series, connect the first LED's negative electrode to the positive electrode of the second LED. Then connect the second LED's negative electrode to the positive electrode of the third LED, and so on.)

STEP 2 Mark evenly spaced spokes 2 inches (5 cm) from the rim of the wheel. Placing the LEDs the same distance from the rim will create a glowing circle when the wheel spins.

STEP 3 Measure the distance between an LED and the hub of the wheel. Cut two wires per LED to this length and strip both ends.

STEP 4 Twist one end of wire around each LED's longer leg (positive end) and one end of a resistor around its shorter leg (negative end). Connect the loose resistor end to the other wire that you cut in Step 3 for each light.

STEP 5 Solder the assembly together, mark its positive end, and cover the exposed joints with electrical tape and/or heat-shrink tubing. You can use a lighter to tighten the tubing—just make sure not to burn the components.

STEP 6 Twist the positive ends of each LED assembly together and solder them to the positive wire of the 9-volt battery connector. Do the same for the negative ends and the negative wire. Cover the exposed wires with tubing and/or tape.

STEP 7 Firmly attach the 9-volt battery to the hub with duct tape and a zip tie. Leave room for the 9-volt battery connector to snap on.

STEP 8 Use duct tape and zip ties to securely attach the LEDs and their wires to your wheel's spokes. Snap the battery connector on to the battery and give your wheel a spin!

WARNING

When working with electronics, take care not to burn or electrocute yourself. When biking with electronics, follow the road rules and wear a helmet!

212 Ride with a Grease-Free Pant Leg

STEP 1 Dig up an old toe strap from a pair of retired bike pedals. Apply a strip of adhesive reflective tape to the strap; it'll keep you safe during night rides.

STEP 2 Gather your chain-side pant leg, or roll it up to about mid-calf.

STEP 3 Wrap the toe strap around your calf, thread the buckle, and tighten. Adjust on the fly.

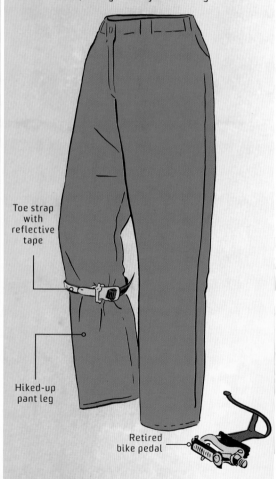

Toe strap with reflective tape

Hiked-up pant leg

Retired bike pedal

213 Reinforce Your Tire with a Seat Belt

STEP 1 Head to the junkyard or second-hand store and find an old seat belt.

STEP 2 Use scissors to cut off the buckle and latch plate.

STEP 3 Lay the belt inside your bicycle tire and cut it so that the ends don't overlap.

STEP 4 Insert your tire tube as you normally would and stretch the tire back onto the rim, making sure the tube still fits well inside the tire.

Seat belt

Tire

Tube

Discarded seat-belt ends

214 Stay Safe with a Beer-View Mirror

STEP 1 Obtain a piece of mirror that fits into your bottle cap. (Or use a glass cutter to score and punch out a small circle from a larger mirror.)

STEP 2 Using a drill bit that matches the diameter of a bicycle spoke, drill two holes in the rim of a bottle cap. The holes should be directly opposite each other.

STEP 3 Thread the spoke onto the cap. Once the spoke is through both sides of the cap, secure it by placing putty on the spoke's end.

STEP 4 Squeeze some glue into the back of the bottle cap and set the mirror down into it. Arrange the cap so the mirror will face you when it's installed on the helmet. Bend the cap and mirror on the spoke about 90 degrees, then wait 24 hours for the glue to dry completely.

STEP 5 Take a good look at your helmet to devise a proper mounting method. If your helmet has holes, you'll need to thread the spoke through one of them and then use needle-nose pliers to bend the spoke's end into a loop, then secure one end of the loop through the helmet's hole. Other helmet styles will call for other tactics—just make sure it's mounted in a way that won't poke you.

STEP 6 Hold the spoke in front of your helmet and determine how much length you'll need, given your mounting method and how far you'd like it to extend in front of you. Cut it to this length.

STEP 7 Secure it to your helmet and ride safe.

Spoke — Helmet

Mirror

Bottle cap

215 Keep Your Handlebar Grips Tight

STEP 1 If your handlebars start to slip around, remove the rubber grips. Wipe out the inside of the grips with a soft cloth.

STEP 2 Spray a few pumps of hair spray—the non-aerosol kind works best—inside the grips.

STEP 3 While the hair spray is wet, slide the grips into place on your handlebars.

STEP 4 Let the hair spray set overnight. Enjoy your no-budge grips.

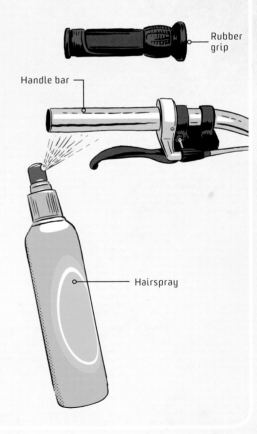

Rubber grip

Handle bar

Hairspray

216 Bring the Party with a Bike Speaker

Everyone knows that bike rides are best when they come with a soundtrack.

COST $$$

TIME 🕐🕐

EASY ●●○○○ HARD

MATERIALS

10-inch (25-cm) speaker with cable

Bike with a rear rack

Marker

Drill

Four bolts with washers and nuts to fit

Saw

2-by-2-inch (5-by-5-cm) wood board

Small screws

Waterproof plastic container

Foam

Tripath-based amp

Bike-light mount

Media player with clip holder

Superglue

STEP 1 Set the speaker on your bike rack and mark places for four holes on its underside for bolts.

STEP 2 Take the grille off the speaker and remove the woofer. Drill the holes you marked and put the bolts in so that they stick out from the speaker box's bottom.

STEP 3 Cut the 2-by-2-inch (5-by-5-cm) board to the size of your speaker's bottom. Make two holes in each board for the bolts in the speaker.

STEP 4 Put the woofer and the grille back into the speaker box, and use the washers and nuts to bolt the speaker to the board on the rack.

STEP 5 Screw the waterproof plastic container onto the speaker's top. Drill two holes in one side of the container and line its bottom with foam. Place the amp inside.

STEP 6 Connect the speaker to the amp's right channel with the speaker cable, threading it through one of the holes in the container's side.

STEP 7 Attach the bike-light mount to your handlebar, and glue on your media player's clip holder. Slide your media player in.

STEP 8 Thread your media player's cord through the second hole in the plastic container's side to connect it to the amp. Press play and put the top on.

STEP 9 Watch parties erupt as you ride by.

Waterproof plastic container with tripath-based amp inside

10-inch (25-cm) speaker

Board on rack

Media player

Cord to amp

217 Stay Warm on Chilly Rides

STEP 1 Wad or fold newspaper to the length of your chest.

STEP 2 Insert the paper into your jacket and zip it up. Add more if you want extra warmth.

STEP 3 Ride on in the cold.

218 Make a Unicycle Out of a Bike

Turns out unis aren't so tricky to make, but they're still just as tricky to ride.

MATERIALS

Old fixed-gear bicycle with a straight fork

Hacksaw

Metal file

Allen wrench

Steel pillow blocks

STEP 1 Remove the bicycle's front fork. Use a hacksaw, if necessary, to cut the frame where it's attached to the fork. File the edges of the cut pieces to smooth them.

STEP 2 Remove the handlebar and stem from the front fork using the Allen wrench.

STEP 3 Remove the rear wheel and crank. To do this, take the chain off the gears of the rear wheel and unfasten the bolts that hold it to the frame.

STEP 4 Attach the front fork to the wheel axle by clamping the steel pillow blocks on each side of the fork and attaching the blocks to the axle at the spacers, using the bottom lock nut. Reattach the crank and pedals.

STEP 5 Insert the seat post into the front fork and unicycle away. (Just spare us the clown suit.)

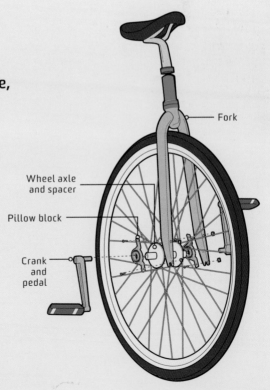

Fork

Wheel axle and spacer

Pillow block

Crank and pedal

TRANSPORTATION & FITNESS

219 Navigate with an Old-Fashioned GPS

Because the best bike adventures lack cell reception.

COST	$
TIME	🕐
EASY ● ○ ○ ○ ○ HARD	

MATERIALS

Bicycle

Scissors

Sturdy plastic mesh

Large zip-top storage bag

Two Velcro strips 6 inches (15 cm) in length

Velcro strip 5 inches (12.5 cm) in length

Map

STEP 1 Cut the plastic mesh so that when you slide it inside the storage bag it lies flat.

STEP 2 Remove the mesh and make four slits in it just large enough for the Velcro strips to fit through. Two horizontal slits go in the upper corners; two vertical slits go in the center (where your bike's top tube is).

STEP 3 Slip the mesh inside the bag and adjust it so that it butts up against the zipper. Mark the location of the top slits on the back and front of the bag. Mark the location of the center strips on the back of the bag only.

STEP 4 Remove the mesh from the bag. Cut slits along the bag's markings.

STEP 5 Pass the Velcro strips through the slits in the bag. Wrap the 6-inch (15-cm) strips around the handlebars and the 5-inch (12.7-cm) strip around the top tube, and fasten them into loops. Insert the mesh back into the bag.

STEP 6 Open the bag and slide a printout of your route inside it.

STEP 7 Start riding, referring to your map when needed.

Velcro

Plastic mesh

Zip-top storage bag

220 Make Your Bike's Tires Snow Proof

Brave the winter with DIY snow chains for your bike.

STEP 1 Make sure your bike has a coaster brake, a disc brake, or, if it's a fixed gear, no brake. (This particular trick won't work with rim brakes.)

STEP 2 Gather two zip ties for each spoke gap on both of your bicycle's tires.

STEP 3 Wrap a zip tie around the tire and rim, positioning the zip tie's head halfway between the outside of the tire and the rim. Fasten it shut.

STEP 4 Continue placing zip ties in the spoke gaps, alternating the side on which the head faces and leaving enough clearance between the zip ties and your fenders.

STEP 5 Trim the end of each zip tie just to the head. Ride off into the slush.

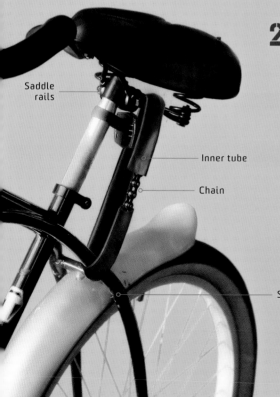

Saddle rails

Inner tube

Chain

Seat stay

221 Protect Your Bike Saddle from Theft

Deter bike saddle thieves with simple, persuasive inconvenience.

STEP 1 Making sure your seat post is at maximum height, measure a length of chain long enough to wrap through the saddle rails and seat stays.

STEP 2 Break the chain at your measured loop length and cut a used inner tube to the length of the chain.

STEP 3 Drop the chain through the inner tube.

STEP 4 Thread the chain between your saddle's seat rails and seat stays, then use a chain tool to rejoin the chain.

STEP 5 Never ride home without a saddle again.

TRANSPORTATION & FITNESS

222 Reuse a Busted Bike Tube

A flat tire can really ruin your day. Get revenge on it with these simple reuse ideas.

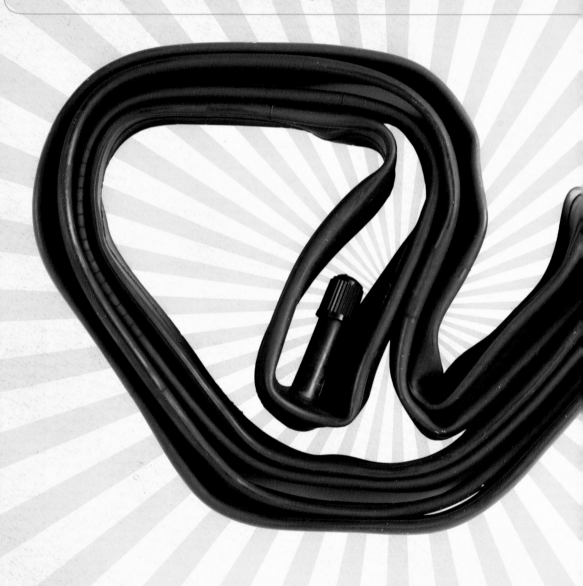

SUPER-SIZE RUBBER BANDS
Cut them into long strips and use them to secure all sorts of things. You can also make a really big rubber-band ball, or shoot them into the sky. (If you shoot them at people, you didn't get this idea here!)

GET A GRIP
Wrap a tube around the handle of common household tools (such as screwdrivers, brooms, rakes, and hammers) to improve your grip.

KEEP PAINT LOOKING SPIFFY
Protect the paint on vulnerable areas of your bicycle—such as where your lock rubs against the frame—by wrapping inner tubes around those areas.

EMERGENCY HEADLIGHT
If your bike light dies and you've got a flashlight handy, fish a spare inner tube out of your bag. Cut a piece that is 2 inches (5 cm) longer than your flashlight, then make a hole near each of the tube's ends. Run the tube under your handlebar so that it is perpendicular to the bar, and thread the flashlight through the holes with the light pointing forward. Turn it on and go.

BUNGEE CORDS IN A PINCH
Cut a sliver of inner tube and use it as a zip tie or bungee cord to lash whatever's loose.

223 Shred on a Fan-Propelled Skateboard

COST	$$$
TIME	☺☺☺
EASY	● ● ● ● ○ HARD

Why cruise on a regular skateboard when you can blast by on this model?

Fast is cool, but few would disagree that faster is even better. This skateboard build has you adding the engine, propeller, and remote-control transmitter from a model airplane (which you can pick up as independent parts in a hobby shop, or salvage from a spare model plane near you) for a version that'd make even Marty McFly jealous.

STEP 1 Blow the template at right up to size so it's about 4¹/₂ feet (1.35 m) in length and trace it onto your piece of wood. Use a jigsaw to cut out the board, and sand the edges so they're splinter-free. Drill holes so you can mount the trucks and risers.

STEP 2 Cut out and sand the two pieces from the remaining wood that will serve as mounting planks for the fan, gas tank, and engine, as well as create a compartment for the electronics. Make the mounting planks tall enough so that they'll provide clearance for your fan model's cage, keeping it off the ground and the skateboard bottom.

STEP 3 Apply adhesive-backed grip tape in your desired colors to the board and mounting compartment pieces.

STEP 4 Screw the trucks and risers to the board using the predrilled holes.

MATERIALS

4¹/₂ feet (1.35 m) of 1-by-10-inch (2.5-by-25-cm) wood

Jigsaw

Sandpaper

Drill

Adhesive-backed skateboard grip tape

Screws and washers

Skateboard trucks and risers with wheels

Wire

Remote-control transmitter with bundled receiver and servo

OS 1.60 FX model airplane engine

Battery for transmitter

Hose clamp

950-cc gas tank and gas

Fan cage

Three-blade propeller

Standard glow starter with meter

12-volt starter motor

Fan cage

Model airplane engine

Glow plug

Gas tank

Skateboard covered in grip tape

Electronics compartment

Trucks and risers

Three-blade propeller

STEP 5 Screw the two mounting planks securely into the back end of the board from the underside, after predrilling holes for them with a smaller bit. Cut another piece of scrap wood the width of the space between the mounting planks. Screw it in between the planks near their tops as a roof for the compartment that will house the electronics.

STEP 6 Wrap a short piece of wire around the servo's horn (the part where the arm screws on), and wrap the other end around the engine's throttle lever.

STEP 7 Plug the servo's connector into the receiver, then hook the battery to the receiver. Next mount the engine above the electronics compartment, screwing through the engine mount holes into the tops of the mounting planks. Secure the servo, receiver, and battery inside.

STEP 8 Screw a hose clamp to the outside of the mounting planks, then tighten the hose clamp around the gas tank to mount it. Connect the gas tank to the engine.

STEP 9 Unscrew the cage from a fan and insert the propeller. Slide the propeller onto the engine, tightening the propeller's bolt, then secure the cage onto the electronics compartment's roof with screws and washers.

STEP 10 Plug the glow starter into the engine's glow plug and use the starter motor to rotate the propeller. Once it's started up, set aside the starter motor, remove the glow plug, and give the remote to someone you trust. Zoom off.

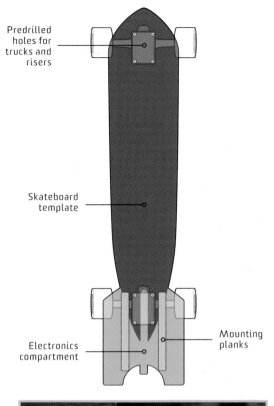

Predrilled holes for trucks and risers

Skateboard template

Electronics compartment

Mounting planks

YOU BUILT WHAT?!

A MOTORIZED SKATEBOARD

If you ever see a grown man whizzing by on a skateboard doing 20 miles per hour (32 km/h), that would be John Carnett, and in case you don't get a good look, his ride is a souped-up, motorized board he built from the ground up. He wanted to create a skateboard that would be superior to commercial models—a fast, hot-looking board that ran on all terrains. He cut an aluminum deck and bent the ends and side rails, then he outfitted it with axles and 8-inch (20-cm) knobby tires. Then there was the matter of installing a disc-braking system and a 500-watt electric motor. It's the sweetest ride on the road—or off it.

224 Give Your Motorcycle a Futuristic Vibe

Ride straight out of the movie *TRON* with this illuminated motorcycle trick.

COST $$$
TIME ☺ ☺ ☺
EASY ● ● ● ○ ○ HARD

MATERIALS

Motorcycle
Flexible LED light strips
Heavy-duty tape
Wire strippers
Two clamp connectors

Soldering iron and solder
18-gauge black wire
18-gauge red wire
Zip ties
On/off switch

STEP 1 Locate your motorcycle's battery—it's probably under the seat.

STEP 2 Place the LED strips where you want them along your motorcycle's frame. If the strips themselves are not adhesive, secure them with tape, and run the wires through the frame body toward the battery.

STEP 3 Using the wire strippers, strip some of the insulation from the ends of all the LED strips' wires. Place the negative wires into a clamp connector and the positive wires into another clamp connector.

STEP 4 Solder the black 18-gauge wire to the clamp housing the black LED wires, and the red 18-gauge wire to the clamp housing the red wires.

STEP 5 Gather the wires and secure them with a zip tie.

STEP 6 Mount the on/off switch somewhere you can easily reach while you're riding. Strip the ends of the black and red 18-gauge wires. Connect the red 18-gauge wire to the on/off switch, soldering on another length of 18-gauge red wire to extend to the battery.

STEP 7 Connect the black 18-gauge wire to the battery's negative terminal and the red 18-gauge wire to the battery's positive terminal.

STEP 8 Start your motorcycle, flip the switch into the "on" position, and make sure all the LED strips light up—if they don't, check your connections.

STEP 9 Suit up and ride off into an alternate reality.

225 Light Up Your Motorcycle Helmet

Make your helmet extra safe—and extra cool, too—with conductive paint.

MATERIALS

Fine sandpaper
Motorcycle helmet
Paper towel
Pencil
Masking tape
Conductive paint
Paintbrush
9-volt battery snap
9-volt battery
Wire strippers
Electrical wire
Soldering iron and solder
On/off switch
Wooden sticks for mixing and
  applying epoxies
Epoxy
LEDs
Conductive epoxy
Clear spray enamel

STEP 1 Sand the surface of your helmet where your design will go and then wipe it with a damp paper towel.

STEP 2 Draw a circuit directly onto the helmet. Trace components (such as the LEDs, battery, and on/off switch) onto the helmet and mark positives and negatives.

STEP 3 Apply masking tape to the area around your circuit that will contain the conductive paint.

STEP 4 Paint inside the tape, mapping your circuit. Make sure to stir the paint thoroughly and often, as the particles tend to settle. Apply multiple coats, if needed.

STEP 5 Let the paint dry for a few minutes and carefully remove the masking tape. Then let dry for 24 hours.

STEP 6 Snap the battery snap onto the 9-volt battery. Strip the ends of two pieces of wire and solder positive and negative leads to the snap's positive and negative ports. Then solder these leads to the positive and negative terminals of your on/off switch.

STEP 7 Use wooden sticks to mix and apply epoxy, then affix the on/off switch and battery to the helmet. Let dry.

STEP 8 Trim the leads of the LEDs. Use conductive epoxy to attach the LEDs where you want them, and then affix the switch wires.

STEP 9 Let dry for 24 hours, then seal over and around the conductive paint with epoxy to waterproof.

STEP 10 Tape off areas of your helmet you want to protect—like fabric parts or LED bulbs—and spray your helmet with clear spray enamel.

STEP 11 To turn the lights on, flip the on/off switch.

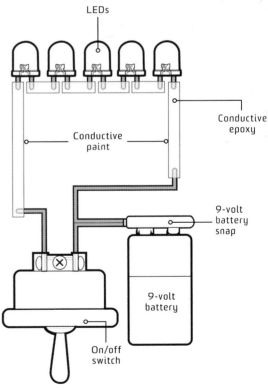

LEDs

Conductive epoxy

Conductive paint

9-volt battery snap

9-volt battery

On/off switch

226 The Vrooming Hot-Rod Hauler

An old logging truck is transforr into a sleek street racer.

Randy Grubb couldn't get it off his mind. For years been driving past an old logger's place near his hom rural Oregon, and one of the long-haul trucks in the yard kept catching his attention. In late 2008, Gru finally stopped for a closer look, and the toothless, chomping trucker let him rev the engine. He was so he had a big change in mind: He was going to trans into a hot rod.

The 49-year-old Grubb had built a number of othe vehicles out of forgotten engines in his backyard sh But making a dragster out of this ancient truck—a Peterbilt Model 351 with a giant 12-cylinder, two-s diesel engine—was unlike any of his past jobs. The engine hadn't been used in a decade, so he found a mechanic to help him tune it up, replaced the origi 13-speed transmission with a four-speed automati normally used in Greyhound buses, installed new f lines, and then polished every cubic inch. Next cam the body. He shortened the truck's grille by 10.5 inc (26.25 cm), took the front and rear axles from anot truck and narrowed them to hot-rod scale, and mac and welded all the connective hardware to complet transformation.

Grubb refers to the car—dubbed Piss'd Off Pete bec it's a Peterbilt with attitude—as an aluminum sculp In fact, the vehicle will most likely soon be in a priva collection. But he hardly treats it like a museum pie As soon as he was finished, he drag-raced it at mor 100 miles an hour (160 km/h).

OFF THE SCRAP HEAP
Piss'd Off Pete runs on a 12-cylinder engine Grubb calls "the biggest, baddest diesel ever made." Just how much did making it cost him? $100,000.

227 Mount a Rad Hood Ornament

STEP 1 Use epoxy to glue a plastic figurine of your choosing to a circular magnet with a center bore.

STEP 2 If your car has a hood ornament, remove it. Thread a screw through the magnet of your new one and turn to secure the screw to the ornament.

STEP 3 Screw it onto your car's hood in the old ornament's hole, or just use the magnet to hold it in place.

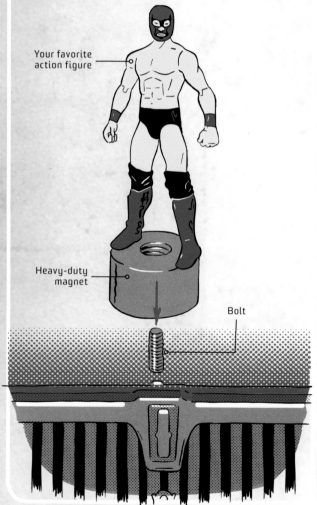

Your favorite action figure

Heavy-duty magnet

Bolt

228 Hang a DIY Air Freshener

STEP 1 Cut out a T-shirt image you like and trace it onto a sheet of fabric softener and a piece of fabric.

STEP 2 Staple the dryer sheet in between the two pieces of fabric.

STEP 3 Punch a hole in the top and insert a rubber band; knot the band to secure it.

STEP 4 Hang it up in your car to cover up stink.

Rubber band

Rad image source

Second fabric source

Dryer sheet

229 Black Out Your Taillights

STEP 1 Remove your taillight lenses by unscrewing the bolts holding them onto the car.

STEP 2 Clean them, and then cover the lights entirely with strips of masking tape, pressing the strips into the grooves with a pen.

STEP 3 Draw your design onto the masking tape.

STEP 4 Cut out your design by tracing your drawing with a razor blade or a craft knife. Remove the excess tape.

STEP 5 Put tape around the light's edges.

STEP 6 Lightly sand the unmasked surfaces.

STEP 7 Spray the taillight with black paint in quick passes. Do two to three coats, allowing them to dry in between.

STEP 8 Apply a coat of clear spraypaint. Gently remove the tape.

STEP 9 Reinstall your badder-than-before taillights and hit the streets (after investigating how your local law enforcement will feel about them).

230 Install Air Horns in Your Car

STEP 1 Open up your hood and detach the battery's negative terminal with a wrench.

STEP 2 Locate the factory-issued horn at the front of the engine and disconnect the power harness from it, starting with the ground wire. (The power harness is the bundle of wires that keeps the horn juiced, and it will power your new horn and air compressor.)

STEP 3 Remove the old horn from the mount. Using the brackets that came with your air horn kit, mount your new horns in the same place as the factory-issued horn. Aim the new horns slightly downward.

STEP 4 Find a clear spot under the hood and along the firewall (the sheet metal that separates the engine from the passenger section). Mount the air compressor here using the mounting bolts that came with the kit.

STEP 5 Connect the wiring harness's hot wire and the air compressor's hot wire to a relay.

STEP 6 Ground the relay's ground wire to a bolt, then connect the relay's hot wire to the car battery.

STEP 7 Run a tube from the compressor to the horns.

STEP 8 Reconnect the negative terminal to complete the circuit. Let those bad boys blast.

Black spraypaint

Design cut out of masking tape

Taillight lens

Masking tape

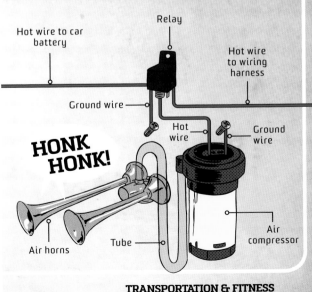

Hot wire to car battery

Relay

Hot wire to wiring harness

Ground wire

Hot wire

Ground wire

HONK HONK!

Air horns

Tube

Air compressor

231 Fend Off Fender Benders with a Sonic Distance Sensor

Back up with confidence thanks to a device that beeps when you're about to crash.

COST	$$
TIME	☺☺
EASY ● ● ● ○ ○ HARD	

MATERIALS

Electrical wire
Ping ultrasonic distance sensor
Arduino Uno
Buzzer
Epoxy

STEP 1 Wire the Ping sensor to your Arduino according to the circuitry diagram.

STEP 2 To hook up the buzzer, wire its positive end to the Arduino's pin 8, and the negative end to a ground pin.

STEP 3 Load up the Arduino code for the Ping sensor, which you can find at www.popsci.com/thebigbookofhacks.

STEP 4 Mount the sensor on the back of your car with epoxy, running the wires through the trunk to the inside of the car.

STEP 5 Mount the buzzer with epoxy somewhere inside the car where you'll be able to hear it.

STEP 6 When the sensor comes within 1 foot (30 cm) of an obstacle, the buzzer will sound to warn you. You may now parallel park without fear.

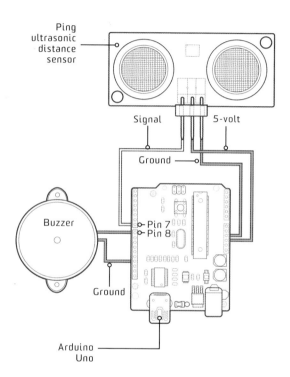

232 Hack an Emergency USB Charger

On the lam without your car charger? Splice some wires and be on your way.

MATERIALS

Knife

USB cable for your device

Any 5-volt car cigarette lighter adapter

Tape

STEP 1 Cut the USB end off the cable for your device and strip the insulation. You'll use the black and red wires to connect to the adapter. Twist together the other two wires.

STEP 2 Cut off the end of the cigarette lighter adapter that does not plug into the cigarette lighter. Use the knife to strip the insulation to reveal the black and red wires.

STEP 3 Twist the two red wires together and the two black wires together. Wrap tape around the joints to insulate them.

STEP 4 Plug it in and charge up your phone in the car.

5 MINUTE PROJECT

233 Shift with a Custom Gear Knob

STEP 1 Pry off your old shift knob. Measure the size of the knob's mount.

STEP 2 Choose an object to use as a new shift knob (resin, wood, and plastic work well).

STEP 3 Drill a hole in the object's bottom to fit the knob mount.

STEP 4 Glue your new knob onto your shifter using epoxy. Upshift in style.

234 Hit the Trail with a Solar-Charging Bag

Mod a basic bag and charge your gadgets with the sun's rays.

COST	$$
TIME	☺ ☺ ☺
EASY ● ● ● ○ ○ HARD	

MATERIALS

Grommeting kit

Messenger bag

Clear vinyl sheeting

Superglue

78M05 voltage regulator

Project box

0.47F 50-volt electrolytic capacitor

0.1F 50-volt tantalum capacitor

Electrical wire

Soldering iron and solder

Scissors

USB cable with female connector

Photovoltaic panel

Digital multimeter

A device to charge that connects to the USB cable

STEP 1 Use the grommeting kit to punch holes in your bag. (These holes are for the wires connecting the photovoltaic panel to the voltage regulator and your device.) Reinforce the holes with grommets.

STEP 2 Use clear vinyl sheeting to create a pocket for the photovoltaic panel. Glue it in place over the grommets so it's on the bag's outside.

STEP 3 Mount the voltage regulator inside your project box, then follow the circuitry diagram to hook up the capacitors and voltage regulator. Solder these connections.

STEP 4 Snip off the male connector from the USB cable. Open the cable end and separate the four wires: red, black, green, and white. Connect the red wire to the output lead of the 78M05 voltage regulator and the black wire to the voltage regulator's ground lead.

STEP 5 With the photovoltaic panel in the clear pocket, connect its positive terminal to the input lead of the voltage regulator. Connect its negative terminal to the voltage regulator's ground lead, threading the wires through the holes in the bag.

STEP 6 Place the photovoltaic panel in direct sunlight and test the voltage readings with a digital multimeter at four points: the photovoltaic panel terminals, the voltage regulator input, the voltage regulator output, and the USB pin 1 + 4. The readings at the first two points should both be approximately 7 to 8 volts. The readings at the last two points should be exactly 5.15 volts.

STEP 7 If everything checks out, hook up a suitable device and charge out there.

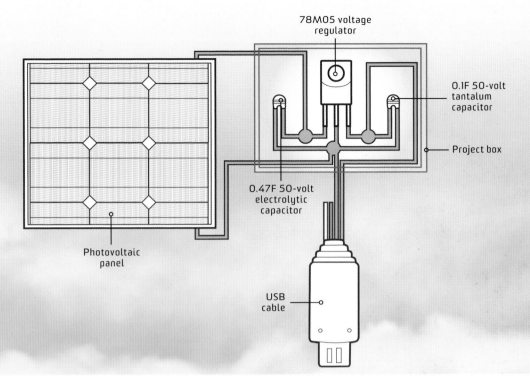

78M05 voltage
regulator

0.1F 50-volt
tantalum
capacitor

Project box

0.47F 50-volt
electrolytic
capacitor

Photovoltaic
panel

USB
cable

235 Create Emergency Candles On the Go

That butter would be better if you lit it on fire.

Good for an emergency if you lack candles or a flashlight, this hack will work with a wide array of grease, wax, or oil-based fuel sources that are solid at room temperature or remain in a solid container that can support the wick. Try it out with other greasy, oily household products, such as lip balm or canned fish in oil. Careful, though! Don't use volatile, flammable household products that warn you about introducing a flame. You might find yourself in a much greater emergency than you prepared for.

MATERIALS

Tissue paper (or similar lightweight, absorbent paper product)

Stick of butter (or another source of fuel, such as wax, grease, or oil, that is solid at room temperature)

Nail, pin, or toothpick

Match or lighter

STEP 1 Twist the tissue paper into a tight roll. This will serve as a makeshift wick.

STEP 2 Place the stick of butter (or alternative fuel source) in a container. Rub the makeshift wick across the stick of butter (or alternative fuel source) to transfer the flammable hydrocarbons onto the wick.

STEP 3 Use a nail, pin, or toothpick to push the wick deep into the fuel source. This will ensure a small but reasonably bright flame that will not consume the fuel source too quickly.

STEP 4 Use a match or lighter to ignite the wick.

STEP 5 Watch as the makeshift wick draws fuel from below into the flame via capillary action, illuminating your immediate surroundings.

236 Take Aerial Photos with a Weather Balloon

Keep your drone envy in check with a rig that snaps shots from the sky.

COST	$
TIME	☺
EASY ● ○ ○ ○ ○ HARD	

MATERIALS

Digital camera

3,500 feet (1,070 m) of heavy-duty nylon string

Gaffers tape

Box cutter

Large plastic bottle

Weather balloon

Helium

Rubber band

Computer with photo-editing software

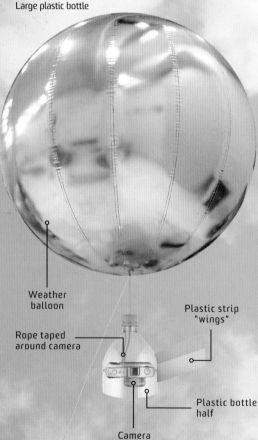

Weather balloon

Rope taped around camera

Plastic strip "wings"

Plastic bottle half

Camera

String

STEP 1 Choose a camera with a large SD card (at least 4 GB) and a continuous setting.

STEP 2 Make a 3-foot (90-cm) loop of string, wrap it around your camera, and knot it securely against the camera body, with the excess creating another loop.

STEP 3 Secure the string around your camera with gaffers tape. When you dangle it by the loop, your camera should be supported on either side of the lens. (Don't skimp on tape and buy the cheap stuff, or you'll pay for it later.)

STEP 4 Cut a large plastic bottle in half. Put the camera inside the top half of the bottle, lens facing down, with the loop of string sticking out through the neck of the bottle.

STEP 5 Cut out two 8-by-2½-inch (20-by-6.25-cm) plastic strips from the plastic bottle's bottom half. Tape them to the top half of the bottle. (They'll help stabilize the camera during flight.)

STEP 6 Inflate the weather balloon with helium, close it up, and tie the string to the balloon's opening. (If you don't have an especially large balloon, you can make your own by taping two Mylar sleeping bags together and then inflating them.)

STEP 7 Attach the camera in its protective cover just below the balloon using the loop of string that's secured to the camera. Tie the 3,500-foot (1,070-m) string to the balloon as well. The weather balloon should lift the camera easily.

STEP 8 Set your camera to continuous mode and use a rubber band to hold down the camera's trigger. Allow the balloon to rise quickly, letting out the string carefully to avoid tangles.

STEP 9 Head in the direction of the area you'd like to document from above. Avoid trees and other structures that could tangle your string. When you're done, just pull the balloon back in by its string.

STEP 10 Use digital photo-stitching software to create huge, detailed maps of your 'hood.

237 Set a Tiny Helicopter Awhirl

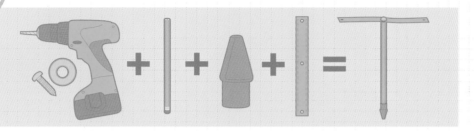

STEP 1 Use a drill with aa 1/16-inch (1.6-mm) bit to hollow out 1 inch (2.5 cm) of a standard-issue pencil. Then put a cap eraser on the pencil's top.

STEP 2 Set a hairdryer to high heat. Hold a plastic ruler in front of the hot air, bending it at its center to create a propeller shape.

STEP 3 Use a screw and a washer to attach the propeller to the pencil via one of the ruler's central holes.

STEP 4 Hold the pencil between your two hands and twist to make it take flight.

238 Launch a Mini Rocket

Combine simple household items to make a rocket propulsion system.

MATERIALS

Paper
Pencil
Scissors
Glue

Empty film canister
Alka-Seltzer tablets
Water

STEP 1 Design your rocket, drawing it on paper. A simple cylinder, nose cone, and a pair of fins will suffice. It should stand around 6 inches (15 cm) tall and be approximately 1½ inches (3.75 cm) in diameter.

STEP 2 Cut out your rocket components (cylinder, nose cone, and fins) and glue them together.

STEP 3 Open the film canister and drop one-half of an Alka-Seltzer tablet into it.

STEP 4 Fill the canister half full of water and snap the canister cap into place. Slide the rocket over the cap, place the assembly cap-down, and get back. Watch the rocket blast off.

TRANSPORTATION & FITNESS

239 Make Your Own Drone

Assemble a drone with basic office supplies and a few cheap electronics!

MATERIALS

Craft knife

Pencil

Eraser

Expired credit card

Drill

15/64-inch (6-mm) drill bit

1/8-inch (3.5-mm) drill bit

Tweezers

Original Hubson H107-A03 main motor set

Soldering iron and solder

Original Hubson H107-A43 circuit board

Hot-glue gun

Original Hubson H107-A35 main blades

Rubber band

Original Hubson H107-A24 battery

Original Hubson H107-16 transmitter

COST	$$
TIME	⊙ ⊙ ⊙
EASY ● ● ● ○ ○ HARD	

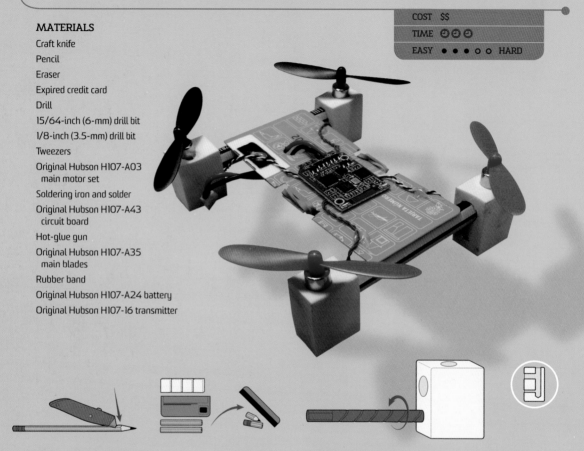

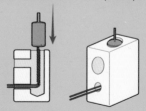

STEP 1 Using a craft knife, cut the point and the eraser off the pencil and the remaining part into two 2⅓-inch-(6-cm-) long pieces. These will serve as the arms of your drone. Now cut the eraser into four separate ⅝-inch (1.5-cm) pieces. Cut an (expired) plastic credit card so that it measures 1½ by 3⅓ inches (3.8 by 8.4 cm). (As an alternative, you can use a piece of hard cardboard or thin piece of wood.) Take care to cut each piece to exact measurements. All parts should be as similar as possible.

STEP 2 Drill the eraser pieces to create the motors' supports. Using a 15/64-inch (6-mm) drill bit, make two large holes in each eraser according to the illustration. Then make a small hole with a 1/8-inch (3-mm) drill bit.

STEP 3 To assemble the motors in the eraser pieces, use tweezers to pass the wires through the 1/8-inch (3-mm) holes. Push the motor inside the larger eraser hole on top.

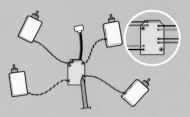

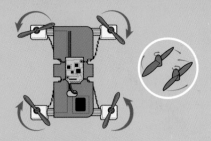

STEP 4 Solder the motor wires to the circuit board, making sure you connect positive to positive and negative to negative.

STEP 8 Attach the propellers to the motors. The top left propeller and bottom right should move in a counter-clockwise rotation. The top right propeller and the bottom left propeller should move in a clockwise rotation.

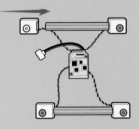

STEP 5 Stick the pencil halves (the arms) into the larger side holes in the erasers.

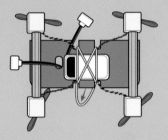

STEP 9 Use a rubber band to secure the battery by weaving it through the slots you made in the card. Position the battery under the card.

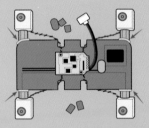

STEP 6 Cut the plastic card and glue it to the pencil arms as you see here. Make a 1/3-inch (8-mm) hole in the plastic card, along with two slots on each side.

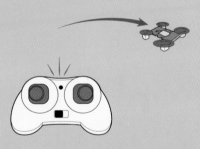

STEP 10 Connect the drone battery, switch on the transmitter, and take to the skies.

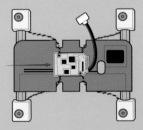

STEP 7 Glue the circuit board to the card, passing the battery plug through the 1/3-inch (8-mm) hole. The card should be resting on the pencil arms.

240 The Incredible Amphibious Tank

Half boat, half car, all adventure.

Avid hunter Stan Hewitt wanted to tackle the prime duck habitat of the Alaskan tundra, an area hard to access using regular vehicles. He knew he needed a tank to do it—one with speed and maneuverability that would be able to handle the water currents there.

Hewitt designed a 21-foot (6.4-m) craft with two wide, tanklike rubber treads that can pivot 180 degrees when afloat. When on the ground, the treads spread the vehicle's weight over a large surface area, improving traction and exerting minimal pressure on the ground. Hewitt installed a simple hydraulic pump to lift and lower these treads vertically in and out of the water. In sea mode, the Chevy TrailBlazer engine drives an outboard propeller. In land mode, the treads drop so the engine can muscle the craft up onto shore. His creation is the first-ever amphibious vehicle with a fully retractable drive assembly—one that needs just 18 seconds to go from sea cruiser to land rover.

The craft can reach speeds of up to 30 miles per hour (48 km/h) and effortlessly trek through mud flats, bogs, rivers, ice, snow, and lakes—and do it with a 1,500-pound (680-kg) load. There's room for a crew of five and all the gear they need for search and rescue, patrol, geological surveying, and other fieldwork. Ironically, though, Hewitt hasn't gotten around to taking it duck hunting yet.

SEA MONSTER
Hewitt increased the cab's ability to resist water by adding foam sandwiched between layers of aluminum to its panels.

241 A Tilting Ping-Pong Table that Throws Off Opponents

A group of young designers reinvent ping-pong. Welcome to "swing pong."

Internships are often mindless, coffee-fetching black holes of boredom. But not at Syyn Labs, a Los Angeles collective that creates unusual interactive art and science projects for commercials and music videos. Last summer, student interns Hoon Oh, Robb Godshaw, and Jisu Choi took it upon themselves to reinvent the sport of table tennis. Their project could pass for an extra in *Transformers*: It's part ping-pong table, part machine, and so difficult to play that it reduces pros to the level of rank amateurs.

Oh came up with the idea of doing a ping-pong project because the game is a staple of so many cultures around the globe, and is normally relatively easy to play. They wanted to make the game more social than competitive, so they eliminated the potential for humiliating one-sided contests by building a table that tilts on demand and makes it tough for even highly skilled players.

They started by scrounging for parts in the Syyn Labs warehouse. A rectangular piece of Plexiglas that had once been used in an illuminated dance floor became the tabletop. To drive the tilting surface, Godshaw suggested using pneumatic pistons left over from a commercial for a Google science fair. Choi worked on the drive system and other aspects of the design, while Oh wrote software to control the pistons and switch the table from level to off-kilter. The group found that getting the angles correct was tricky. "We wanted to make it tilt at a dramatic angle but not hit anybody in the jaw," Godshaw says.

They were right about leveling gameplay—when table-tennis pro Adam Bobrow visited Syyn Labs, he won his match by only a single point. In fact, the game is such strange, absurd fun, Godshaw says, that competition is an afterthought: "Most games never make it to nine."

242 Make Your Own Prescription Swimming Goggles

See as clearly underwater as you do on land.

Wearing your glasses in the water is never a good idea, and contacts tend to pop out when swimming. Using an old pair of prescription glasses, you can customize your swim goggles for just a few bucks.

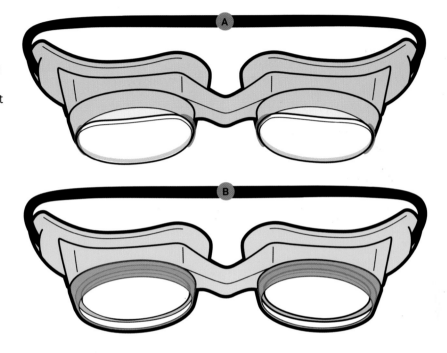

MATERIALS

Eyeglass screwdriver

Pair of old prescription glasses that you longer use

Pair of swimming goggles

Fine-grit sandpaper

Silicone adhesive

STEP 1 Using an eyeglass screwdriver, remove the lenses from your prescription glasses. (If your glasses don't have screws, carefully pop them out with your hands.)

STEP 2 Test fit the lenses onto the goggles. The lenses should at least overlap the frame of the goggles on the left and right sides, and they should be close to the same distance from your eyes as they were in your glasses. Make sure you can still see through them!

STEP 3 If you're using plastic prescription lenses, sand the edges that overlap the goggle frames for better adhesion. You should also lightly sand the parts of the goggle frame that the sanded edges of the lenses will touch.

STEP 4 Wipe down the lenses and goggles' frame, then use silicone adhesive to glue the lenses to the goggles—go easy with the glue, as excess will smudge and impede your vision. You will have to glue the lenses on differently depending on whether they are very curved or flat.

• If the lenses are curved (see Drawing A), apply the glue only at the left and right edges of the goggles' frame where the lenses will touch the frame. The top and bottom are left open for water to flow between the glasses' lenses and the goggles' lenses. Position the lenses onto the frames, and hold in place until the glue hardens.

• If the lenses are flat and they fully overlap the goggle frames (see Drawing B), apply the adhesive all the way around the edges of the frame where the lenses overlap. To prevent fogging from moisture getting trapped in this sealed space, work in a dry environment, or you can apply some antifog to the lenses on the inside of the space.

STEP 5 Take care to fill in any gaps. Hold the lenses in place until the glue hardens.

STEP 6 Let the goggles set overnight so the adhesive can fully cure. Then strap them on and go for a swim to test them out!

243 Hack an Oversize Air Hockey Puck

STEP 1 Cut a hole in the top of a smoke-detector case. Make sure the hole is large enough to mount the propeller and motor from a remote-controlled plane or helicopter.

STEP 2 To protect the smoke detector's outer surface, coat it completely (except for the bottom rim and the hole) with rubberized foam coating.

STEP 3 Connect six AAA batteries in series using aluminum-foil duct tape. Glue the cells onto a round piece of plastic with ventilation holes, making sure that the weight is evenly distributed.

STEP 4 Wire the motor, an on/off switch, and the battery together, and attach the cap to the smaller end of the smoke detector with hot glue.

STEP 5 Place the larger end on the floor. The air should be sucked up through the detector vents.

STEP 6 Enjoy air hockey beyond the confines of the tabletop version.

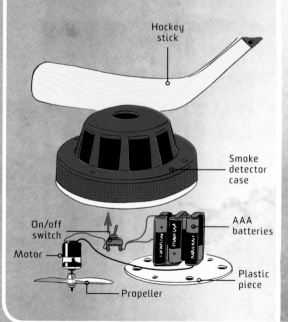

Hockey stick

Smoke detector case

On/off switch

Motor

AAA batteries

Plastic piece

Propeller

244 Score with Ping-Pong Paddle Gloves

STEP 1 Using a handsaw, cut the handles off two Ping-Pong paddles.

STEP 2 Cut two pieces of plywood into wedges. The widest part should measure 3 inches (7.5 cm) in width; the narrowest should measure 1 inch (2.5 cm) in width. Both should be 4 inches (10 cm) long.

STEP 3 Drill a hole in each of the two plywood pieces, one that's large enough for your thumb, and one that's large enough for your fingertips to protrude.

STEP 4 Sandwich the wood pieces between the paddles so that the glove fits your dominant hand and the thumb and finger holes align. Secure with wood glue.

STEP 5 Dominate at the table.

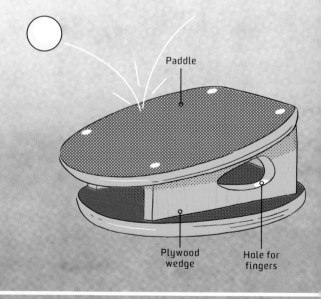

Paddle

Plywood wedge

Hole for fingers

245 Assemble a PVC-Pipe Soccer Goal

STEP 1 Use a handsaw to cut twelve lengths of 1½-inch (3.75-cm) PVC pipe so that you have four 2-foot (60-cm) sections, four 6-foot (1.8-m) sections, two 8-foot (2.4-m) sections, and two 10-foot (3-m) sections.

STEP 2 Put the goal together without glue first, using six 1½-inch (3.75-cm) rounded PVC elbows and four 1½-inch (3.75-cm) T-style PVC connectors. Make sure that all the pieces fit together correctly.

STEP 3 To glue, pull apart one joint at a time and spread PVC glue on the inside of the connector and the outside of the pipe. Reconnect the joint. (If you want to keep your soccer goal portable, leave a few joints unglued.)

STEP 4 Once you've glued all the joints, leave the structure to set.

STEP 5 To make the net, wrap netting around the goal and cut it to size, leaving a bit of extra netting around the edges. Attach the net using zip ties wrapped around the frame every 6 inches (15 cm).

STEP 6 Find a goalie to stand in front of your soccer goal, and get kicking.

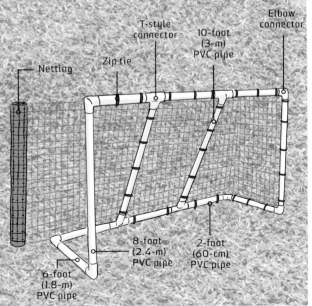

Netting — Zip tie — T-style connector — 10-foot (3-m) PVC pipe — Elbow connector — 8-foot (2.4-m) PVC pipe — 2-foot (60-cm) PVC pipe — 6-foot (1.8-m) PVC pipe

246 Transform a Bike into a B-Ball Hoop

STEP 1 Detach the entire front section of the bicycle frame, from the handlebars down to the fork.

STEP 2 Adjust the handlebars to a horizontal angle, then mount the detached section of the frame to a large piece of wood using three U-clamps: one directly under the handlebars, two at the fork's top.

STEP 3 To use an old bicycle wheel for the hoop, remove the tire and clip off the spokes with wire cutters, leaving the hoop empty in the middle.

STEP 4 Set the hoop in the center of the handlebars, then use hose clamps to attach it. Make sure that the hoop rests parallel to the ground when the backboard is vertical.

STEP 5 Attach a net using zip ties or wire.

STEP 6 Shoot some hoops.

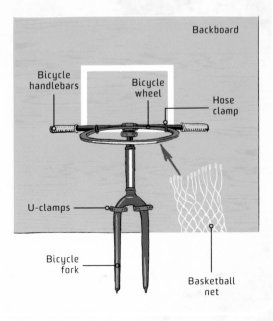

Backboard — Bicycle handlebars — Bicycle wheel — Hose clamp — U-clamps — Bicycle fork — Basketball net

247 Serve Up a Tennis Ball

This is one piece of sporting equipment that's useful both on and off the court.

STEALTHY SHOOTER

Poke a hole in a tennis ball and fill it with water for an instant squirt gun.

SUPER GRIP

Slice a tennis ball in half and use one half as a grip to twist off pesky stuck lids on jars.

HAMMER TIME

Protect surfaces while you hammer nails by cutting an X into the ball and sliding the head of the hammer inside it.

LIGHTBULB MOMENT

Got a broken lightbulb that you need to remove? With the light's switch and breaker turned off, clear the shards away from the bulb, press the tennis ball against the socket, and unscrew with the ball protecting your hand.

DOOR STOPPER

If you've ever had a doorknob smash through a wall when someone flung the door open, you know it can really hurt your chances of getting your apartment security deposit back. Cut a hole in a tennis ball and put it over the doorknob—it'll help keep your drywall intact.

248 Wear a Heart (Monitor) on Your Sleeve

Its LEDs will flash a symbol of affection with your every heartbeat.

COST	$	
TIME	⏲	
EASY	● ● ● ● ○	HARD

To contract the heart muscle and pump blood, waves of electricity spread through the organ. Two electrodes on the chest, one on either side of the heart, can pick up these electrical impulses. (A third—often placed on the right leg—increases accuracy.) Heart rate monitors typically feed this data to a screen that shows the signal, such as an EKG. Instead, you can send it to a heart-shaped LED display that will pulse along with every beat.

MATERIALS

AD8232 single-lead heart rate monitor

Drill

Glue

Seven red LilyPad LED micros

Soldering iron and solder

Wire

Scrap of 1 1/8-by-1 3/8-inch (2.85-by-3.5-cm) clear plastic

Screwdriver

Three 1/2-inch (2.5-cm) 4-40 machine screws and nuts

Seven 1/4-inch (6.35-mm) round spacers

LilyPad coin-cell battery holder

Three sensor pads

Sensor cable with attached electrodes

CR2032 coin-cell battery

Sheer sock or stocking

Safety pins

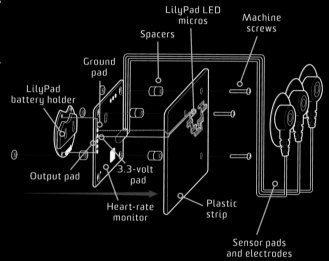

LilyPad LED micros

Machine screws

Spacers

Ground pad

LilyPad battery holder

Output pad

3.3-volt pad

Heart-rate monitor

Plastic strip

Sensor pads and electrodes

STEP 1 Place the clear plastic scrap over the heart rate monitor, mark it at three of the four points where there are holes in the monitor, and drill 1/8-inch (3.2-mm) holes at these marks. Then use a dab of glue to arrange the seven LED micros in a heart shape on the clear plastic. The heart rate monitor's LED should appear in the center.

STEP 2 Solder a piece of wire through all of the positive terminals of the LED micros, and connect it to the OUTPUT pad on the monitor. Solder another wire through all of the negative terminals and connect it to the GND pad.

STEP 3 Mount the clear plastic over the monitor with three screws. Slip two spacers around each screw to prevent the plastic from directly touching the heart rate monitor.

STEP 4 Attach the LilyPad battery holder to the back of the heart rate monitor with one of the three screws, slipping one spacer between the holder and the monitor. Then solder a wire from the battery holder's positive terminal to the 3.3-volt pad of the monitor and another wire between the holder's negative terminal and the GND pad.

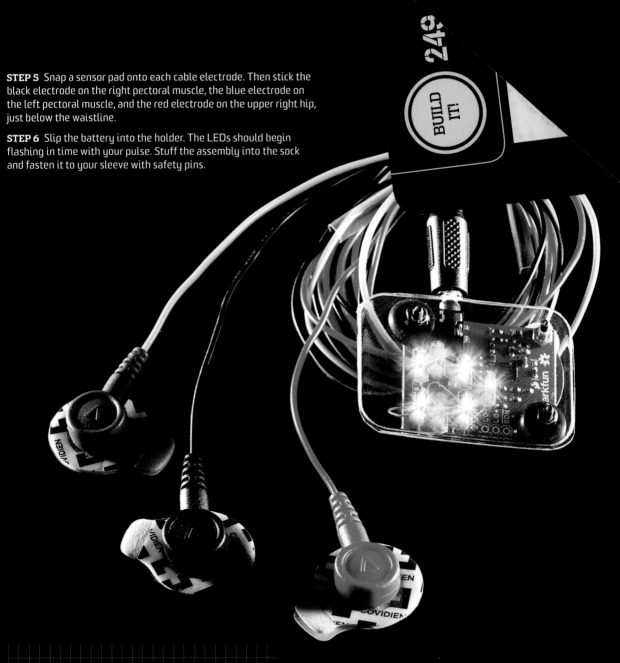

STEP 5 Snap a sensor pad onto each cable electrode. Then stick the black electrode on the right pectoral muscle, the blue electrode on the left pectoral muscle, and the red electrode on the upper right hip, just below the waistline.

STEP 6 Slip the battery into the holder. The LEDs should begin flashing in time with your pulse. Stuff the assembly into the sock and fasten it to your sleeve with safety pins.

BUILD IT!

249

WARNING
This project is not intended for medical use. If your heart skips a beat, go see your doctor!

| COST | $ |
| TIME | 🕐 🕐 |
| EASY ● ● ● ● ○ HARD |

MATERIALS

Adafruit FLORA main board (the UV sensor does not work with Gemma or Trinket, so a FLORA is required!)

Adafruit FLORA UV index sensor

Piezo buzzer

500mAh Li-poly battery

Sunhat

Pin

Scissors

Plain thread

Sewing needle

2-ply conductive thread

Pliers

Clear nail polish

Hit the pool with a hat that eliminates the guesswork—and your sunburn.

Remember to reapply your sunblock by building a reminder right into your hat. This sewable circuit uses an Adafruit FLORA sewable microcontroller and compatible UV index sensor to sense the sun and play a tune on a piezo buzzer when it's time to refresh your SPF.

You can use any battery pack 3-9 volt, though we recommend a 500mAh rechargeable Li-poly battery for a good balance of long battery life and portability.

STEP 1 Wire up your circuit, including connecting the FLORA main board, UV index sensor, and piezo. Connect the piezo to FLORA GND and FLORA TX (digital pin 1). It does not matter which leg goes to which pin.

The UV index sensor connects as follows:
FLORA 3.3v → sensor 3V
FLORA SDA → sensor SDA
FLORA SCL → sensor SCL
FLORA GND → sensor gnd

STEP 2 Find a good spot on your hat for the circuit. You want the sensor to face the sky, and the piezo to be near your ear on the underside of the hat. The FLORA needs to be as close as possible to the other components—behind the ribbon on top of the hat is best. Just make sure you can access its USB port.

STEP 3 Pin the ribbon in place while you attach the circuit to the hat. Cut a length of plain thread and use it to tack the FLORA loosely to your hat through the RX hole.

STEP 4 Use an arm's-length strand of conductive thread to stitch a few times around FLORA's GND pad closest to the battery port. Leave a 4-inch (10-cm) tail. Tie the working thread and tail in a double knot inside the hat. Do not trim the tail yet.

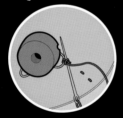

STEP 5 Twist the leads of the piezo with pliers so they're easier to stitch around. Use a running stitch to make your way to the location of the piezo, which should be facing down near your ear on the inside of the hat, and stitch many times around one leg of the piezo. Tie a knot and cut the working thread, leaving a tail.

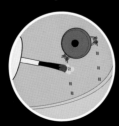

STEP 6 Repeat to attach the FLORA TX pin to the other leg of the piezo. Pull thread tails taut and apply a tiny bit of clear nail polish to the knots. Test your piezo by loading up the mario code from the Wearable Piezo Tones guide (www.popsci.com/thebigbookofhacks).

STEP 7 Following the circuit diagram, add the UV index sensor. Stitch conductive traces between all four connections to the UV index sensor (3V, SDA, SCL, and GND). Use the same technique as with the piezo, leaving tails on your knots at each end of all four threads. Apply nail polish to all eight knots. Allow to dry, and then tug test before snipping the thread tails short.

STEP 8 Follow the instructions on the UV index guide for testing your sensor—upload the demo code and verify with the serial monitor that the sensor is returning readings. Attach the battery under the hat's ribbon using plain thread.

STEP 9 Upload the code found at www.popsci.com/bigbookofhacks to your FLORA, ensuring you have the UV index sensor library installed properly. This code is well-suited for testing your complete circuit indoors, near a window. The UV index threshold is set very low (0.05, achievable by pointing the circuit toward an open window), with a reminder interval of ten seconds. You can also open up the serial monitor while it's running to check out the readings and timer.

STEP 10 Wear it! As you work on your tan, your hat will buzz a tune when it is time to reapply sunscreen. Remember this circuit is not waterproof, so don't get it wet! Leave it on your towel when you're going for a dip, hopefully within earshot. Watch out for humidity from your wet hair.

250 The Motorized Easy Chair

Getting to class just got a little faster.

Chris McIntosh's first recliner was not your standard La-Z-Boy: It was electric-powered and capable of going 15 miles per hour (24 km/h). After he finished making it, he pulled a doughnut on his high school's front lawn, circled the gym during a pep rally, and ruled the street near his home in Orinda, California.

McIntosh spent his youth building ad hoc vehicles (he once made a mini hovercraft out of a leaf blower), so when the chair's paltry electric motor burned out, he decided it was time for a monster makeover. "I wanted to go fast," he says.

To upgrade the recliner, he removed the electric motor he had installed, the motor's controller, a pair of batteries, and other parts. He bought a 9-horsepower, four-stroke dirt-bike engine, which fit perfectly in the space beneath the seat, and welded on a fixed rear axle so that the engine could power both rear wheels instead of just one. Bike engines need to be kick-started, but the recliner's lever snapped when he tried to use it. He welded on a motorcycle kick-start lever instead.

Then there was the danger of the vehicle catching on fire. The dirt-bike engine's exhaust pipe got so hot that it sometimes glowed red and threatened to set the upholstery (and McIntosh) ablaze. To avert disaster, he rerouted the pipe, mounting it farther from the underside of the chair, and covered it with fireproof wrap. His parents were pleased.

Still, the first test drive was frightening: McIntosh immediately popped an accidental 45-degree wheelie. He added 30 pounds (13.6 kg) of weights near his feet to keep the front down, along with a roll bar and harness for safety. The chair has no suspension at all. "The ride gets a bit bumpy," McIntosh says. "But then again, there's plenty of padding."

He says he has now mastered climbing hills and turning corners, although he's planning to add a rearview mirror to reduce the large blind spot behind the backrest. The newly completed gas-powered version now goes 40 miles per hour (64 km/h) and, just as important, he says, "It sounds like a Harley."

STREET ILLEGAL
McIntosh figured the chair wouldn't be street legal, so he designed it to fit in the back of his hatchback. To load it, he slides off the backrest, leans a ramp against the back of his car, and pushes the heavy frame up and in. He typically uses it in parking lots, but he does occasionally take it around local streets and even took it to USC's homecoming parade.

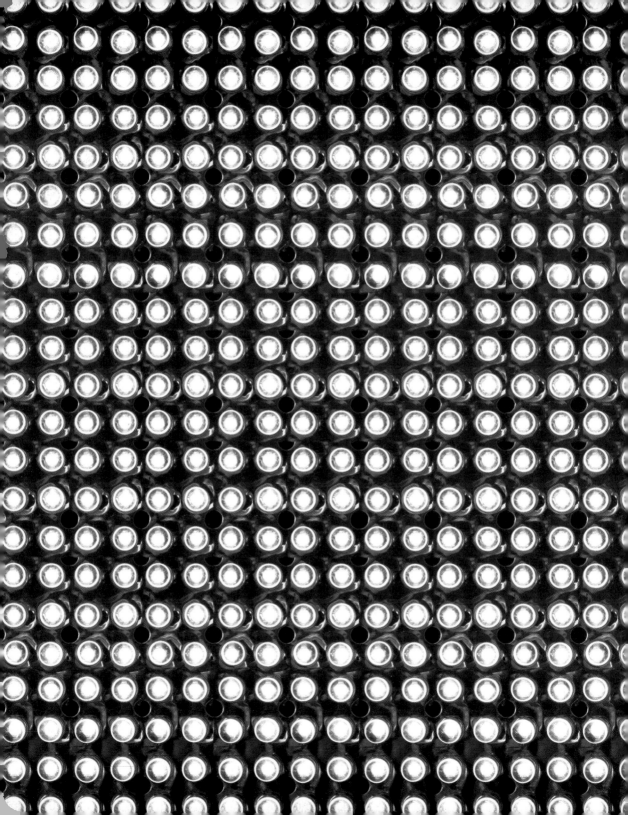

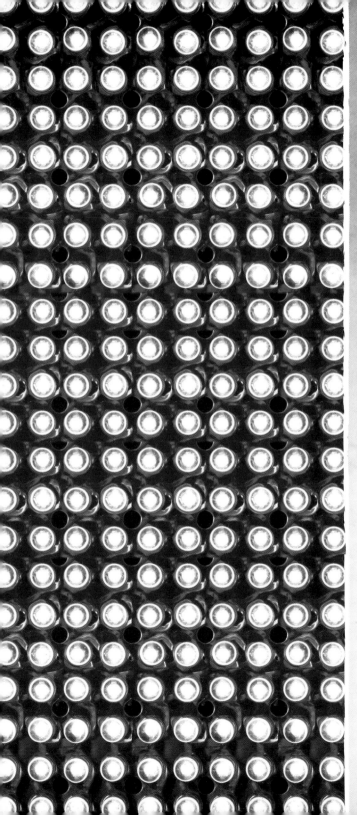

RESOURCES

GLOSSARY

ALLIGATOR CLIP Spring-loaded clip that can be used to connect a component to a wire in a temporary circuit.

ALUMINUM FLASHING Thin sheet of aluminum; often used in weatherproofing to prevent water from flowing through a joint.

AMPLIFIER Component that augments the power of a signal. In circuits, an amplifier is usually used to increase the voltage or current.

ANTENNA Wire, thin metal pole, or other device that can transmit or receive electromagnetic waves, such as TV or radio waves.

ARDUINO Common, open-source microcontroller. There are various types of Arduino microcontrollers, but all can be programmed using the same programming language.

BLACK LIGHT Type of lamp that gives off ultraviolet light. Many substances emit fluorescence that can be seen under a black light, but not in normal lighting conditions.

BREADBOARD Base used to set up temporary circuits and test them out before soldering components together.

BREAKOUT BOARD Electrical component that allows you easier access to tightly spaced pins on a microchip or densely bundled wires. The device connects the hard-to-reach pins or wires to an easier-to-access interface.

BUSHING Connector used to join pipes of different diameters; one end has a smaller opening, the other end a larger one. A bushing can also be called a *reducing coupling*.

CAPACITOR Electrical component that stores energy within a circuit. Unlike a battery, a capacitor does not produce energy, it simply contains or filters the energy already flowing through the circuit.

CIRCUIT Closed loop through which electrical current flows. A circuit is often used to power an electrical device.

CIRCUIT BOARD Thin, insulated board on which electrical components are mounted and connected together. A printed circuit board has thin conductive strips printed on the board, allowing connections to be made between components largely without the use of wires.

CLAMP Device used to hold an object tightly in place. Clamps can vary widely in size and construction, and can be intended for temporary or permanent use.

COAXIAL CABLE Cable with a central conductive wire, surrounded by an insulating layer, which in turn is surrounded by a conductive tube. A coaxial cable is often used to transmit radio or cable television signals.

COIN BATTERY Also called a button cell, a coin battery is a small, flat, disc-shaped battery that is often used to power portable electronic devices.

CONDUCTIVITY Capacity to transmit an electrical current; it can also refer to the measure of a substance's ability to transmit electrical current.

CONTACT Point where an electrical component is connected to a wire or circuit board.

COUPLER Short section of piping used to join two pipes together.

CRAFT KNIFE Small, fixed-blade knife used to make precise cuts.

DESOLDERING Removing solder to detach components from a circuit or circuit board. Desoldering can be used to fix a fault in a circuit, or to replace a component.

DIODE Electronic component with one terminal that has high resistance, and another terminal with low resistance. A diode is used to allow current to flow in one direction but not another.

DRILL Tool used to cut holes in a variety of materials. A drill is usually powered by electricity, and comes with an array of interchangeable bits in different sizes.

ELECTRICAL TAPE Type of tape covered in an insulating material, often used to cover and connect electrical wires.

ELECTRICAL WIRE Insulated strand of conductive material used to carry electricity.

ELECTRODE Conductor used to transmit current to a non-metallic material. Electrodes are used in arc welding to fuse objects together.

EPOXY Adhesive made from a type of resin that becomes rigid when heated or cured.

EXHAUST FAN Fan used to ventilate a workspace; it is particularly important to use an exhaust fan when working with materials that emit toxic fumes.

FIBER OPTIC CABLE Cable made up of thin fibers that transmit light from one end of the fiber to the other. A fiber optic cable can carry signals and provide illumination.

FLASH DRIVE Small data-storage device that can be connected to a computer, often via a USB port.

FRESNEL LENS Thin lens made of a number of smaller lens segments. A Fresnel lens magnifies a light source, and is often used in projectors and spotlights.

GROUND WIRE Wire in a circuit that provides a return path for current, often leading to the earth. A ground wire can prevent the buildup of dangerous static electricity in a circuit.

HACKSAW Fine-toothed saw held in a frame. A hacksaw can be used to cut metal or other hard materials.

HEAT-SHRINK TUBING Tubing that contracts when heated; often used to insulate wires or to create a protective seal.

HEAT SINK Device that channels heat away from an electronic system, keeping it cool enough to operate properly.

HOLE SAW Cylindrical saw blade, used to cut holes of uniform size. A hole saw is usually used in a drill, in place of the drill bit, to create a large hole.

HOLOGRAPHY Technique that allows for the capture of a lifelike 3D image. The resulting hologram looks different when viewed from different angles, much as a real-world scene would.

INSULATION Material, such as the nonconductive coating around an electrical wire, that prevents current or heat from flowing.

INTEGRATED CIRCUIT Also called a *microchip*, this small, thin device is a complete circuit etched or imprinted on a semiconductive surface. An integrated circuit allows for complex circuitry to be condensed into an extremely small space, and is vital to the operation of many modern electronic devices, notably computers.

JIGSAW Tool (usually a power tool) with a long, thin saw blade. A jigsaw is useful in cutting curves and irregular shapes.

JOINT The point at which two objects are connected together. In woodworking, creating a join may involve cutting a notch or angle into the pieces of wood to be joined; in metalworking, the process often involves soldering or welding.

LASER Device that emits a tightly focused beam of light. Lasers vary widely in intensity, and can be as weak as a laser pointer, or strong enough to cut through extremely hard and thick materials.

LCD MONITOR Display that uses liquid crystals to bend and shape light to create an image. In an LCD monitor, the liquid crystal material is sandwiched between two electrodes and filtered through a layer of polarizing film.

LEAD A wire extending from an electronic component that is used to connect that component to another electronic part.

LED Diode that gives off light. They are usually more energy-efficient than incandescent light sources, and can be much smaller.

LITHIUM-ION BATTERY Type of rechargeable battery often used in consumer electronics. A lithium-ion battery commonly carries a large amount of energy for its size, and loses charge relatively slowly when not in use.

MICROCONTROLLER Tiny dedicated computer, contained on a single chip that can be embedded within a larger device.

MULTIMETER Device that measures electrical current, resistance, and voltage. A multimeter is very helpful for monitoring and identifying problems in circuits.

O-RING Circular seal used in joining cylinders together. An O-ring is usually seated inside a joint to prevent leaks.

OHM Unit of measurement of electrical resistance.

OPTICAL MOUSE Computer mouse that uses an LED to sense motion, as opposed to the rolling ball used by a mechanical mouse.

PARTICLEBOARD Composite wood-based material manufactured from small chips or shavings of wood joined together by resin.

PEG-BOARD Plank or sheet of wood pre-drilled with a grid of evenly spaced small holes, A Peg-Board is useful for mounting hooks and tools on a wall.

PHOTOCELL Device that produces a flow of current when exposed to light. A photocell can detect the presence (or absence) of light or other radiation.

PLEXIGLAS Hard, transparent plastic; looks like glass but is more lightweight and durable.

POLARIZING FILM Sheet of material, often used in LCD monitors, that allows only light polarized in a specific direction to pass through.

PORT Point of interface between one device and another. On computers, common ports include Ethernet ports and USB ports.

POTENTIOMETER Three-terminal electrical component that acts as a variable resistor. These adjust the flow of current through a circuit, and are often used in dimmer switches or volume controls.

PROGRAMMING LANGUAGE Language used to convey instructions to a computer or other machine. Many distinct programming languages are used for different purposes and types of hardware.

PROJECT BOX Box designed to contain the components of a circuit; useful for mounting and protecting the elements of a device.

PVC PIPE Type of durable, lightweight plastic pipe often used to carry liquids in plumbing.

PVC PIPE CEMENT Adhesive designed to connect pieces of PVC material together.

REBAR Ridged bar of steel, often used in construction to reinforce concrete or masonry.

RECIPROCATING SAW Power tool that cuts with the back-and-forth motion of a saw blade.

REED SWITCH Switch composed of metal reeds enclosed in a tiny glass container. The reeds react to the presence of a magnetic field by either opening or closing the switch.

RESISTOR Two-terminal electrical component that resists the flow of an electric current. A resistor is used in a circuit to control the direction and strength of the current flowing through it.

ROTARY TOOL Power tool with a wide variety of interchangeable bits that can be used for different purposes. A rotary tool can cut, polish, carve, or grind, and is particularly good for detail work.

SAFETY GOGGLES Glasses that shield the eye area from heat, chemicals, and debris.

SCHEMATIC Two-dimensional map of an electrical circuit. A schematic uses a set of symbols to stand for the components of a circuit, and shows the connections between components.

SKETCH When working with Arduino microcontrollers, a sketch is a program that can be loaded into an Arduino.

SLAG Scrap metal that results from the welding process.

SOLDERING Connecting two metal objects together by melting solder (a type of metal) with a soldering iron to create a strong joint between the objects.

SUGRU Type of silicone-based putty that can be molded for about 30 minutes after it is removed from its packaging. Sugru cures to a solid but somewhat flexible state after 24 hours.

SWITCH Component that can stop the flow of current in a circuit, or allow it to continue. These include push-button switches, rocker switches, toggle switches, and many other devices.

TABLE SAW Machine that cuts wood or other materials with a rapidly spinning serrated metal disc. A circular saw is usually powered by electricity, and often mounted within a safety guard.

T-CONNECTOR Short section of pipe with three openings; used to connect lengths of pipe into a T shape.

TERMINAL End point of a conductor in a circuit; also a point at which connections can be made to a larger network.

TOUCHSCREEN An electronic display screen that users interact with by touching with their fingers; the screen detects touch within the display area.

TRANSFORMER Device that transfers current from one circuit to another. A transformer can also be used to alter the voltage of an alternating current.

TRANSISTOR Semiconducting electrical component with at least three leads; can control or amplify the flow of electricity in a circuit.

USB Universal Serial Bus; an extremely common type of connector for computer and other electronic components.

VISE Type of clamp, often affixed to a table, that uses a screw to hold an object tightly in place.

VOLT Unit of measurement for electrical potential.

WELDING Process of joining pieces of metal together by melting them slightly and introducing a filler material at the joint.

WIRE CUTTER Pliers with sharp diagonal edges used to cut lengths of wire.

WIRE STRIPPER Device composed of a set of scissor-like blades with a central notch; used to strip the insulation from the outside of electrical wires.

ZIP TIES Self-closing fastener. When the end of a zip tie is inserted into the slot at its head and tightened, it creates a loop that can't easily be loosened.

INDEX

THANKS TO OUR MAKERS

Lots of inventive people contributed their ideas and how-to tutorials to the pages of this book. Look them up to find out more details about their projects, as well as any new cool stuff they're up to.

MAKER BASICS

14: Pocholo Manalac 17: Sean Michael Ragan 18–19: Blaine Dehmlow 20: Matthew Griffin

GEEK TOYS

21: Pocholo Manalac 22: Susan E. Matthews 23: John B. Carnett (carnettphoto.com) 24: Elizabeth Hurchalla and Kent Hayward 26: Alessandro Lambardi 28: Kip Kedersha (kipkay.com) 30: Jamie Price (jamiepricecreative.com) 31: Paul Adams 32: Scott McIndoe 33: Kyle Pollock 34: Evil Mad Scientist Laboratory (evilmadscientist. com) 36: Sean Michael Ragan and Evil Mad Scientist Laboratory (evilmadscientist.com) 37: David Haxworth 38 (potato gun): Spudtech (spudtech.com) 38 (pumpkin gun): Gary Arold and John Gill 40: R. Lee Kennedy, Associate Professor, Department of Drama, University of Virginia 41: Michel Mota da Cruz 42: Bob Munz 44: Mike Andersen, Grant Elliot, Schyler Senft-Grup, and Scott Torborg (scotttorborg.com) 45 (Rubens' tube): Nik Vaughn 45 (fireball gun): Vin Marshall (te-motorworks.com) 46: campfiredude.com 50: waterzooka.com 52: Inspired by a tutorial by Instructables username hunrichs; furthered by Emelie Griffin 53: Rainworks 54: Emelie Griffin 55: Liz Kruesi with Ankur Mehta and Benjamin Shaya of MIT 56: Anthony Le (masterle247.wix. com) 59: William Gurstelle 62: Harout Markarian 63: Daniel Wolf (cookrookery.com) 64: Jason Wilson 65: Robert Waters 68: Dave Prochnow 69: Sean Michael Ragan 70: Kip Kedersha (kipkay. com) 71: Levi Sharpe 72: Christopher Marley 74: Andrew Lim (cofounder of Recombu.com) 75: Aram Bartholl (deaddrops.com) 76: Lindsay Lawlor (electricgiraffe.com) 77: Scott Garner 78: illphabetik.com 83: Tim Lillis 84: Michael Greensmith (steampunkwayoflife.blogspot.com.au) 85: David Sheinkopf 87: Stephen Yin with Jay Silver 88: Dave Prochnow

HOME IMPROVEMENTS

89: Kip Kedersha (kipkay.com) 96: Eric Dyer and Maggie Hoffman (radiohole.com) 99: Daniel Julian 104 (graffiti laser): Chris Poole 105: Scott McIndoe 107: Dave Prochnow 113: Ben Diaz 115: Damon Hearne 118: Patrick Lalonde 119: Dan Poff (tophatlabs.wordpress.com) 122: Vine user oh so tracy 124: Perry Watkins (perrywinklecustoms. co.uk) 125: Dave Prochnow 129: Juan Francisco Paredes 134: Melanie Rapp Mimikry 135: Ed Lenz (windstuffnow.com) 136: Dave Prochnow 137: Dave Prochnow 139 Jeremy Blum (jeremyblum.com) 140: littleBits 141: John B. Carnett (carnettphoto. com) 143: Dean Segovis (hackaweek.com) 144 (lawnmower): Korey Atterberry (atterberry.net) 144 (golf cart): Bill Rulien (beavercreekgolfcarts. com) 147: Kai Grundt

GADGET UPGRADES

148: William Finucane (adapted with permission from his original guide in the Mad Science World on wonderhowto.com) 153: Wallace Kineyko 154: Zach Supalla 155: Dylan Hart (householdhacker. com) 159: Kip Kedersha (kipkay.com) 161: Jennifer Lee (jen7714.wordpress.com) 163: Phil Herlihy (braindeadlock.net) 164: Jeffrey Davies 167: Evil Mad Scientist Laboratories (evilmadscientist. com) 169: Instructables username unclesam 170: Ian Cannon 172: Dave Fortin (failsworld.com) 174: Toma Dimov (outfab.com) 175: Bard Lund Johansen 179: Ian Cannon 180: Jani "Japala" Pönkkö (editor of metku.net) 182: Ingo Schommer (chillu.com) 184: Pamela Stephens (pbjstories.com) 189 (portable X-ray machine): Adam Munich 190: Bionerd23 (youtube.com/user/bionerd23) 191: Sarah Charley (courtesy of Symmetry magazine) 192: Felix Rusu 194: Dave Mosher 195: Dave Prochnow 196: Markus Kayser (markuskayser. com) 197: Sean Michael Ragan 201: Larry Towe (getawaymoments.com) 206: Justin Quinnell 207: Chris Voigt and his team at MIT 209: Public Lab (publiclab.org)